# FOUND magazine:

## THE EARLY YEARS!

# ATTENTION BOOKSELLERS

## Important Announcement

The title stenciled on this carton is fictitious and was used for security reasons.

The books in the carton — *I Want to Tell You* by O. J. Simpson — are what you ordered.

Please put them on sale immediately.

Thanks.

# CONTENTS:

Dedicated to Woody Hilboldt

## FOUND MAGAZINE IS:

Davy Rothbart, Sarah Locke, James Molenda, Brande Wix, Peter Rothbart, Al McWilliams, Andy Schwegler, Anna Stasek, Jason Bitner, Arthur Jones, Brett Loudermilk, Hakim Selby, Andrew Cohn, and the Story Pirates, plus dozens of friends who have contributed their time and energy so generously these past 13 years, and thousands of finders worldwide!

SEND IN YOUR FINDS!

FOUND MAGAZINE

3455 charing cross - ann arbor, mi - 48108

foundmagazine.com

This drawing FOUND by Brianna Barnes, Santa Cruz, CA.

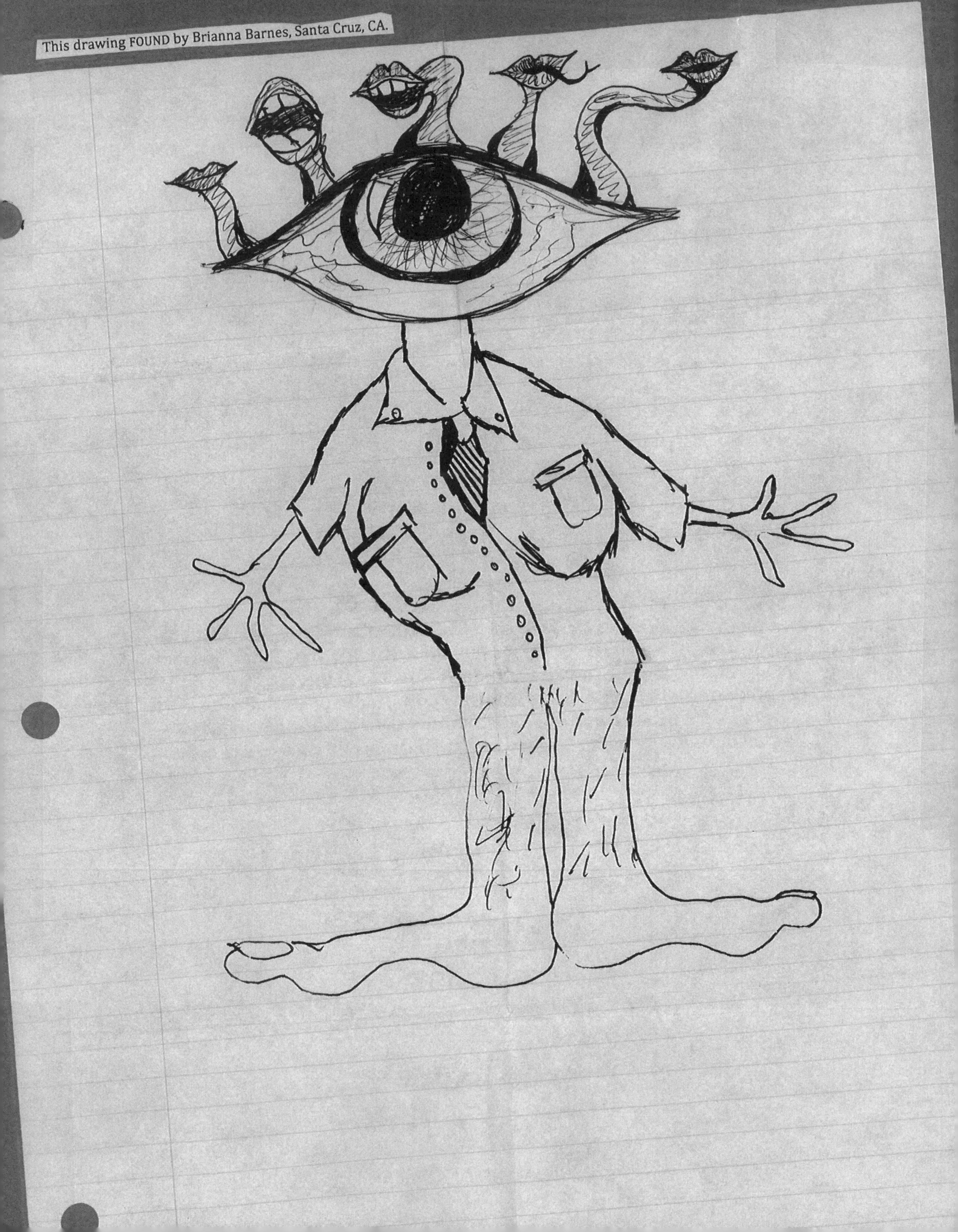

# INTRODUCTION

## by Davy Rothbart

## I.
## P.S. PAGE ME LATER

LATE ONE NIGHT in Chicago, in February of 2000, I went out to my car and found a folded note tucked under my wiper blade, addressed to someone named Mario. Apparently, someone had confused my Toyota Camry for someone else's. I looked around, but the street was empty—nary a Mario to be seen. So I unfolded the note and read it:

> Mario,
> I fucking hate you you said you had to work then whys your car HERE at HER place??
> You're a fucking LIAR I hate you
> I fucking hate you
> Amber
> PS Page me later

Amber's bewildering swirl of emotion—anger, jealousy, longing, and hopefulness—captivated and intrigued me. Her bitterness at Mario seemed tempered by that sweet, unexpected postscript: *P.S. Page me later.* I only wished Amber had left her phone number so I could've paged her to let her know that she'd mistaken my car for Mario's! Then again, I figured, Mario wasn't entirely off the hook—he must've done something in the past to earn her distrust.

In the days that followed, I began to share the note with my friends around Chicago, and what surprised me was not only how fascinated people seemed by the note itself, but also the fact that everyone seemed to have their own fascinating finds to share with me in return. These were love letters, To Do lists, Post-It notes, kids' drawings, and Polaroid pictures they'd plucked from the gutter, which they'd kept taped to their fridge or pinned above their desks. Although I'd always collected found scraps of paper—anything that gave a glimpse into other people's lives—I'd never realized how many people shared my weird hobby. It seemed a shame that so many incredible finds were taped up on people's refrigerators, to be seen only by visitors to their kitchen. I'd always loved reading zines, and one day on a road trip with friends I had an idea: What about making a zine called FOUND, where everyone could share their most interesting finds with everyone else?

A simple idea, and my ambitions were small. I made a bunch of flyers that said "FOUND Magazine needs your help," and included a copy of the Mario and Amber note and a brief explanation of my idea, inviting people to send me their finds, and began posting the flyers in bars and cafés, and handing them out to friends in Chicago and Michigan, and even to strangers on the street during trips to New Mexico and California. Friends passed me some gems, and thrillingly, a few were sent to me by total strangers around the country who'd seen a flyer or had heard about the project through someone else. After a year, between the finds I'd received and my own longstanding collection, I had enough to fill the first issue of the magazine.

For three nights in May of 2001, a handful of friends and two of my teenage cousins joined me at Tix-N-Flix, the combination ticket broker-and-video store where I worked, and with scissors, Scotch tape, and an old-school Xerox copier, we quickly assembled FOUND Magazine #1. At the end of the third night, around four A.M., my cousins and I went to a nearby Kinko's, planning to make fifty copies. But this young punk rocker working the night shift took one look at what we'd put together and said, "You guys, this is awesome—let's make eight hundred!" That sounded way beyond our budget, but he told us he could make the copies on the cheap. Eight hundred copies it was.

My friend Rob Doran, an art student and bassist for the fledgling band Alkaline Trio, designed a cool and stately FOUND logo, and spent days silk-screening it one at a time onto eight hundred pieces of heavy-stock paper that we used for the magazine covers. My brother Peter rolled into town from Ann Arbor, along with a few of our other friends, and together we collated and stapled the thousands of loose pages we'd picked up from Kinko's, and then hand-decorated each magazine, taping individual found notes and pictures to the covers. Finally, the night of June 10th, we held an official release party for FOUND #1 at a small music venue in the South Loop called The Hot House.

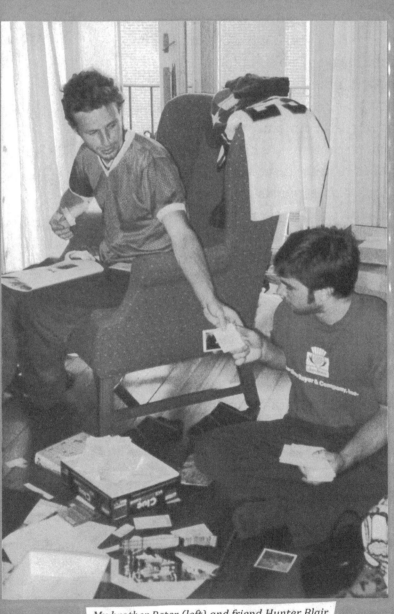

*My brother Peter (left) and friend Hunter Blair hand-decorate the first batch of FOUND #1.*

*Collating FOUND #1s in my Chicago kitchen, early June, 2001.*

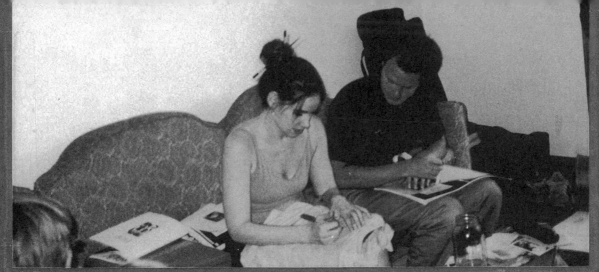

*Friends Aimee McDonald and Aaron Dennis hand-decorate T-shirts and the initial batch of* FOUND #1.

A jazz quartet composed of Michigan friends performed for those first to arrive, while on the street outside the Hot House, a bunch of my colleagues in the ticket-scalping business hawked passes to our show, as though we were the Rolling Stones: "Who needs two? FOUND Magazine release party—who's got 'em, who needs 'em?" Eventually, about fifty people filed in and filled the chairs inside; they'd each paid a five-dollar cover, which also entitled them to a free copy of our debut issue. For about fifteen minutes I stood at the front of the room and read some of my favorite finds featured in the magazine. My friend Jason Bitner, who'd constructed a website for FOUND, spun records. The highlight of the night came when Peter and a couple of his roommates from Ann Arbor took the stage as The Sweatpants, performing energetic covers of a series of homemade booty rap anthems that they'd discovered on an audio-cassette a friend of theirs had found lying in the grass at a park, left behind, presumably, by one of the teenagers who'd recorded the songs: "Wave Yo' Booty In The Air," "Taste That Booty Flava," "The Booty Don't Stop," and "Yo' Shit Be Up In My Face." Classics, one and all.

The night was a success, and to my surprise a *Chicago Tribune* reporter had even shown up to see what we were up to; his article the next day described FOUND as "quite literally, a trashy magazine." The only problem was, my apartment was now filled floor to ceiling with box after box containing the remaining 750 hand-decorated copies of FOUND #1, and I was leaving in a couple of days for a six-week trip to Guatemala and Honduras that I'd planned months before. My roommate, Tim McIlrath, lead singer of a newly-formed punk band called Rise Against, was a super friendly dude, but understandably, he was pissed off about the apartment being so crammed full of magazines that you could barely move from room to room. "Let me see what I can do," I told him.

I brought a stack of zines over to Quimby's Bookstore and asked if they might be willing to stock FOUND. The guy working there that day was Al Burian, one of my favorite writers and musicians, known for his zine *Burn Collector*. "Can I take a look at those?" he asked me. I passed him the stack, and he pivoted and placed them on the nearest shelf. "There you go," he said. "Now they're for sale."

There were still 725 magazines left at my apartment. I apologized to Tim and told him I'd have to deal with it when I got back to town. Six weeks later, back from Central America, Tim greeted me inside our empty apartment. All of the magazine boxes were gone. I figured he'd either thrown them all away or stuffed them in the storage unit in the basement, which often flooded. "No," he told me. "I sold them all! Quimby's kept calling, asking me to bring more boxes of magazines over. I brought boxes to Chicago Comics and Reckless Records, and they're selling them now. Same with Tix-N-Flix." He went on: "And then so many of our friends were coming by, ringing our doorbell morning, noon, and night, wanting to buy one copy, three copies, five copies for their friends... the neighbors actually called the police—they thought I was selling drugs out of the apartment!"

I was totally shocked, overwhelmed, and thrilled. I'd never have guessed that there'd be so many people who were just as fascinated by these little found scraps of paper as me. "Well, shit," I said. "I guess there's only one thing to do: print more!"

*Jazz saxophonist Tim Haldeman (right) and a friend at the FOUND #1 release party, June 10, 2001.*

*FOUND shipping and distribution manager Brande Wix inspects a copy of FOUND #1 at the Hot House.*

## II.
## D.I.Y. OR DIE

THE MORE MAGAZINES that found their way into people's hands, the more finds we began to receive in the mail—they came from all over the U.S., and from dozens of countries around the world: Singapore, Senegal, Sweden, Chilé. For someone who'd always loved discovering a found note or letter tumbling down the street, it was an incredible joy to go to the mailbox every day and find it stuffed with brand-new finds, each one more heartbreaking or hilarious than the one before.

It had never occurred to me that our little handmade zine would interest folks in the media, but they suddenly seized on FOUND. NPR's *On The Media* called, *The Chicago Sun-Times* wrote a lengthy story, as did several alt-weeklies, and Yahoo featured FOUND as its site of the day. The reach of these outlets was far beyond anything I could've achieved with flyers and duct tape. People were writing to us from all over the place, sending us finds, and asking how to subscribe to a magazine that didn't even really exist yet, other than the original copies we'd printed at Kinko's.

We found a printer in Winnipeg, Manitoba called WestCan, run by a guy named Chris Young, who was known for his work printing awesome comic books and graphic novels like *Eightball* by Daniel Clowes. Chris offered to run off another few thousand copies of the magazine at a great price, and even had some suggestions for stores around the U.S. and Canada that might want to carry it.

At the time, there was a girl in Vermont named Liz I'd been trading soulful letters with for three years, ever since a single chance meeting at a party one night in Chicago. Finally, that spring, we'd had a magically romantic week-long road trip, and hatched a plan to move together in the fall to some small town down south—we figured we'd just keep driving until we found the right place (the kind of plan that you'll make when you're 26). But over the summer, things dissolved between us, and Tim and I had already given up our apartment in Chicago, since I'd planned to head south with Liz. Not sure what my next move should be, I loaded up my old '73 Ford LTD and headed back to my folks' house in Ann Arbor until I could sort it all out. It was there that I had Chris Young ship the reprint of FOUND #1. A big rig rumbled up the dirt road I'd grown up on and dropped two pallets full of magazines on our front lawn—a total of 84 boxes, which I carried down to the basement a box at a time, over several hours.

I began calling indie bookstores around the country, explaining the idea behind FOUND to them, and asking if they'd be down to carry the magazine. Some folks hung up on me, repelled by what might've seemed like just another sales call, but others instantly vibed to the premise of FOUND and asked me to ship them a box. Within a couple of months, there were 20 or 30 stores around the country stocking the magazine.

I'd always admired the way all my Chicago friends who played in bands would spend a year writing and recording an album and then hit the road in a van for a couple of months to share their work with people. I wasn't sure what kind of show I'd put on, exactly, but the idea of a tour for the magazine made a lot of sense to me: I could spread word about FOUND, Johnny Appleseed-style, and also collect new finds from people as I traveled, to be included in the next issue.

Leaning on help from plenty of far-flung friends, I pieced together a 17-city tour in November of 2001 that wound its way through the Midwest and up the East Coast, booking events at bars, cafés, bookstores, and art spaces, and posted the dates on the FOUND website. My friend Brande Wix offered to join me, and we hit the road in a cheap rental car loaded with boxes of magazines.

# FOUND Magazine

## TOUR 2001 >> COMING TO A CITY NEAR YOU!!

- **cleveland – thursday, november 1– 7pm**
  mac's backs paperbacks (1820 coventry rd. cleveland heights 216.321.2665)

- **philadelphia – friday, november 2 – 9pm & wednesday, november 7 – 7pm**
  november 2, 9pm: the book trader (514 bainbridge st. 215.925.0219)
  november 7, 7pm: robin's bookstore (108 s.13th st. 215.735.9600)

- **atlantic city – saturday, november 3 – 10pm**
  FOUND magazine's annual o.g. ball – for info write us at foundmagazine@hotmail.com

- **boston - sunday, november 4 - 8pm**
  three cheers bar (290 congress street, near the south station t stop, 617.423.6166)

- **providence – monday, november 5 – 7pm**
  white electric (150 broadway  401.453.3007)

- **new haven - tuesday, november 6, 7:30 pm**
  the book trader cafe, (1140 chapel street, 203.787.6147)

- **baltimore – thursday, november 8 – 7pm**
  atomic books (1100 west 36th st. 410.662.4444)

- **new york city - friday, november 9 – 7:30pm**
  niagara (a bar at 7th street and avenue A in the east village, 112 avenue A.)

- **washington, d.c. - sunday, november 11 - 7pm**
  brickskeller inn (1523 22nd street, between p + q, dupont circle metro stop,  202.293.1885)

- **grand rapids - wednesday, november 14**
  11am-2pm, grand valley state u., for info write us at foundmagazine@hotmail.com
  7:00pm, argo's bookstore (1405 robinson rd, S.E. at lake drive, 616.454.0111)

- **madison – thursday, november 15 – 7:30pm**
  canterbury bookstore (315 west gorham 608.258.9911)

- **chicago – friday, november 16 – 8pm**
  quimby's bookstore (1854 w.north ave. 773.342.0910)

- **ann arbor – saturday, november 17 – 7:30pm**
  shaman drum bookstore (311 s.state st., 734.662.7407)

- **bay area, l.a., sacramento, santa cruz, san diego** – these will be after thanksgiving,
  dates and locations TBA

foundmagazine@hotmail.com         **foundmagazine.com**         3455 charing cross road,
ann arbor, MI 48108-1911

*A flyer we passed out to audience members on the inaugural FOUND tour, outlining our tour schedule.*

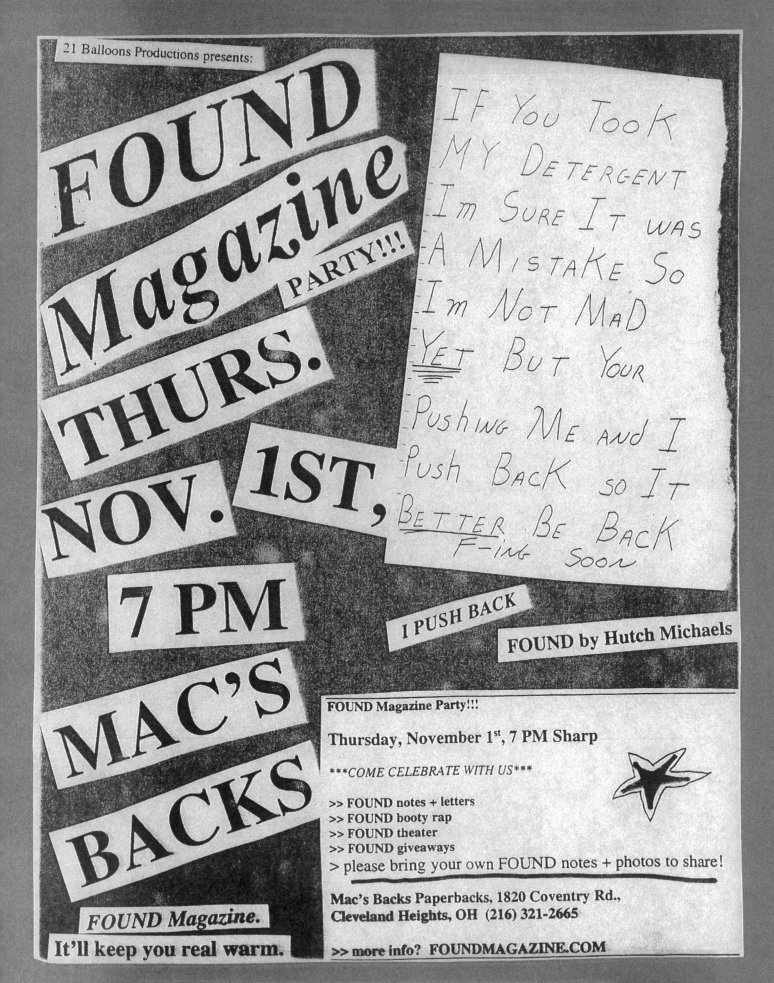

A flyer for the first-ever FOUND Tour event, November 1, 2001, at a bookstore in Cleveland.

Our first stop was a quaint used bookstore in Cleveland. When we saw that only a handful of people had shown up, we recruited a dozen teenage skaters from the street out front who'd asked us to buy beer for them. We said we'd be happy to, as long as they'd come check out our event, so they all crowded in, sipping from Budweiser cans in paper bags. Completely nervous, with no idea what I was doing, I simply read my favorite finds from FOUND #1 out loud, as I'd done at the Hot House, starting out a bit shyly. But, as I've learned over the years, the finds themselves are so rich, incredible, and unexpected, any crowd will respond warmly to them, once someone gives voice to them. Perhaps it shouldn't have been a surprise that everyone in that bookstore found the notes as moving, affecting, and hilarious as me, but I emerged from that night transformed, newly aware of the power the finds possessed.

We rolled on to Philadelphia, New York, New Haven, Providence, and Boston. In some cities, only three people showed up; in others, we had as many as twenty or thirty. But in every city we left a box of magazines behind with some new friend to distribute to local bookstores, and most nights people handed us beautiful, weird, funny, and fucked-up finds to take home to Michigan. We ended the tour with shows at bookstores in Madison, Chicago, and Ann Arbor; over the course of the tour, the crowds had grown—almost overnight, word about the magazine seemed to be spreading.

Waiting at home were three crates of FOUND mail that had arrived in the month I'd been gone. This was better than Christmas! I invited a few friends to come over to my folks' house that night and we dug right in.

## III.
## NATION OF MILLIONS

SOMEHOW, WITHOUT REALLY meaning to do it, I'd moved back in with my parents. Living there rent-free, I figured, would allow me to keep working full-time on FOUND Magazine. Eventually, I'd look for a new place in Chicago, but this would do for now. As a bonus, my Mom often helped me send out magazines to people who'd ordered them, and my Dad made occasional post office runs when a bookstore in Milwaukee or Seattle needed another box of FOUND #1.

Right after my 27th birthday, some clumsy ogre pulverized my foot in a pickup basketball game, and I spent the summer of 2002 on crutches. It was bad enough having to tell girls at the bar that I was 27 and lived in my parents' basement, but now, hobbled from the injury, it was a struggle to even get to the bar to get dissed by girls. Then, somehow, my luck changed, and I was introduced to a beautiful, friendly, upbeat girl who'd just graduated from the University of Michigan and was named, quite appropriately, Emilie Goodhart. She was in town for the summer before starting a job in New York that fall writing for *The Nation*; for now, she had plenty of time on her hands to help me put together the new issue of FOUND.

We carpeted the living room of my parents' house with our favorite finds, covering every available surface, and used the dining table to put the magazine pages together, again using only scissors and tape, along with a clunky office copier we bought for 25 bucks out of the classified ads in the back of the *Ann Arbor News*. This time we put the pages together a bit more intricately, and since it was just the two of us, it took several weeks to finish the magazine.

We designed four separate covers for FOUND #2—one featured a found photo of a shirtless guy holding a street sign; another had two men in suits holding a giant, colorful Easter Egg. My favorite was an old '70s photo of a teenage couple all decked out at their high school prom. A company had agreed to distribute our magazine to hundreds of new stores, and it was a thrill to know that the D.I.Y. zine we were slapping together at my parents' dining table would soon be available at indie bookstores and record shops around the country, and Borders and Tower Records outlets worldwide.

I'd listed the magazine's price as $5 on each of the covers, except on one—the guys with the Easter Egg—where I'd foolishly said, *"FREE for subscribers."* My thinking was that we'd mail these ones to subscribers, and the magazines with the other covers would be shipped to stores. But WestCan wasn't able to separate our shipments in the way I'd imagined, and the magazines with the 'FREE' cover price were widely sent out to stores. You can imagine how many people walked off with these ones, believing they were giveaways. Clerks would actually chase people down in the parking lot and accuse them of shoplifting, only to have the customers point to where it said 'FREE' on the cover. "I don't want to see the word 'FREE' ever again!" the magazine distributor told me. "Don't even use that word *inside* the magazine!"

# FOUND magazine #2

## EGG ARTISTRY

GENERAL PUBLIC — STILL 5 BUCKS!!

SPECIAL SUBSCRIBERS' EDITION!! FREE

# FOUND magazine #2

Love is... you and me

STILL 5 BUCKS

# FOUND magazine #2

5 BUCKS

# FOUND magazine #2

← 400 W 300 →
MARKET STREET

5 BUCKS

*The four covers of FOUND #2, including the problematic 'FREE' version, top left.*

ATOMIC BOOKS → 10 COPIES
(RACHEL WHANG)                    7/22/01
THANKS FOR CARRYING

# FOUND
## MAGAZINE

___

When you sell your copies please
send me a check, $3 per mag + we split mailing costs.
Here's a worksheet to make the
math easier:

# of copies [10]    x $3.00 each = [30]

50% of mailing cost [   ]
(you might want to fill
in this box now while
you have the package with the postage amount on it) → + [1.32]

___

CHECK AMOUNT [31.32]

Checks payable to FOUND MAGAZINE
Mail to :    FOUND MAGAZINE
             PO BOX 14364
             CHICAGO, IL 60614

___

CALL ME WHEN YOU RUN OUT SO I
CAN SEND MORE COPIES PRONTO!
(510) 393-6343    Thanks! DAVY

A DIY invoice from 2001 with an order from Baltimore's Atomic Books,
one of the first stores to carry FOUND.

Live and learn. I had bigger concerns—Emilie had left for New York, which essentially meant the end of our budding relationship, and I was busy putting together an ambitious 47-city fall tour that would help me spread word about FOUND from coast to coast. I called it FOUND's Nation of Millions Tour, after a favorite Public Enemy album, and on October 1st, a few days after copies of the new issue had arrived from Manitoba, I held a small release party at a café in Ann Arbor, and then hit the road.

It was a couple of the wildest months of my life. After a year holed up in my parents' basement and a summer spent crutching around their house, it was a thrill to be in a new city every day, meeting kindred spirits who loved found stuff as much as I did and shared my insatiable curiosity about other people's lives. After each event, people brought me heaps of incredible finds, and invited me back to their apartments to have a few drinks and crash on their floor or sofa.

In St. Louis, I went train-hopping through downtown, right past the Arch, with a couple of kindly punks, and stayed overnight at their squat—an abandoned, boarded-up house—where they cooked me a delicious late-night meal on a rickety camping stove. In Louisville, I met a pair of high school kids who told me with amazement that they'd seen their hard-ass principal in attendance at the FOUND event; later, they explained in an email, when they went to the principal's office to ask why he'd been there, they learned he was an old-school Dumpster diver who'd collected found stuff all his life, and they all made plans to go Dumpster diving together. In Chicago, as we set up for an event an art gallery called Intuit, the truck driver delivering beer for the night's brouhaha glimpsed the front cover of FOUND #2 and did a double-take: crazily, almost unbelievably, the kid in the prom picture was *him*, twenty-five years earlier! For a minute he was completely discombobulated, but once we explained the idea of FOUND Magazine, he dove joyfully into the story of that less-than-magical night, back in Ohio, twenty-five years before; apparently, his date had ditched him immediately after the picture was taken, but he'd still had a fun time with his friends. In Manhattan, one of my favorite *New Yorker* writers, Tad Friend, weaved around the East Village with me on foot as we searched the ground for interesting finds, and he wrote a piece about FOUND for the magazine's Talk of the Town section, which frankly blew my mind. The crowds at the events continued to swell. Some weeks I'd drive on my own from town to town; other weeks, one of my friends—Brande, Mike Kozura, Shawna Lee, or Samantha Grice—would join me on the road, sharing the adventure with me.

One night in Houston, right after an emotional phone call with Emilie Goodhart back in New York, a guy named Woody Hilboldt rang me up, calling from the tiny town of Ozark, Alabama. In a rich, dripping, Southern drawl, he told me that his daughter, a journalist in Florida, had asked him for a copy of FOUND Magazine for the holidays, but he wasn't sure how to order it online (this was 2002), and he'd tracked down my number to ask what could be done. Somehow, we ended up talking for almost an hour. Woody was a mortician and county coroner, a kind soul with an inquisitive mind. I promised to send him the first couple of issues of FOUND, and by the time we got off the phone, any pain about Emilie had been largely diffused.

My whole life, I'd been fascinated by talking to strangers, and now, rolling around the country, I was having the chance to do just that, night after night. People I never would have had the chance to connect with, ordinarily—folks like Woody Hilboldt—were now appearing in my life and sharing their stories with me. I couldn't have felt any luckier. I owed Mario and Amber a mountain of thanks. The West Coast still lied ahead.

## IV.
## MY NEW SIMBOL

ONE EXCITING DEVELOPMENT from the fall 2002 Nation of Millions tour was meeting a wonderfully smart and eclectic editor from Simon & Schuster named Amanda Patten. She signed me up to produce a FOUND book that would have the same exact feel as the magazine, but three times the length, and be distributed by S&S to every bookstore in the country. With money from the book contract, I'd also be able to keep printing future issues of the magazine (and settle some outstanding bills with WestCan). Beyond that, I could afford to move out of my parents' basement. A few friends of mine had an open bedroom in a beautiful, creaky old mansion they'd been renting in downtown Ann Arbor, built in 1873 by a local brew master. It was right near the train station and across the street from my favorite basketball court, Wheeler Park. In January, 2003, I moved in.

The best thing about the house, in my opinion, was its enormous basement. Though it was stacked high with debris—bricks and cinderblocks, broken windows, old bike tires, and piles of wood—I saw its potential as an office for FOUND Magazine. For a full week, a few friends helped me clear it out, and once we added a few desks and tables and Oriental rugs that we'd nabbed at garage sales, plus a black light and a Bruce Lee poster, we had ourselves a legit (if somewhat dank and dungeon-like) place to work. Gone were the days of my Mom processing orders with me—Brande Wix and Mike Kozura, my friends since grade school, began clocking in daily, helping me manage the operation. Meanwhile, in Chicago, my friend Jason Bitner kept the FOUND website humming along, posting brand-new finds every day of the week.

I'd been working with the public radio show *This American Life* for a couple of years, doing occasional stories for them, and in the spring of 2003, host Ira Glass invited me to join him on a U.S. "Lost and Found"-themed tour, along with frequent T.A.L. contributors David Sedaris, Sarah Vowell, Jonathan Goldstein, and Starlee Kine, and musical acts Jon Langford and OK Go. We played enormous auditoriums, and I found myself, surreally, reading the same found notes I'd been reading eighteen months before for a crowd of three, now for a crowd of three thousand.

*Chicago Theater marquee on May 31, 2003, from This American Life and FOUND Magazine's "Lost In America" Tour.*

After our live show aired nationally on T.A.L., the finds poured in by the crate-load, and I had Chris Young at WestCan on speed dial. New shipments of magazines came every couple of months, and Brande, Mike and I would shoot baskets in the park, waiting for the giant semi to pull up the street, then spend a few hours carrying boxes down to the basement, into a hidden room we called "The Cave," where the brew master was rumored to have stashed liquor during Prohibition.

*Publicity shot from the 2003 "We Are Nighttime Travelers" FOUND Tour with my brother Peter and Devon Sproule.*

In early summer, I did a smaller 30-city tour with my brother Peter, who'd been honing his skills as a singer-songwriter. Peter had written a number of songs based on individual notes from the pages of FOUND Magazine—some outrageous, some quietly beautiful. We were joined on the road by a talented young folk singer from rural Virginia named Devon Sproule. It was a treat to get to see two of my favorite musicians perform every night, and to continue to build friendships I'd made on previous swings across the country.

The rest of the summer, and on through the fall, I worked on putting together the FOUND book, with help from Peter, Mike Kozura, and other friends. We had plenty of material to choose from, since incredible finds kept arriving from all over the globe. Reading the FOUND mail, I could see the effects of our live events—a huge proportion of the stuff we received came from cities we'd hit on tour, where we'd had a chance to personally beseech people to keep their eyes on the ground and send us their finds. Some finders were newly deputized recruits; others had been finding stuff their whole lives. Many of the finds we received had been carefully tucked away for years and years—sometimes longer than I'd been alive—and had now been sent to us so we could put them in the magazine, FOUND book, or website, and share them with a wider audience.

For me, the effect of reading hundreds of found notes every week, peeking intimately into such a wide range of lives, was immensely powerful. Though I'd always considered myself a compassionate person, the notes drew me so deeply into the pain, sorrows, joys, and triumphs of thousands of souls I'd never get to meet in person, I found myself discovering new levels of empathy and understanding. Once, reading a series of letters written by a young man dying of AIDS, I felt moved to tears. Other times, reading a FOUND journal—passionate, intense, novelistic in its level of detail—I'd feel like I was falling in love with the unknown woman who'd written it.

By winter, the FOUND book was done, and it was time to move on to the new issue of the magazine, FOUND #3. A student from Bennington College named Genevieve Belleveau had asked if she could move to Ann Arbor for a couple of months during her school's Field Work Term to volunteer with FOUND. I wanted to make sure that she knew what she was getting herself into—that our office was not a typical Condé Nast magazine office, but the spooky, brick basement of an old haunted-looking house. We often fell under siege by bats, I explained. Undeterred, she drove to Ann Arbor and spent January and February of 2003 putting the new issue together with me.

"My new simbol" find from the cover of FOUND #3.

As we sifted through a year's worth of finds, there were two we fell in love with the most: A red notebook that had belonged to a cook in Portland, Maine, struggling to overcome a heroin addiction, filled with his ideas for new recipes, pained yet determined journal entries (it appeared he'd been instructed to write in the notebook every time he felt beset by the urge to shoot up), and shopping lists, which, humorously, always contained the item "One pound of heroin." Our other favorite was a tiny drawing of a fractured heart with flames fanning out in either direction; written underneath, in cursive, it said, "My new simbol" (the misspelling was theirs). Perhaps a sketch for a planned tattoo? We used the broken heart drawing on the front cover, along with the cook's red notebook (his journal pages went inside); on the back cover, a collage of pictures of happy couples where one person had been cut out, ripped off, or stabbed with a cigarette—it was kind of crazy how many of these we'd received. We called FOUND #3 the Love & Heartbreak issue and organized a release party at the Blind Pig, a rock club in Ann Arbor, for mid-April, 2004, just two weeks before the FOUND book was to be released, and Peter and I were to leave on a sprawling, months-long, 50-state, 136-city tour. That night, at the Blind Pig, we met a girl who'd become a core member of the FOUND team for more than a decade to come: Sarah Locke.

# V.
# SLAPDANCE ACROSS AMERICA

HONOLULU, HAWAII. ANCHORAGE, Alaska. Fargo, North Dakota. It boggled my mind that the note meant for Mario that Amber had mistakenly left on my windshield had in some weird way delivered me to odd corners of the country, where I'd climb up on stage and read from pieces of paper that other people might reasonably view as trash. Peter and I had bought an old van off eBay and covered it with FOUND stickers. We dubbed the tour "Slapdance Across America," based on a particularly crude and graphic find about a guy who liked to jump up and down naked, his penis slapping against his belly. It tickled us to hear NPR announcers say the words "Slapdance Across America," knowing the find it referenced.

The 50-state tour was both the time of my life and also hard and lonely work. Some nights turnout would be dismal, and I'd go to sleep in our van in say, Sioux Falls, South Dakota, listening to rain whip the roof and windows. Other nights we'd rock a packed theater and I'd spend the night gallivanting around a city I'd never been to with new, wonderful friends. The year became a blur—sound checks; performing on stage; breaking down our gear; folks handing us amazing and ridiculous new finds in every city; sleeping on sofas, floors, in the van, and in the woods; local morning TV shows; Letterman; plenty of Maker's Mark; and driving, always driving, through mountains, desert, prairie, corn fields, and lush forests, admiring our country's insane natural beauty. Peter warmed up his voice each night by singing Bon Jovi's "Wanted Dead or Alive," and though we were nowhere close to rock stars, in our own indie, D.I.Y. way we'd built a life on the road for ourselves, and hearing the song always made me feel a well of emotion.

Meanwhile, back home in Ann Arbor, Brande and Mike held down the FOUND office, joined now by Sarah Locke, who was just 19 years-old but easily as smart, energetic, cheerful, and capable as the rest of us combined. I looked forward to getting to work with her on a new issue of the magazine, once I finally made it home.

In mid-December, in a small town in Wyoming, Peter and I reached the end of our 50-state Slapdance tour and performed our last FOUND show of the trip, then loaded up the van one last time. Dazed, feeling aglow, proud, and at the same time a bit lost and set adrift, I wandered out into a snowy field, holding a glass of whiskey and a bottle of beer, for a moment of quiet reflection on the year that had passed. That's when my phone rang—it was my old buddy Woody Hilboldt, the mortician from Ozark, Alabama, calling to check in, and to order the latest FOUND stuff as a Christmas present for his daughter. For all the new friends I'd made on the road and incredible people who'd come into my life the past couple of years, it felt somehow fitting that I was celebrating the end of our 50-state tour with a friend I'd made through FOUND but hadn't yet met in person. At his home in Ozark, Woody poured himself a drink, and we each raised our glass for a toast, a couple thousand miles apart.

# FOUND magazine's SLAPDANCE ACROSS AMERICA TOUR "2004!"

we're loading up the van with finds and coming to visit you -- this year, FOUND parties in all 50 states! what happens at a FOUND party?? FOUND madness!! davy shares our favorite finds of all-time and gets rowdy and rambunctious and generally acts a fool, peter bangs out new tunes based on FOUND notes, and we ask you to share your own finds!

- september 9, 2004 -- **toronto, on** » moved to november 5th (see details below in nov. listings)
- september 10, 2004 -- **kingston, on** » the sleepless goat, 9 pm, 91 princess street, 613.545.9646
- september 11, 2004 -- **montreal, qb** » casa del popolo, 9 pm, 4873 boul. st-laurent, 514.284.3804

- september 12, 2004 -- **burlington, vt** » radio bean coffeehouse, 8 pm, 8 n. winooski ave, 802.660.9346
- september 13, 2004 -- **portland, me** » SPACE Gallery, 8 pm, 538 congress street, 207.541.3842
- september 14, 2004 -- **newmarket, nh** » the stone church, 8 pm, 5 granite street (zion hill), 603.659.6321

- september 15, 2004 -- **lawrence, ma** » essex art center, 7 pm, 56 island st, 978.685.2343
- september 16, 2004 -- **boston, ma (brookline)** » brookline booksmith, 7 pm, 279 harvard st., 617.566.6660
- september 18, 2004 -- **montague, ma** » lady killigrew @ bookmill, 8 pm, 442 greenfield rd, 413.367.9666
- september 19, 2004 -- **new haven, ct** » art space, 7 pm, 50 orange street (at crown), 203.772.2709
- september 20, 2004 -- **hartford, ct** » hartford stage, 7 pm, 50 church st., 860.525.5601
- september 20, 2004 -- **bridgeport, ct** » the green room, 10 pm, 3442 fairfield ave, 203.384.2233
- september 21, 2004 -- **princeton, nj** » small world coffee, 7:30pm, 14 witherspoon street, 609.924.4377

- september 23, 2004 -- **new york** » the tank, 9 pm, 432 w. 42nd street, 212.563.6269
- september 24, 2004 -- **new york** » the tank, TWO SHOWS! 10pm & 12 mid, 432 w.42nd st., 212.563.6269
- september 25, 2004 -- **new york** » the tank, TWO SHOWS! 8pm & 10pm, 432 w.42nd st., 212.563.6269

- september 26, 2004 -- **ithaca, ny** » ithaca college, 2 pm, phillips hall, call meg @ 607.273.1757
- september 26, 2004 -- **buffalo, ny** » medaille college, 8 pm, main building, jerry @ 716.884.3281 x.174
- september 27, 2004 -- **rochester, ny** » bullwinkle's, 7:30 pm, 622 lake ave, kelli @ 585.271.3361 x 352

- september 28, 2004 -- **cleveland, oh** » mac's backs paperbacks, 7 pm, 1820 coventry rd, 216.321.2665
- september 28, 2004 -- **oberlin, oh** » details TBA
- september 29, 2004 -- **columbus, oh** » wexner center for the arts, 6 pm, 1871 n.high street, 800.678.6264
- september 29, 2004 -- **dayton, oh** » wright state U, 9 pm, student union (E156), call jim @ 937.470.0758
- september 30, 2004 -- **bowling green, oh** » grounds for thought, 8 pm, 174 s. main street, 419.354.3266

slapdance

across

america

- october 3, 2004 -- **ann arbor, mi** » the blind pig, 9:30 pm, 208 s. first street, 734.996.8555
- october 4, 2004 -- **indianapolis, in** » the melody inn, 9 pm, 3826 n. illinois st., 317.923.4707
- october 5, 2004 -- **bloomington, in** » boxcar books, 7 pm, 310A s. washington st., 812.339.8710
- october 6, 2004 -- **champaign, il** » cowboy monkey, 7 pm, 6 taylor street, 217.398.6665

- october 7, 2004 -- **milwaukee, wi** » alverno college (the mug), noon, 3390 s. 43rd st, 414.382.6317
- october 8, 2004 -- **milwaukee, wi** » club garibaldi, 9 pm, 2501 s. superior street, 414.483.6335
- october 9, 2004 -- **beloit, wi** » details TBA
- october 9, 2004 -- **madison, wi** » orpheum theater, 10 pm, 216 state street, 608.255.8755

*A flyer from the Fall half of 2004's "Slapdance Across America" Tour.*

- october 11, 2004 -- **sioux falls, sd** » blacksheep coffee, 8 pm, 1007 w. 11th street, 605.339.7207
- october 12, 2004 -- **lincoln, ne** » duffy's tavern, 9 pm, 1412 'O' street, 402.474.3543
- october 13, 2004 -- **des moines, ia** » vaudeville mews, 7 pm sharp! 212 4th street, 515.243.3270
- october 14, 2004 -- **iowa city, ia** » gabe's oasis, 9 pm, 330 e. washington st., 319.354.4788

- october 15, 2004 -- **louisville, ky** » rudyard kipling, 8 pm, 422 w. oak street, 502.636.1311
- october 16, 2004 -- **nashville, tn** » springwater, 10 pm, 115 27th ave. N, 615.320.0345
- october 17, 2004 -- **lexington, ky** » the icehouse, 8 pm, 412 cross st. (directions? click here), 859.489.8200
- october 18, 2004 -- **cincinnati, oh** » shake it records, 8 pm, 4156 hamilton avenue, 513.591.0123

- october 20, 2004 -- **pittsburgh, pa** » future tenant, 7:30 pm, 801 liberty ave., 412.325.7037
- october 20, 2004 -- **morgantown, wv** » 123 pleasant st, 10:30 pm, 121 pleasant st, 304.292.0800
- october 21, 2004 -- **washington, d.c.** » staccato, 9 pm, 2006 18th street NW, 202.232.2228
- october 22, 2004 -- **richmond, va** » chop suey books, 7:30 pm, 1317 w. cary street, 804.497.4705
- october 24, 2004 -- **charlottesville, va** » gravity lounge, 8 pm, 103 s. 1st street, 434.977.5590

- october 25, 2004 -- **durham, nc** » regulator bookshop, 7 pm, 720 9th street, 919.286.2700
- october 26, 2004 -- **chapel hill, nc** » the cave, 8 pm, 452 1/2 franklin street, 919.968.9308
- october 28, 2004 -- **asheville, nc** » vincent's ear, 10 pm, 68 n. lexington avenue, 828.259.9119

- october 29, 2004 -- **south carolina** » new brookland tavern, 6 pm, 122 state street, 803.791.4413
- october 30, 2004 -- **athens, ga** » details TBA
- october 31, 2004 -- **decatur, ga** » ashton's, 8 pm, 314 e. howard avenue, 404.378.6310

- november 1, 2004 -- **gainesville, fl** » the atlantic, 9 pm, 15 n. main street, 352.337.1188
- november 3, 2004 -- **coral gables, fl** » books & books, 8 pm, 265 aragon avenue, 305.442.4408
- november 4, 2004 -- **delray beach, fl** » dada, 8 pm, 52 n.swinton avenue, 561.330.3232

- november 5, 2004 -- **toronto, on** » details TBA

- november 6, 2004 -- **tampa, fl** » covivant gallery, 9 pm, 4906 n. florida ave, 813.234.0222
- november 7, 2004 -- **birmingham, al** » details TBA
- november 8, 2004 -- **oxford, ms** » details TBA
- november 9, 2004 -- **jackson, ms** » lemuria books, 12 noon, 202 banner hall, 4465 I-55 N, 601.366.7619
- november 10, 2004 -- **new orleans, la** » masonic lodge, 8 pm, 619 carondelet, 504.451.4842
- november 11, 2004 -- **baton rouge, la** » ak photography/oculus gallery, 8 pm, 421 third st, 225.389.9099
- november 12, 2004 -- **houston, tx** » diverseworks, 8pm, 1117 east frwy (I-10 @ n.main), 713.223.8346

Super special event! FOUND vs. The Aurora Picture Show!!
- november 13, 2004 -- **houston, tx** » 8pm, 800 aurora street, 713.868.2101
- november 14, 2004 -- **houston, tx** » 1pm, 800 aurora street, 713.868.2101

- november 14, 2004 -- **san antonio, tx** » details TBA
- november 16, 2004 -- **austin, tx** » alamo drafthouse, 9:30pm, 409 colorado street, 512.476.1320
- november 17, 2004 -- **dallas, tx** » conduit gallery, 7:30 pm, 1626 C hi line drive, 214.939.0064
- november 18, 2004 -- **denton, tx** » art prostitute, 8 pm, 210 e.hickory, 940.381.1526

- november 19, 2004 -- **oklahoma city, ok** » galileo bar & grill, 9 pm, 3009 paseo, 405.415.7827
- november 20, 2004 -- **fayetteville, ar** » details TBA
- november 21, 2004 -- **columbia, mo** » ragtag cinema, 8 pm, 23 north 10th street, 573.443.4359
- november 22, 2004 -- **lawrence, ks** » hawk's nest (KU union), 6:30 pm, 1301 jayhawk blvd, 785.864.7469
- november 24, 2004 -- **albuquerque, nm** » guild cinema, time TBA, 3405 central ave. NE, 505.255.1848

- november 27, 2004 -- **honolulu, hi** » the arts at marks garage, 7:30 pm, 1159 nuuanu avenue, 808.521.2903

- december 3, 2004 -- **las vegas, nv** » 1st friday (@ funk house), 8 pm, 1228 s casino ctr, 702.767.6676
- december 4, 2004 -- **long beach, ca** » 2nd city council gallery, 8 pm, 435 alamitos ave., phone TBA
- december 5, 2004 -- **los angeles, ca** » gallery nineteen eighty-eight, 7 pm, 7020 melrose ave, 323.937.7088
- december 7, 2004 -- **san francisco, ca** » details TBA

- december 9, 2004 -- **salt lake city, ut** » slc public library, 7 pm, 210 east 400 south, 801.322.8133
- december 10, 2004 -- **jackson hole, wy** » details TBA
- december 15, 2004 -- **ypsilanti, mi** » henrietta fahrenheit, 8 pm, 126 w. michigan avenue, 734.484.3833

*slapdance across america*

found magazine

50 STATES or BUST!
for more details please visit
www.foundmagazine.com
www.poemadept.com

*A flyer from the final stretch of 2004's 50-state "Slapdance Across America" Tour.*

## VI.
## COME INTO OUR WORLD.

"WE NEED MORE grass!" I cried.

Not marijuana—actual grass. It was the summer of 2005, and Sarah and I were putting the finishing touches on the cover of FOUND Magazine #4. My idea was to have a grass-filled cover, to replicate what it felt like to glimpse an intriguing photo lying in the weeds. I'd asked two student interns, Moira and Angela, to glue grass and leaves from my back yard onto the piece of cardboard we were using for our cover, which would later—delicately—be scanned and sent to WestCan.

The cover photo we'd chosen had been found in Sacramento—three high school kids flashing "West Side" hand signs in front of a glitzy cityscape backdrop. What I loved most about the picture was what someone (one of the kids, I imagined) had written on the back with a marker: *Come Into Our World*. Really, wasn't that the invitation extended by all found notes, letters, and pictures—the chance to explore the world of someone you'd never met?

With so many finds at hand, Sarah and I had been able to stuff the issue with all kinds of jewels, including personal letters written by *The Twilight Zone*'s Rod Serling and a student's letter to her college professor, proposing an illicit, if well-organized affair. We included an interview with a woman whose two adopted children had literally been found in a bush, as babies. And *Zippy The Pinhead* artist Bill Griffiths created a *Zippy* comic strip based on one of our favorite finds.

As always, we were careful to change any names or identifying info in each of the finds to help preserve the anonymity of whoever had written it—these were all real notes written by real people, and the last thing we wanted to do was to put someone in an embarrassing or awkward position. Fortunately, Sarah proved adept at matching people's handwriting, and we managed to carefully change names and phone numbers without interrupting the flow of each letter.

My friend Vinh Nguyen helped us scan each painstakingly-constructed page, and we sent the files to Chris Young at WestCan, celebrating the completion of another issue by setting off fireworks on the train tracks across the street from my house, watching the bright lights explode across the night sky.

*Peter and I with the FOUND Tour van in the Colorado Rockies.*

That was almost ten years ago. Wow.

In the years since, with help from Sarah and Brande, along with newer friends like James Molenda and Al McWilliams, we've published two more FOUND books and five more magazines at a pace of about one magazine per year, a pace we hope to sustain for years to come. We still put each issue together with scissors and tape; FOUND #10 is in progress now and will be out soon. Peter and I have continued to tour around the U.S. nearly every year, and we also completed our first-ever European tour, hitting 30 cities in 12 countries over six weeks back in 2008, when a new FOUND book was released overseas.

I've also had time to explore some of my other interests: I've continued to contribute work to *This American Life*, and wrote a book of short stories, *The Lone Surfer of Montana, Kansas*, and a book of personal essays called *My Heart is an Idiot*. With my friend Andrew Cohn, I directed a documentary called *Medora*, about a small, struggling town in rural Indiana and its high-school basketball team, which aired on the PBS series Independent Lens. A couple of years ago, I moved out to L.A., and have assembled the last couple issues of FOUND partly at my apartment here in Echo Park, partly back in Ann Arbor. New friends now live in what has come to be known as the "FOUND House," and the basement there still holds our FOUND archives, while new FOUND mail continues to arrive day after day at my parents' house in Michigan (the official mailing address we've used since the fall of '01).

For several years, a theater group in New York called the Story Pirates has been working with Sarah and I to create a full-on FOUND musical, based on the magazine's early years; the play, written by Hunter Bell, Lee Overtree, and Eli Bolin, debuts this fall off-Broadway at the prestigious Atlantic Theater Company. Watching early versions of it, I felt like I was tripping on mushrooms—how weird to see a bizarro version of my own life, and the world of FOUND, reflected back to me through a funhouse mirror! But it's also a thrill to see new crowds continue to be introduced to the project, potential recruits for our FOUND army. And the chorus of one song in particular really strikes a chord: *"I just want to do something that I love/ and do it with people that I love."* I'm so grateful for the group of awesome, dedicated friends who've carried FOUND forward with me over the past 13 years. It's been a total D.I.Y. labor of love, and the magazine only exists because of their energy and selflessness.

Looking back, it's not hard to see just how fully FOUND has changed my life. Through the finds themselves, I've explored what it means to be human; from our time on the road, I've made lifelong friends and found endless adventure. If life is about finding connection with the people we share the world with, I'm counting my riches.

I want to thank every person who's sent us a find, read one of our magazines, sold one of our books at their store, been to one of our events, and showed us kindness in our travels. And for those of you discovering FOUND for the first time, I hope you'll join in, keep your eyes to the ground, and send in your finds.

The book in your hands contains our favorite pages from the magazine's four early issues: FOUND #1, FOUND #2, FOUND #3, and FOUND #4. After putting out 50,000 to 100,000 copies of each, we're retiring these issues from print, but they'll live on here. Enjoy!

I've dedicated this book to my buddy Woody Hilboldt in Ozark, Alabama, who I've still never met in person, but speak to every year around the holidays, an annual tradition that gives me more satisfaction than I can really explain. I look forward to having a drink with Woody in person one day, and I'll tell you what, dear readers and finders, I also look forward to one day having a drink with you.

 PEACE—  DAVY

*FOUND Magazine's Brande Wix and Sarah Locke join me in the FOUND House basement, July 2014.*

Davy —

Brandy Hilboldt Allport here. (My father is Woody from Ozark, Alabama.) Y'all "met" a few years ago when I read about Found in some odd place — this was before the article in the N.Y. Times - etc. What you were/are doing sounded so, well, neat (that sounds as nerdy as neat-o). — It's hard to write to someone who reads letters all the time. — Anyway, I mentioned it to him, and that Christmas I opened a wrapped package to find a pile o' Found-related stuff. Your books are easier to find now, and a lot more people know about them, but Daddy likes to say "he knew you when." You are a regular part of our family's Christmas season now. "Don't forget to call Davy." The sticker is on my calendar (no PDA or blackberry for me, and the T-shirt you signed gets worn, too. I always forget exactly what it says until someone behind me in line reads it aloud "Brandy rocks." It is so nice to hear that out of the blue.

---

*Part of a letter from Woody Hilboldt's daughter Brandy from 2009.*

# FOUND

## magazine

## #1

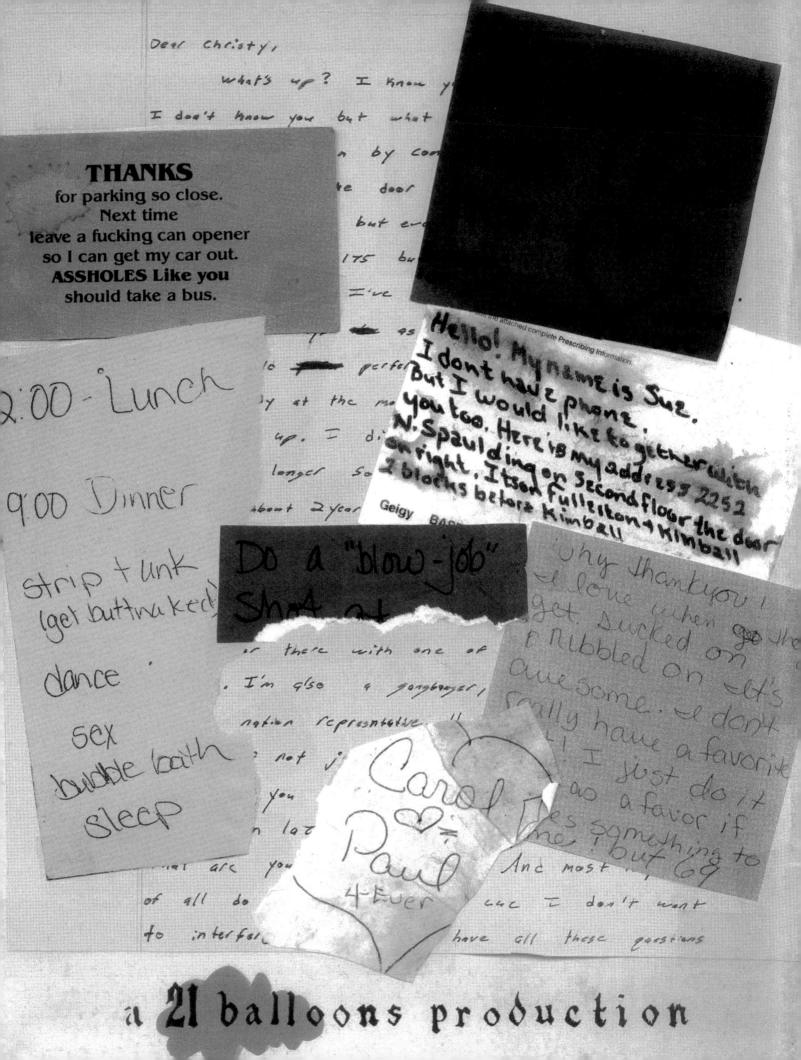

a 21 balloons production

248.4
C

To my parents
Matsu and Vernon Crawford
who have taught me much

And to my wife, Sylvia
who adventures with me in this
complex sphere of Christian life

ADVENTURES

FOUND by Davy Rothbart

i found this on the basketball court at 18th and state, chicago.
i like the idea of an author and his wife as a pair of adventurers.

27

# FOUND Magazine

WEB-SITE DESIGN by JASON BITNER

JOSH FENTON
USHER

ELDAD Z. MALAMUTH
BLUE BOMBER

LARRY TACKUS
TREASURE HUNTER

JOHNNY GRUBB
RHYME SAYER

JIM THOMPSON
NIGHT WATCHMAN

BRANDE WIX
THE GOOD DOCTOR

SONNY TURSKI
THE TERROR

VONTEEGO CUMMINGS
POSTER BOY

JOSEPH MOTON
PASTOR

AARON DENNIS
SPIRITUAL ADVISOR

LOVE-BLISSFUL DIVINE PERSON

COVER DESIGN by WOUND CRUST PRESS CHICAGO

LIAM MURPHY
MOTIVATIONAL SPEAKER

MATT LIVIDINI
NIGHT WATCHMAN

STARLEE KINE
SCOUT

A.J. WILHELM
KODACHROMES

JULIE SHAPIRO
CROUPIER

SETH WENIG
BALL BOY

JOSH NOEL
EMERGENCY LIAISON

RACHEL FREY
BARBER

MARLIN FLORIDA
SCALPER

PAUL REDMOND
BOSS

POPCORN PETE
PROMISED GOD-MAN

NICOLE SCHUDE
TRIPLE AGENT

DOUG BAIR
CLOSER

GULLIVER GOLD
STUNT DRIVER

GABE NOEL
NUMEROLOGIST

BARBARO GARBEY
DESIGNATED HITTER

ELIZABETH SANGER
NAVIGATOR

DAVY ROTHBART
POINT GUARD

TONY LIGAMENT
SHUT THE FUCK UP GODDAMN BITCH!!!

A 21 Balloons Production.

What up. Welcome to FOUND Magazine!

Why do I love FOUND stuff? I get high off driving around this country and talking to people, watching them, listening in on their conversations. *Feeling* them. There's no better way to really feel someone than to read a note they've written filled with subtle shades of what they really want and what they're most afraid of. FOUND stuff can be at once hilarious, beautiful and heartbreaking.

So read on. These are things people found. We'd love for you to join in—find stuff and send it to us! Pick up every scrap of paper you see tumbling down the street; four out of five won't be anything too interesting, but I promise you that fifth one is always something amazing.

Madd love to everyone who's helped out with this first issue. Special shouts to my D.C. playaz, the Ace Deuce + Ypsi Zoo, New Mexico crew, all my Chi-town Hustlas, everyone reprezintin' out in Cali (Ed in L.A.—good lookin' out with *80 More Days*), and 21 big ups to the East Coast—what up New York, what up Philly.

Hope you enjoy this. Write or e-mail us! Holla holla!

Peace out for now. DAVY —*DAVY ROTHBART*, point guard, FOUND Magazine

2: alex

look, U need to drop it, Vanessa is making you do this, if She want's to box, wont she bring it on, in front of the school, That spooked ass bitch. look alex U were nice and now this one girl made U change, I suggest U leave her, cause she is going to make something happen to one of yo family, cause my cousin does witch craft and she said that vanessa just wants U to be hurt. if U don't change I'm never Speaking to U.

DROP IT!

FOUND by Jorge Just

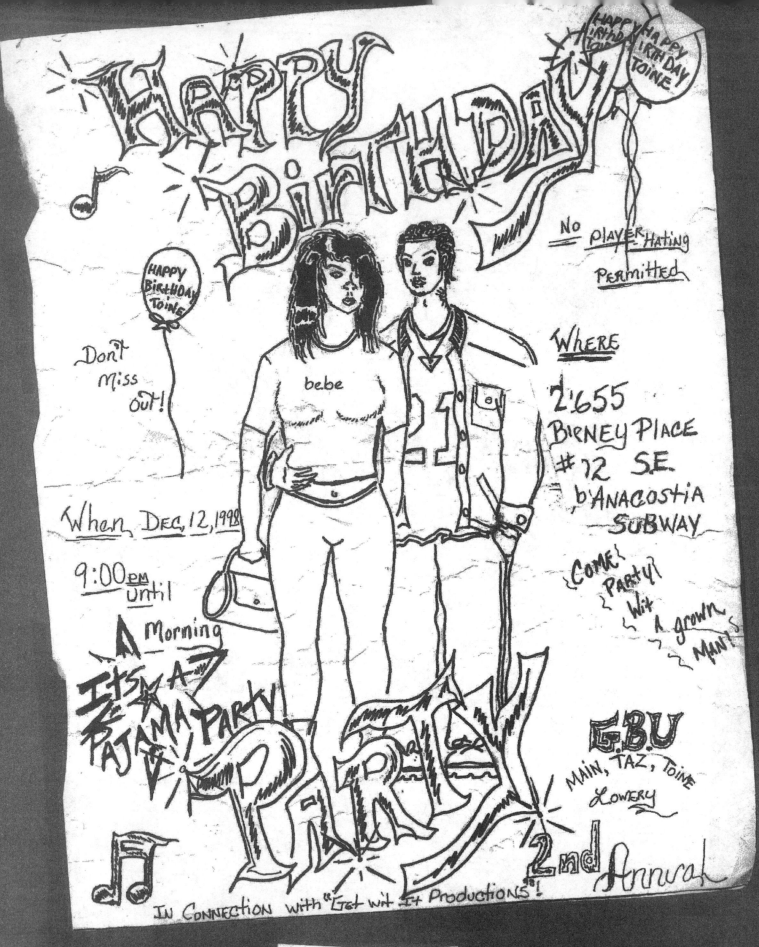

**A GROWN MAN**

FOUND by Gulliver Gold

South-East Washington, D.C.

I found this flyer taped up next to a drinking fountain on the U. of M. campus in April of 1998. O.K., I know it would be really easy to make fun of this dude, and I'm not too sure if I like his tone at times -- "I have a hearty sense of humor (those who do not, need not apply)" -- but all the same I've got to say that in a strange, desperate way, wallpapering every stairwell and kiosk on campus with these personal ads feels to me a courageous act.

FOUND by Gulliver Gold

# Looking for love?

## (I sure am.)

But what is love anyway? Is it just the physical nature of the beast? Perhaps. But more so, it's being able to watch a scary movie with someone knowing that if something happens, you'll be there to protect them. It's being able to call that person in the wee hours of the morning "just cuz" and know that person won't get angry at you for calling so late. It's brushing that stray piece of hair from their face, not because it bothers you, but because it hides their true beauty.

Sure, that's what I want. It's so easy isn't it? If it is that easy, I wouldn't have to write this......

So here goes. I'm 5'8"(-ish) Asian guy looking for someone to watch a movie and eat ice cream with. You like sports? I like sports. Pool, darts, rock climbing, racquetball, snowboarding, ultimate, skating, you name it. I have a hearty sense of humor (those that do not, need not apply), and I like aminals. If anything, we can always go have hot chocolate(since I never got used to the taste of coffee) and reminisce about the 80's.

There I said it.

- lovelost@umich.edu

31

# CHEESEBURGER IN PARADISE

FOUND by Carly Ptak

THE AUTHOR OF THIS travel log was probably mortified when she realized she had forgotten it on the airplane that brought her home. There wasn't much reason to be. Aside from a few afternoon screws with "Eric," astonishingly little happens during this eight-day trip to Hawaii, which includes four trips to McDonald's, four more to a place called Cheese Burger in Paradise, lots of shopping and plenty of touristy gawking (even if they missed half the Kodak Hula Show because they had a hard time finding it).

## Hawaii
### Feb. 9-17th 1999

THOUGH THESE PAGES prove the author enjoyed Hawaii, this log is an indictment of sorts. It is filled with details of where and what she ate and description of the junk she bought ("a little wood totem pole guy for my nic-nak shelf"). Mix in a few references to "making love" and watching TV (they returned to the hotel one night to watch *ER*) and you have the very America the rest of the planet rails against. There is hardly an observation of the external world in these pages except when the author says that every American should see Pearl Harbor, though now that the movie is out, she would probably figure that's good enough. If we rely solely on this log, we would presume that nothing interesting happened to this couple for their eight days in Hawaii except the morning when Eric awoke "with one of his headaches."

SO WHY is the log itself interesting? Because it is true. Because it meant so much to the author. In these pages, her dreams comes true, even if they are mundane. Toward the end, Eric announces they can return to Hawaii in five years ("yea!"). They're gonna work their asses for five years to get back here, eat more food they could eat at home and buy more crap? Sigh. Whatever makes you happy I suppose.

*--Josh Noel*

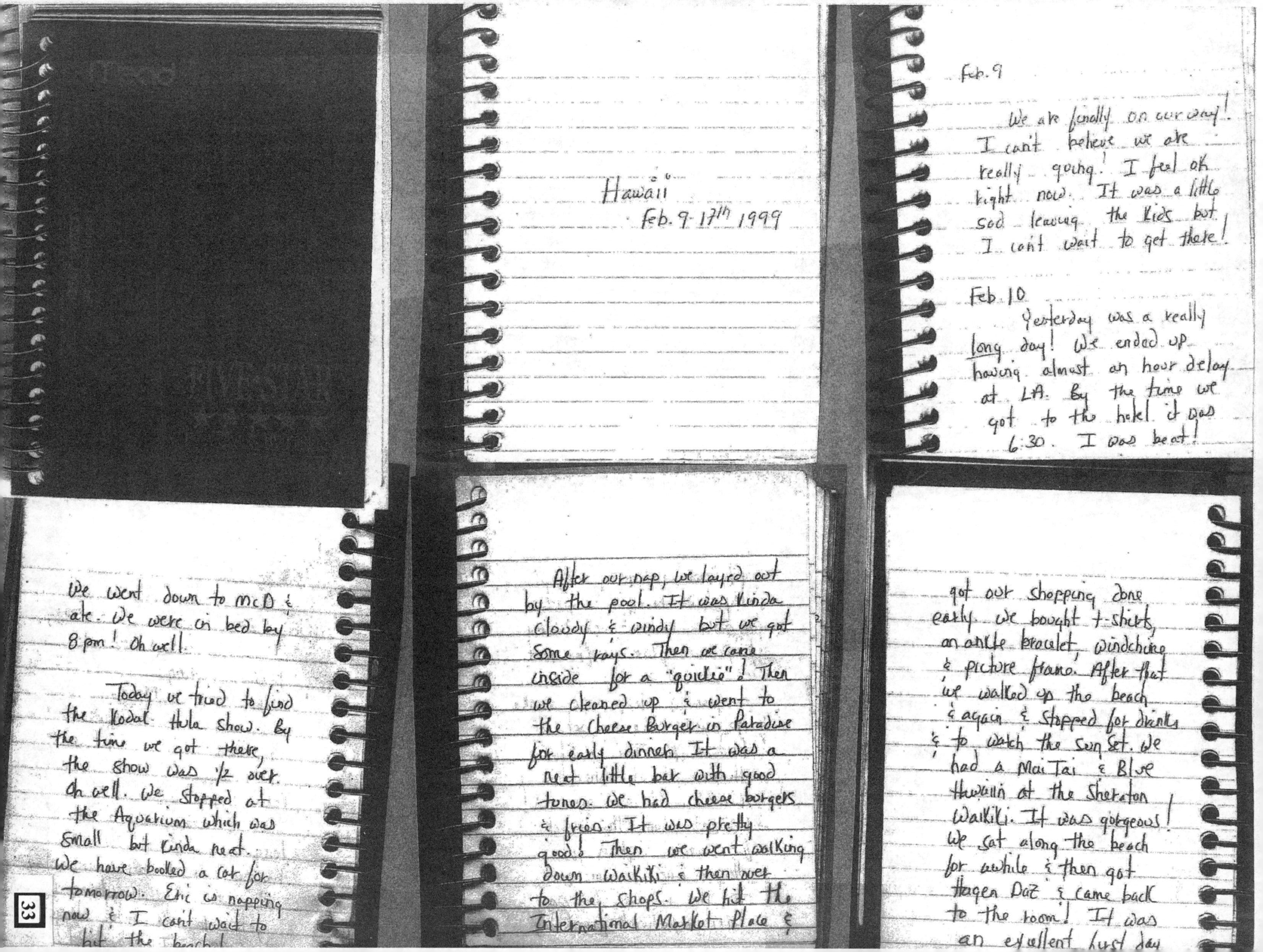

Feb. 9

We are finally on our way! I can't believe we are really going. I feel ok right now. It was a little sad - leaving the kids but I can't wait to get there!

Feb 10

Yesterday was a really long day! We ended up having almost an hour delay at LA. By the time we got to the hotel it was 6:30. I was beat.

**Hawaii**

Feb. 9-17th 1999

We went down to McD's at. We were in bed by 8pm! Oh well.

Today we tried to find the local hula show. By the time we got there, the show was 1/2 over. Oh well. We stopped at the Aquarium which was small but kinda neat. We have booked a lot for tomorrow. Eric is napping now & I can't wait to hit the beach

got our shopping done early. We bought t-shirts, an ankle bracelet, windchime & picture frame. After that we walked up the beach & again & stopped for drinks & to watch the sun set. We had a Mai Tai & Blue Hawaii at the Sheraton Waikiki. It was gorgeous! We sat along the beach for awhile & then got Hagen Daz & came back to the room! It was an excellent first day

After our nap, we layed out by the pool. It was kinda cloudy & windy but we got some rays. Then we came inside for a "quickie"! Then we cleaned up & went to the Cheese Burger in Paradise for early dinner. It was a neat little bar with good tunes. We had cheese burgers & fries. It was pretty good! Then we went walking down Waikiki & then went to the shops. We hit the International Market Place &

33

Dinner & the sunset was awesome. The band played "tiny bubbles" twice. I had a drink called a Scorpion & it was really really good. We ok already back in the room getting ready to watch ER.

Feb 12
Today we went back to Cheese Borget in Paradise for breakfast. It was ok. After that we went

---

Started w/ introducing the King & Queen. Then they took the pig out of the ground. Then we sat on the ground at low tables to eat. The food was good but I was afraid I'd get a tummy ache so I ate cautiously. After dinner was the Hula Show. That was neat! Then we took the bus back & got home around 10:30. It was long!

---

quick breakfast at McD & we were off to Pearl Harbor. I think this was my 3rd time. Still sad & something every American should see. After that we headed for the North Shore. We spent the afternoon at Sunset Beach. It was gorgeous but the waves weren't very big. Now we are off to a Sunset Dinner at Sheraton Moreana. (p2)
                                    Moreana

---

we played out on Waikiki & then came back with & McDs & ate on Deck. Then we made love & I just got out of the shower. Tonight we are going to a Luau

The Luau was cool but chilly. I have never been cold in Hawaii but I was last night! We got to the site right at sunset. We got our picture taken & had a drink. Then it

---

& I have finally settled down a little. It has started to become the vacation I always dreamed it would be!

Feb. 11
Happy b'day to me! What a way to turn 28. It doesn't even feel like my b'day!
We were up at 7am to get ready. We caught the car rental shuttle at 8am to get our car. Then we had a

---

shopping again at International Market Plate. We bought another frame we're going to put one to Meg. Some perfume that Nikki wanted me to get, & a flowered shirt for Eric. We also bought a little Good Luck Hula guy for my nic-nel shelf. After that we played video games & then changed into our suits. We also called home & Meg said all was well.

This morning we tried to go to breakfast at a little place I remembered from last time. However, when we got there, the line was out the door! We ended up at the Sunset Terrace at the Outrigger Waikiki. It was very good & we sat practically on the beach. After that we did some more shopping & got our pictures taken by some guy with exotic birds.

The pictures are funny. Eric's turned out better than mine but we bought all of them anyway. Then we went to the Honolulu Zoo. It was pretty nice for the middle of a city. It's gorgeous but it may again. After that we layed out by the pool & read. The hotel arcade has Ms PacMan so I played a few games. Now we are ready to go to dinner but the

lock box in the room is broken so we are waiting for maintenance. I hope they don't take too long.

Well, it took long enough that we decided just to go back to Cheese Burger in Paradise. Then we sat on Waikiki & took songs pictures. Then we walked down to Sunset Terrace where we saw earlier they had happy hour Mai Tai's for $2.50. They were

We got up fairly early today & had breakfast at Denny's. Then we decided to catch the Bus for Hanauma Bay. We got there around 11:00 we layed out all afternoon. I considered snorkeling for the very first time! It was fun but cold & hard to maneuver everything. I got a toe cramp & it was hard not step on the coral. But it was really neat &I

Saw some pretty fish. We bought a couple more t-shirts there & then were back by 3:30. I got tired at from just walking up that hill? That place has got to be the most beautiful place I have ever seen! When we got back I fell asleep for a little bit. Then we got ready & went to dinner. We were going to go to this Italian place M.O.E.T. had been to before but

good too. So we had a few of these & walked back & sat on the beach for a while longer. What an excellent vacation!

Feb. 15

Today Eric woke up with one of his headaches. He went back to sleep until 9am. I got up then & went to McD's. I brought breakfast to him while he layed down. We stayed in the room until 11:00. I finished my second book. After that we walked the strip again. Shopping shops & eating lunch at Taco Bel. We talked about going home. I miss the

pets but I am not ready to leave. He said we could come back in 5 yrs. if I wanted. Yea! After that we layed out on our last time on Waikiki. It was gorgeous & the wind finally died down. I even went in the water for a few minutes. We just got (cleared up & are deciding on where to go for dinner.

We went to the Lovers St. Fish (o. Those were lined up outside at 6pm but he got seated right away. I had lobster & steak & a Maitai. It was really good. Then we got ice cream at Baskin Robbins & headed to the beach for the sunset. It was spectacular of course. We walked along the beach for awhile & then played those games for a little bit. Now we ate an out

when we got there it was booked! Luckily some guy on the street handed us a thing about another Italian place called Spencers. It was excellent! It was a great little place with excellent food. We played Jimmy Buffet on the jukebox & Dean Martins "That's Amore." I had incredible cheese ravioli w/ mushrooms & Eric had chicken parmician. We are going back one more before we leave. Then

bathed & the sunset & took pictures. Then we came back to the room early to make love.

I have only one full day left! I am so sad. I don't want to leave. It is way too wonderful here!

Pi's. Surprisingly I didn't get a tummy ache after the lobster & food deal.

Feb. 16
I am so sad! Our time here has come to a close! I got a little fatty eyed but I haven't cried yet!

This morning we woke awake early. Luckily Erica's headache was gone. We got up & had our last breakfast at Cheese Burger in Paradise. One of my plans to live here included getting a job there! After that we used to

the beach for a few minutes to collect more sand. Then we decided to hang out in the room as long as we could. Check out was at noon. We made love, took showers & packed. Then we checked out & put our luggage in storage for the day & caught the bus to Sea Life Park. It was a long ride, but we decided it was the most beautiful side of the island. We

wished we'd have known earlier & we'd have kept the last 6 day to go back. It was gorgeous! The scenery was incredible & park was neat. It was sorta a mini Sea World. There was a lighthouse, whales & parasailers. The park itself was neat but kinda small. It looked gorgeous & guard but there wasn't much to it. We took pictures & saw two dolphin

shows & we're done in a couple hours. We came back & had our last dinner at Spinners. Cheese Ravioli. Excellent! Then we watched our last sunset (boohoo) took our last pictures & got some ice cream. Now we are all changed, re packed & waiting for the airport shuttle. It was a fabulous vacation & I am very sad to leave!

Ankle Bracelet $5.00
3 t-shirts $10.99
2 Frames
1 fish
1 fish chime
Perfume
Hawaiian Shirt
1 CD
2 t-shirts (Hananea)
1 totem pole guy

These ten musical gems came to me by way of Greg Warner in Phoenix. A few years back Greg's friend Nigel Morgan found an unmarked cassette-tape on the street in Ypsilanti, Michigan which contained a string of minute-long booty-rap anthems. Apparently some thugged-out white kids with a drum machine had put together a demo tape.

I've given these dudes the name Ypsilanti All-Starz and titled each of the songs. My favorites are "Yo' Shit Be Up in My Face," "Yo' Ass is So Fine" and "Wiggle on the Flo'."

What's remarkable to me is the earnestness with which these songs are performed. Some folks disagree with me but I don't think the Ypsilanti All-Starz are aware of their comic brilliance.

This tape circulated around south-east Michigan for two years, copied and recopied. Then Greg played it for someone who said, "I know these guys!" This person said it was not a satire, these guys were out to make it big. They were fully confident they'd sell a million records. If it means anything to the Ypsilanti All-Starz, I'd buy one.

– Davy Rothbart

THE YPSILANTI ALL-STARZ

FOUND by Nigel Morgan

1. Wave Yo' Booty in the Air (Bounce)
2. Yo' Ass is So Fine
3. Ass-Whomp Bustin' Out of Yo' Back Pocket
4. Yo' Shit Be Up In My Face
5. Wiggle On the Flo'
6. Booty Time
7. Taste That Booty Flava'
8. Booty Shake (a capella)
9. Your Booty Don't Stop
10. (She Got a) Big Fat Booty
11. Wave Yo Booty in the Air (remix)
12. Yo' Ass is So Fine (heartfelt remix)
13. Ass-Whomp (re-dux)
14. Yo' Shit Be Up in My Face (abandoned)

**80 MORE DAYS**

Larissa found this note in Los Angeles outside a night-club that caters to transvestites. I absolutely love the author's willingness to go anywhere as long as she/he can be with Yevette. This is about the most beautiful FOUND note I've ever come across. –D.R.

FOUND by Larissa Williams

Yevette,                                    2-19-01

   Girl, when I left your House I trued to Go to the Store and Got arrested in the perking Pot, I dudn't Even Get to Get in the club. I'm Sorry if I Got on your narves but Girl you Know how your baby Sister Get after I take a hit. Yevette, if you decide to Go back to North Caralina I want to Go too Even jirst if I have to be moved out I tired of being a Gay-Boy. and yes I'll leave my Lover jor it. at lease I stell hpd 300.00 dollars left when I Got cought. Don't worrie I have All 4 eyes on the feauture. Girl I Brough Some Blue contacts and they look Good. Also if you Need Some money to move let me know. I might Gee out in 80 more days. So wait for my Next Letter to find out what happends. Big Sis I love you and Happy-Birthday and hang in their you a very strong Woman.

                              Love You Baby Sis

                                 Diva ♥

The following are cars that appeared to be pursuing me. From time to time I took down the license plate numbers. Yesterday April 5, 1999 was interesting as I came home from work, a man drove from around the corner at approximately 165th Woodlawn the license plate read:

April 5, 1999 - SWATOSH

Aorll 6, 1999 - XS N OS

Feb 29, 1998

45B 1449 - Indiana

December 7, 1998

RIETVLD

I've decided that I must tell my story. Though, there are some who hope that I remain silent. If I do, they will have won. My story has to be told, so that this madness does not continue. It is for my students that I tell my story. It is for.my family, that I tell my story. It is for my sanity, that I tell my story. Many will try to convince you that I am having illusions, but if you dig deep you will get the true story. I am only one person going against several reputable systems. But nevertheless, I must tell my story. I am a public school teacher, with the Chicago Board of Education. My husband is also. We had lived quietly in the Village of South Holland for the past five years, until last year.

F177-477.

November 3, 1998

NVR SLP 2

EZ 1375

PAY IT UP

DEcember 3, 1998

PMT 197
D 914 899

XCK 937

PU SSE 24

SLAMMEN

MS MC D 1

JCN YG 8

Y SA 379

761 RWD - Michigan

45K 6263 - Indiana

Y BEBRIJ

CRN 806

B 406 -695

XPK 197

5480 NL

## VANITY PLATES

### FOUND by Dave McGuire

The 40-page letter that accompanies this list of license plates is the most bizarre, ludicrous, and chilling thing I've ever read. An upcoming special issue of FOUND Magazine will be devoted entirely to this license-plate woman. If you're intrigued and you want to read the whole thing, contact us!     -D.R.

People with vanity licence plates that read KKKK, KKX269 DY B, DY J, DEAD 995, Princs DY, McVay, BMB and today, a licence plate drove in front of me that said AVENGER.

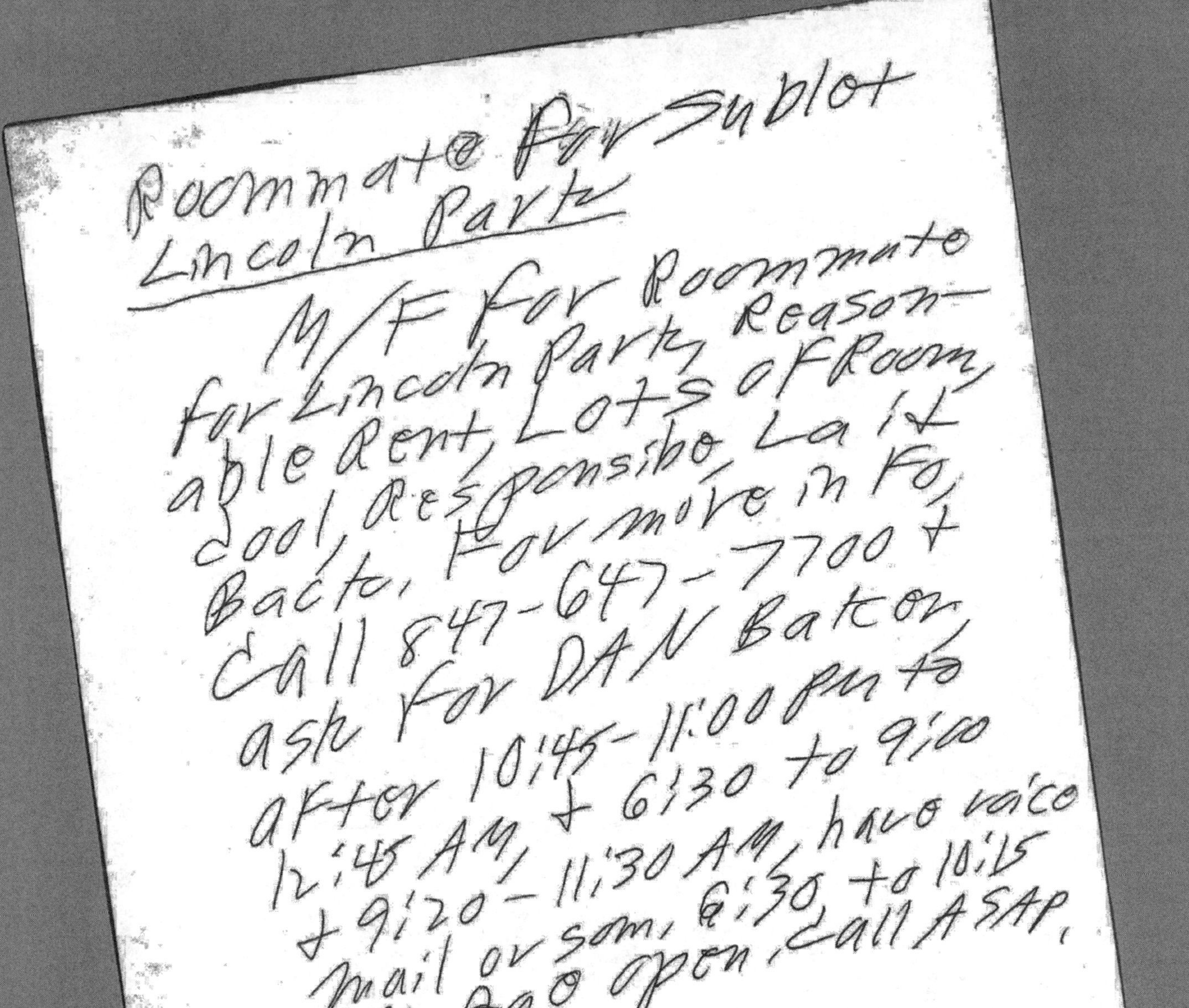

Roommate For Sublot<br>
Lincoln Park<br>
M/F for Roommate<br>
for Lincoln Park, Reason-<br>
able Rent, Lots of Room,<br>
cool, Responsibo, La it<br>
Backa, For move in Fo,<br>
Call 847-647-7700 +<br>
ask for DAN Baker,<br>
after 10:45-11:00 pm to<br>
12:45 AM, & 6:30 to 9:00<br>
& 9:20-11:30 AM, have voice<br>
mail or som. 6:30 to 10:15<br>
AM, Ago open. Call ASAP.<br>
8 1/4

***MY VERY PRIVATE QUALITY TIME***

FOUND by Gulliver Gold

There's a few strange things going on here but my biggest question is this: what exactly does this guy *do* every morning from 9:00 to 9:20?!

Jason,

Congrats!
Tonight's event was just a
tradition of the house. It was
not gay even though you had to
pull down your pants. At least
you don't have to show it to all
the actives! Snot your pledge
master.. the meaning = To
prove your manhood and
that you are not a boy.
But we want to see it
You swear we want was done
You swear we was done it
Your dick.! Everyone
but none of us are gay!
Aside from all this, I've
never seen anyone that I've
never seen come out of you

ET

since 7st
Your 7st Keep up positive
preached, Keep a here a
the effect on it. I tell u cause!
not gay even though your cause?
attitude of things. One you long?
Its all worth it! Just long
Take word for it! I want your
in there it w. me
Take me dinner somewhere
house we are free
so you took few party
when you take better care
It's a great me qualifications
so to know some besting bright
get me to answer I'll go.
for me mean shit.

Love + Respect,

*765

# More Respect

*by Joe L̶̶̶̶̶̶̶̶*

Respect is needed towards MARILYN MANSON, KORN and TOOL which are all underground bands which means they want to make it to the top without being supported by the t.v or the raido but there not the only ones doing this.

Then theres MARILYN MANSON a man of his word in my eyes because I respect him alot because MARILYN MANSON stands for your good side and your bad side like Mariyln Monroe and Charles Mason and thats allhes tring to repusent along with him being the ANTI CHRIST SUPERSTAR which means your against god and the devil but you wirshop yourself. MR. MARILYN MANSON is very racist because his music is intended for whites only and im glad its for white people only because its about time theres something for one race only .

MARIYLN MANSON made over two million dollars alone just by going on the 1996 DEAD TO THE WORLD TOUR.

KORN and TOOL are among alot of other underground bands like THE DEFTONS and PANTERA "but the fans are great to us" says Jon Davis the leader of the five man band KORN. Then theres TOOL a band that tours alot with KORN but both bands feel that there getting the respect they need but in my eyes theres no respect for them where i live but i hope that will soon change.

MORE RESPECT

FOUND by Susannah Felts

43

# Ruchira Avatar Adi Da Samraj

*"I Reveal The Divine Person, Who <u>Is</u> The Heart Itself, and That Is The Real God Within The Heart's Own Felt Bewilderment"*

Avatar Adi Da Samraj is the Love-Blissful Divine Person, Appearing in the world in the form of a human being. He is the <u>Promised God-Man,</u> the Divine Liberator Who has been expected and prayed for throughout the ages. Avatar Adi Da Offers to everyone the Grace of a direct Spiritual relationship with Him -- through the practice of the Way of Adidam.

Enjoy a Multimedia Presentation About the Spiritual Work of Avatar Adi Da Samraj, and the Religion of the Way of the Heart: with longtime devotees
**Anthony Costabile and Eileeen McCarthy**

---

## Tuesday November 14, 2000
## Ann Arbor "YMCA" @ 350 S. Fifth Avenue (near Williams)
## 7 PM in the Zonta Room
## $25 at the door -- $15 for students

## Website: www.adidam.org

44

**PROMISED GOD-MAN # 2**

FOUND by Davy Rothbart

New York, NY

FOUND by dan zatkovich, janice smith, & dan smith

*DAN ZATKOVICH EXPLAINS....* So janice's brother dan comes into town (san diego) for a couple days before leaving for china for a year. we take him to a pizza place in ocean beach and we're just sitting there eating. there's this door near our table that separates the kitchen from the dining area and dan points out the sign on it—CAUTION!! DOOR WILL SWING OPEN AND NAIL YOU! It's pretty funny to all of us. i mean, usually you see a sign like that and it says, "Careful, door opens quickly" or "watch for swinging door." something about the "and nail you" part just seems hilarious. it provides such a concrete image; its so full of malice. janice says, "hey, that would be great for davy's magazine." we have a lengthy debate, the 3 of us, about what exactly constitutes "FOUND." i mean, does it have to be blowing down the street? or can it just be a sign you see hanging somewhere?

eventually we decide that one of us is gonna have to grab the sign. actually, janice and her brother decide that *I* have to grab the sign. so when we're done eating, we're kind of hanging out, waiting for a quiet moment by the kitchen door. for some reason i get real nervous about getting caught. i mean, realistically, they're not gonna have me arrested or anything. but there is a real potential for a big scene and some serious embarassment. finally there's no employees around. i go over to the door and take out the bottom two tacks. janice and her brother are watching from the front door, ready to book out of there if any of the employees swoop in on me.

# AUTION !! DOOR WILL SWING OPEN AND NAIL YOU!

from up close i can see how much time someone put into making the sign—there's pencil underneath, like they did a rough draft, putting it down, erasing, putting it down, and then once they got it right they retraced their letters with a thick pen or thin marker. i've got no idea why I'm so goddamn nervous, but i keep looking all around, making sure the coast is still clear, then i turn back to pull out the top two thumb-tacks and WHAM!!! the door flies open and fuckin *NAILS* me!! a dude comes out of the kitchen with a platter full of food and drinks, and he's like, "oh, sorry," and he walks off toward a table in the next room. my head and my face are throbbing from the blow. i yank the sign down and walk woozily outside—janice and dan are squealing dond collapsing with laughter, practically peeing themselves. looking back on things, now that the bruise has healed up a bit, i can imagine how funny it must have been to them. i got so caught up in how COOL and FUNNY the sign was, i forgot about the practical nature of its message. davy, tell people to be careful collecting FOUND stuff—it could get them killed.

DEAR ELSIE
HI!! WHY ARE YOU SUCH a
WOMEN and THATS EXACTLY
WHAT I NEED A
WOMEN JUST LIKE
YOU. IT LIKE YOUR A HEART
and I'm a soul and together
we cannot function. we were
~~[scribbled out]~~ Brought to this earth
For each other you just don't
Know. But remember I'm here and
willing. XOXO

*YOU JUST DON'T KNOW*

**FOUND by Anonymous**

# LYNDA BARRY

## COLLECTIONS

LYNDA — BARETTE

**Panel 1:** PART OF SCHOOL THIS YEAR IF YOU HAVE MISS RONSON IS YOU HAVE TO START COLLECTING SOMETHING LIKE IT'S YOUR HOBBY. MARLYS IS TRYING TO DECIDE WHAT.

**Panel 2:**

ROCKS? TOO AVERAGE. CERTAIN ANIMAL THINGS LIKE PIG FIGURINES OR FROGS OR EVEN PLASTIC HORSES? ALSO TOO AVERAGE.

**Panel 3:** ONE IDEA SHE HAD WAS, IN MY OPINION, GENIUS: THINGS FOUND ON THE SIDEWALK. I AM A PERSON WHO IS ALWAYS LOOKING DOWN, FINDING THINGS OTHER PEOPLE DROPPED: PENS, COMBS, LETTERS THAT SAY, "I love you so much, please don't leave me."

**Panel 4:**

YOU LIKE THAT IDEA? HAVE IT.
SERIOUS?
HECK, I GOT SO MANY IDEAS. HAVE IT.

**Panel 5:** ON MY WAY. TO WINKY'S LIQUOR STORE TO GET A BOX FOR MY NEW COLLECTION, MY EYES WERE SO EXCITED. I FOUND: A BLUE BARETTE SHAPED LIKE A SCOTTIE DOG, TWO PERFECT CIGARETTES, A STIFF, RUN-OVER GLOVE GIVING THE PEACE SIGN, AND A COUPON – "BUY 3, GET ONE FREE" – FOR CHICKEN DELIGHT.

**Panel 6:**

HOW YOU GONNA ORGANIZE IT?
WHAT DO YOU MEAN?
YOU KNOW, ALPHABETICAL, CRONOLOGICAL, DEWEY DECIMAL.
OLDE SKULL POPPER

**Panel 7:** MARLYS SAYS ORGANIZATION AND PRESENTATION ARE VERY IMPORTANT TO MISS RONSON, IF I WANT A DECENT GRADE ON MY COLLECTION. ALSO WHAT IF THE PEOPLE START CALLING ME "SCROUNGE"? SHE KEPT SAYING THINGS THAT MADE ME FEEL DOUBTFUL UNTIL I FIGURED OUT SHE JUST WANTED HER IDEA BACK.

**Panel 8:**

NO.
WELL, CAN I AT LEAST HAVE ONE OF THE CIGS?

## the FOUND INTERVIEW

**lynda**: I was always pretty much of a scrounge. Part of it might have been bugs. I really really liked bugs and when you are look around at ants on the ground or potato bugs or caterpillers you sort of will run into trash and some of the trash will be interesting. At least in my neighborhood this was true. I remember finding brown paper bags with glue wads inside. The glue sniffer's corner. And a whole block of houses was empty up the street. We all went inside, dug through things. Opened drawers. Bums were there. People set corners on fire. Peed on things. Made out. Places like that totally magnetized me. I loved finding things there that would give me a weird chill. A hairbrush. A pile of letters. And there was a dump, an unofficial dump, actually it was a mile long stretch along a ravine down the hill where people threw things out, and I used to go poking around there, looking for tossed off weirdness. This is when I was really little, like around eight. I would walk down there by myself, digging around in the piles of garbage. Finding suspenders and stoves and photos of people. There was a store called Pay'n'Save near my house and I used to look around their garbage area, trying to find broken things they threw out. Nothing really good comes to mind, I just liked looking. It relieved a certain kind of itch I didn't know any other way to scratch.

**davy:** *what is your attraction to FOUND stuff? what does FOUND stuff mean to you?*

**lynda:** I guess because it gives me something to imagine into both while on the prowl and after I find something. I especially like found notes and I used to keep them all together but my organizing has since exploded. I love conversation notes between two people in class. Two kinds of hand-writing ripping on a teacher. Mainly I like the story that smokes up from certain found things. And I like the collections of things one can put together. I collected playing cards found on the street with the eventual hope of getting a whole deck. A weird sort of life long game of solitare. I still run into the cards all over my house. No organization! When I was in college I nailed rows and rows of nails on one wall and then went out and picked up anything that was U-shaped and hung it on the nail upside down. Everything from tiny little twist-ties in a U shape to an actual letter U that fell off a marquee. I loved being able to pick a shape and look for it. This was twenty five years ago so I can't remember much about it except by the end of the year the wall looked amazing and no one could believe I found all the U- shapes on the street.

## Scrounging had everything to do with why I married a certain someone.

In high school I started to notice shoes in the road, a single shoe laying here or there and I would think about how the hell that happened. Who loses one shoe in the road and how? I used to stop my 1964 Valient and go get the shoe and throw it in my trunk. I loved opening my trunk and seeing all of these shoes that had no mates. I probably did it to be a way-out hippie and impress boys. But usually boys have nothing to do with why I scrounge. Although scrounging had everything to do with why I married a certain someone. I'm married to the KING of scrounging. My husband has furnished our house from dumps and alley-ways. He is always coming home with some insane thing he found. Once he brought home a stuffed grizzly bear head. Someone had cut it off of their bear-skin rug and put it out on the street with the trash. We dig the found lifestyle. I've been with people who were horrified when I bent to pick something up or slammed on the brakes to dig though a pile of trash on the side of the street. "You don't know where that has been" is either a nightmare or a dream statement depending on the person picking up the thing.

I think mainly it's two things that makes me love trash. One is the imagined story that comes with it (like who cut that bear head off the rug? How long did they think about it before they did it? What did they use to do it? Did they think a grizzly bear skin would be less offensive minus the head? What did people say after they saw the rug without the head?") The other is the feeling of rescuing some otherwise over- lookable thing from oblivion. That might be a way that I identify with trash. Understand trash. Empathize with trash. I will call it trash. "Found Object" is a nice term but it reminds me when I was in college and looked down on comics so much that I called what I did "Drawings with Words." Now I'm a cartoonist and a trash lady.

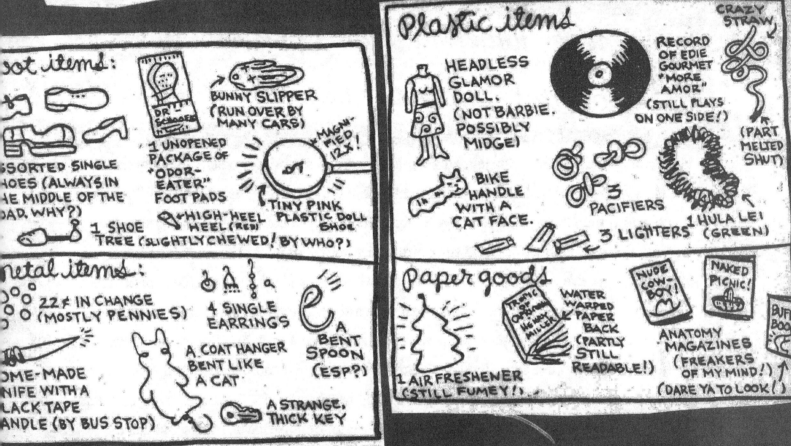

**davy:** *what are some of your favorite + most memorable things youve found?*

**lynda:** Well the first thing that always comes to mind is a tiny bowling bag purse that would have fit in my hand when I was about seven. It was perfect with a little zipper and it had five bucks in it. I found it in the woods, in this totally unexpected area that kids were using to race bikes around piles of dirt. I loved that bowling bag! It was green and white and made me feel huge. I remember finding porn all over the place. It's amazing how much porn is laying around certain neighborhoods. I never understood the migration of porn. How did it leave the indoors for the outdoors. How did it get under the lunchroom portable up at the school? I found a series of notes in a notebook a man and a woman had been writing each other over a year. She worked nights. He worked days. It ends with her writing LIES! LIES! LIES! all over the last pages. In a certain way my favorite or memorable thing is hard to identify because it's been a life of picking up trash. As I look around the room right now I can see that only the computer and stereo and other tech stuff are new. Mostly it's found or church rummage sale which is a paid-for kind of trash. About my favorite kind. My husband Kevin has a thing about push lawn mowers. He finds them set out for the trash man. We have eight of them in the basement, lined up like they were for sale. We do not have a mowable lawn. He has to struggle with himself to keep from picking up more.

*I never understood the migration of porn. How did it leave the indoors for the outdoors.*

He restores prairie. That's his job. He's a plant freak. So sometimes when a development is going in we go over to the planned site right before they start digging and find all the native plants and rescue them. This counts as found, I think, if you consider the rescue aspect of finding. Once I found a migrating song bird in the middle of down town Chicago, just standing in the street. He'd just come over lake Michigan and was pretty tired. I picked him up and put him in my purse because I'd just seen a show about bird smugglers so I knew birds could ride ok in a purse if they were in a small space. I took him home and he was feeling a lot better after some food and water. He was yellow and black. Kevin would have known what he was if he could have seen him but he was gone by the time Kevin got home. As I write this there is another found bird making a lot of noise. "Mr. Birdis" who is a sparrow with a dislocated wing we found in the back yard. We've had him for about a month. I dig Mr. Birdis!

One of the things I used to LOVE to do is take something really eye-catching that I didn't want any more and put it outside somewhere on display and see how long until it was "found". I used to love to take my penny jar and make tall stacks of pennies in funny places in alleys. The kind of places kids might look but adults would not. I loved walking and checking on the pennies. Seeing which of the stacks had been located.

52

3455 Charing Cross Rd.
Ann Arbor. MI 48108

## thought provokers:

PAIR OF PANTS WITH LONG YELLOW ROPE TIED TO THEM

A PAIR OF SUNGLASSES WITH BAND-AIDS ON THE EYES

A CAN OFF CHILI WITH "I'M JEFF'S!" WRITTEN ON THE TOP (FOUND UNDER A MAIL BOX)

A POTATO ON A BROKEN CAR ANTENNA (FRESH)

STUDLEY

A SCHOOL PICTURE WITH "STUDLEY" WRITTEN ON THE FRONT AND "I JUST PSYCHED YOU!" ON THE BACK

AN ASPERIN TIN WITH A TOOTH INSIDE., (SILVER FILLING)

DRAWN ON WITH BIC PEN

A RUBBER GLOVE WITH EYES! (WHY?)

**davy:** *could you talk about those 2 specific comics you did which dealt with FOUND stuff (scroungina). How did you pick marlys' sad post-winter finds?*

**lynda:** Well the name Scroungina came from being friends with a guy named Scrounge. When he phones, he always says, "Hey, it's Scrounge." so I started saying "Hey, it's Scroungina" and that name turned into something in the strip the day I went for a walk and notice all the left over stuff from the most recent thaw. In the midwest where the snow stays awhile and gets added to, there is this wild layering of trash that shows itself only once a year in true splendor. For some people spring is the cherry blossoms. For me it's all the hats, gloves, cans, and things that finally come out of the snow. When Kevin and I were first married his wedding ring flew off while he was sprinkling ashes on the icy walkway out front. A month and half later, he found the ring, right on the side of the walkway. We live on a well-walked street but no one saw it. Kevin's the kind of guy who looks down. My kind of guy.

## You have to be tender with other people's work.

**davy:** *does something qualify as FOUND if you know who it belongs to? like last summer i was staying with my friend at another friends house in michigan who was gone. my friend got drunk and the next morning i found on the dining table all these pained rap lyrics he'd written at 4 in the morning. i mean, i knew it was him who'd wrote them, but still, it felt like a FOUND find because when i read the lyrics new things about him were revealed to me, things i dont think he would have shared with me in any other way. does this still count as FOUND? it might be dangerous if it does qualify because then it might condone snooping: "look, i know you caught me reading your journal, but i FOUND it in your sock drawer!"*

**lynda:** To me that doesn't count as found at all because you know who did it so the story that normally comes from a found thing, *the wondering* which in some weird way is a kind of wondering about ourselves, I don't think that would be there if I knew who wrote it. It would be *something*, but it would be something else. It reminds me of a conversation I heard on the train between two teenage girls. One had the other's cassette and she wanted it back. The one holding the cassette said "I'll give it back to you only if you can give me one good reason besides the fact that it's yours." Your friend's rap makes me think of that. You have to be tender with other people's work. Especially when they write it in the middle of the night and they might have been drunk when they did it. You wouldn't treasure their barf, right? In a way something like that is as private as barf. Why it becomes less private than barf if you DON'T know who did it, I'm not sure, but it's different when you don't know the origin. The things in our house we've gotten from the neighbors aren't as light or lively because I can always feel the "true story" in the object. I know Tammy got that vase from someone she hated, put it on the trash pile, I took it from the trash pile (asking first) but I can always feel Tammy there and that relationship so in a way the vase will never be free of that thing. I like it less than a vase that could come from anywhere and any situation. A good piece of trash has just enough information to make you wonder but not so much to make you stop.

**davy:** *well, thanks a lot, lynda. Send us some FOUND stuff!*

**lynda:** I will! It was fun thinking about this.

*FOUND* Magazine. **A 21 Balloons Production.**

Get rich... Get famous... But also

CONTRIBUTE TO FOUND MAGAZINE

Yeah You!!!!

# FOUND Magazine

## needs your help

We are looking for FOUND stuff: love letters, birthday cards, kids' homework, to-do lists, ticket stubs, poetry on napkins, telephone bills, doodles—anything that gives a glimpse into someone else's life. Anything goes.

You will be credited in the magazine for your find!!!

You will be credited in the magazine for your find!!!

Yeah You!!!!

FOUND by ... YOU!

## How YOU can Help

1. Find Stuff On the city bus, at Kinkos, in recycling bins, on the street, in restaurants, by the printers at the computer center, in the ER waiting room, in the bowling alley parking lot, in the woods, in the prison yard. 2.Write the circumstances of your find. One sentence or a couple of paragraphs Where you found it, What city, the date, any reactions or interpretations you might have 3.Name your find. Your found item is your piece now, give it a name, as you would a piece of art

# 3455 CHARING CROSS ANN ARBOR, MI 48108
USA

It was February of '62' colder than a witches tit ina brass brassiere, and the ship I was aboard was anchored in the harbor of a small coastal town, that was the asshole of the world.

I had recently made PO3 (Petty Officer 3rd Class), and was also on the Chief's (Chief Petty Officer) shit list for what I don't even remember now. So I got stuck with Shore Patrol duty for a replentishment detail that was to meet the trucks full of fresh meat, milk, veggies at the fleet landing for loading into the utility boats.

The wind that day was like a knife that cut right through our heavy winter blues and peacoats. The water in the bay had been whipped into a nasty chop into which the bow of the boat would plunge, thus throwing up an icy spray, that found its way into the boat. It was a bitch of a ride, that made every soul in that fuckin' boat's life miserable.

The boat tied up at the quay and the sailors unassed it to stand around pissin' 'n moanin', and lightin' up smokes. Naturally the trucks were'nt there yet, so we all stood out in that cold wind freezin' our asses off.

Finally the goddamned trucks showed up and the sailors begun unloadin' 'em, 'n loadin' ~~the~~ up the boat. I was busy freezin' my ass off, 'n watchin' the sailors work, when I happened ta spot a couple a ragged assed kids over by one of the old shacks by the quay. They sure were a sad sorry lookin' bunch, but its a sight sailors see all over this mudball we call Earth.

One of the little fuckers hollered to me, "hey Joe ya got american cigarette for me?" So I motioned the little shit over and gave 'em one of my Humps (what we called Camels), the little shit could'nta been 8 or 9, but he could hack that fuckin' Hump. Me 'n the little fucker stood there smokin' for a bit 'n he looked up at me 'n said "I hungry Joe", shit I didn't have nothin' ta give that poor raggedassed kid. I looked over at the trucks and saw the workin' party unloadin' cartons of fresh milk in cases 'n frozen beef, 'n got me an idea. I told the kid ta go stand by the shack 'n wait for me, then walked over ta one of the trucks 'n grabbed a case of milk 'n one of beef, I toted 'em over ta the side 'o the shack 'n gave each 'o those sorry lookin' rugrats a hunk 'o beef 'n a carton a milk, 'n before each one scampered off they thanked me.

Givin' those kids that food was a courtmarshel offense, but fuckit I was'nt caught, 'n it made me feel good!

**HEY JOE**

FOUND by Shorty Smooth Dawson

E. S. (KRAUT) SWAGGER

I found these in one of the classrooms by the library (Cotton Correctional Facility, Jackson, Michigan).

*(Freedom, And why it's important to me.)*

This is really a hand subject for me to write about. Maybe because so much of my freedom has been taken, i can't determen between the two anymore. I can however describe the thing's i used to do and enjoy on a daily bases, and how being in prison has changed that for now.

      I guess you could say for me it's the little thing's i think about the most. Like really being able to drive a car some where. Or how about being able to go out with your friend's say to a club, or to a movie. How about hanging out at the house just you and your lady? Enjoying a little peace and serenity together? See these are thing's you probable don't give much thought to, but i think about evryday. It's like a vast wasteland caught in the middle of time. Your just dormant to the outside around you. Say me for instance I've been away for four and a half year's, you probable haven't noticed much change out there but i bet if i were to get out tomarrow I'd be lost as hell. Here's another example of a little thing you may take for granted useing the bathroom or your own shower for a change. We have to share are shower with 45 other people, and after 12:00am count has been takeing we are made to ask to use the restroom. If you don't ask and just go, well then you are subject to get a ticket which will in the end hurt you more than it will hurt them. Let me explane alittle. When and if you get a ticket you already know that you'll most lickly get seven day's top lock for it some of your good time taken so now your out date ain't what it use to be and you don't go home when you are supose to.

      I sit aroun all day and think about what it would be like to go out to the Mall, or take a walk in a park. Something that you probable look at everyday might mean the world to someone in here right about now. When's the last time you walked out of your house and really looked at what's out there, such as the flower's or the tree's in the front yard. Everyday when i go out side i see another building houseing 190 more people just like me. Not a street with car's diving down it or your friend next door mowing his lawn. Just a concrete jungle that's surrounding me. Ask yourself this when is the last time you hade to be in at 9:00 O'clock at night for good until the next day? Its something we have to do all year around. I guess what I'm trying to say is you, as i once did pretty much take everything for granted includeing life it's self. We get caught up in are everyday thing's that we forget about the flower's and the other little thing's that should mean so much to us. Give yourself a break, take the time to look around and enjoy all life has to offer befor it's taken from you someday.

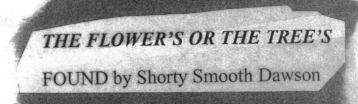

**THE FLOWER'S OR THE TREE'S**

FOUND by Shorty Smooth Dawson

Michigan Department of Corrections

**PRISONER STATIONERY**

4835-3110
CSJ-110

| TO: | | |
| --- | --- | --- |
| NAME | | |
| NO. AND STREET OR R.R. | | |
| CITY | STATE | ZIP |

| FROM: | |
| --- | --- |
| NAME | |
| NO. | LOCK |
| INSTITUTION | DATE |

**IN CORRESPONDENCE, USE NAME AND NUMBER ON YOUR LETTER AND ENVELOPE.**

IN 1979, I WAS residing in SanFransico. Given the pristenLey beautiful weather, I opted To Traverse hone on Foot one Evening.

The sky WAS ArrestingLy beautiFuL; The Night breeze carried the exotic fraygrance of A CINNAMON Tree. The Crisp, Soothing Night Air Served to remind me of other times - other place. I WAS ELated because I had just got paid.

Suddenly, I reached the Golden GAte Bridge. I had the SubLime feeLing that Something WAS Ashaw. upon closer inspection, I observed A MAN reading to JUMP. I Appraoched with caution.

"What's the matter, Sir," I Asked. "I have No income NO Job, Life the desolete man Exclaimed.

Being A SmaLL business man, I offered him A job.

That WAS 3 years ago. Now Bob works gainfuLLy For me. Last week, I promoted him to ASSistant manager.

I WAS glad that I opted To waLk that Night.

The End

By: D. Smith

**PROMOTION**

FOUND by Shorty Smooth Dawson

Dinner's over...

gourmet body paint

**Hotmail®** *trixie55@hotmail.com*                                    Messenger   Calendar   Help

Inbox   Compose   Address Book   Folders   Options

## Folder: Inbox

From:      Gina Gollan <silverone69@yahoo.com> Save Address - Block Sender
To:        trixie55@hotmail.com Save Address
Subject: stupid hotmail
Date:      Sun, 21 Jan 2001 22:46:59 -0800 (PST)
Reply          Reply All          Forward          Delete      Previous      Next      Close

hi.  i'm writing you from this yahoo address because
hotmail is being stupid and not letting me compose
messages.  please respond to the
silverone69@hotmail.com address.  on february 2nd i'm
going to be in the city for a concert.  you've
probably never heard of the band O.A.R.  they're not
something i would usually like, but i love them.  it's
weird.  i have a favor to ask you though.  the show is
an 18 and over show at the house of blues, and
obviously on february 2nd i will still be 17.  would
it be at all possible for me to borrow your id?
please? please? PLEASE?  please let me know soon,
because the concert is in 12 days or something insane.
in other news, kevin and i broke up.  we're 2 days
away from what would be our 19 month anniversary.
it's so fucked up.  i feel really weird.  we're
talking about just gradually seeing less and less of
each other so the change wouldn't be so shocking.  i
don't know how/if it's going to work, but i'm scared.
it's been so long, you know?  i hope i'll be okay
without him!  that's the whole thing though, i want to
know that i will be okay without him.  the oar concert
will be the 2nd concert i've gone to without him, and
the other one was in 1996 or 1997.  it's scary.  i'd
be going with this guy chad from work, and a lot of
other people. one of the problems that have brought
about this breakup is that i kind of like chad.  it
sucks.  it's all foreign to me, i'm nervous.  tomorrow
is the first day of my last semester of high school.
how strange is that?!!  ahhhh!!!  now i'm making myself
freak out.  i'm going to go now.  please write me back
love you, gina

_____

Do You Yahoo!?
Yahoo! Auctions - Buy the things you want at great prices.
http://auctions.yahoo.com/

Reply          Reply All          Forward          Delete      Previous      Next      Close

Move To   (Move to Selected Folder)

## IN OTHER NEWS

### FOUND by Tim McIlrath

This was e-mailed to a friend of mine; it must have been mis-addressed because my
friend had never heard of Gina Gollan. —T.M.

FoR Some RezSon
I zwøke in
happiness
sweethezRt, I hzu
pRemonitiow on
Thzt box—dzRk
pRemonitiow whicc
pRemonitiow itself
has bore itself
oot. Thztpremonitu
expLZint why
we were dezdscattc

This note was flapping down the beach by the North Avenue pier by downtown Chicago. I was with Nicole and Claire. It was a clear, windy day—Thursday, May 11, 2000. The note is written on the back of a blue piece of stationary from a Secretarial-Bookkeeping Service in Kansas City. Of all the cryptic, inexplicable phrases I have found in FOUND notes, I can't think of one more spooky and baffling than *I had premonition on that box*. What the hell is *that box???* There's something very creepy about the handwriting, the use of the word *sweetheart*, and especially *dark premonition which has bore itself out*. Reading this note a few times, I've begun to feel like the sole witness to an extraordinarily grisly murder.

**FOUND Magazine.**
**Everyone can play.**

Hi. Sherry.
write on the back
You have the sexiest eyes!
I'm gonna call you in a minute, and
tell you what I would love to see
you do with those cucumbers.
If its okay with you.

YOUR FRIEND JEROME

IF OKAY SAY OKAY ☐
I HAVE A FANTASY TO TELL
(OVER) YOU. ALL IN FUN (PUSSY)
I would love to eat your (PUSSY)

YOU HAVE beautiful
(BREASTS)
I'm in the bathroom
masturbating.

Maybe one day I can
have you. (Please)

YES              NO
☐                ☐

YOU ARE (VERY) SEXY

Roach Spray
Batteries
Water Mellon

**FOUND by Anonymous**

**SHOPPING LIST #1337**

**SHOPPING LIST #153**

Beer. Meat.
Dog Food
boloney

guy in Chicago wrote to us, said he'd been collecting FOUND stuff for over
0 years, and invited us to check out his collection. We took him up on his
ffer and were blown away by the vastness of his finds. This is a guy who has sorted
nd the incredible range and intensity of his finds. This is a guy who has sorted
is FOUND notes into a bunch of separate folders—'Love Notes Women to
Men', 'Love Notes Men to Women', 'Letters from Prison', 'Juvenalia',
etcetera—and each folder has twenty to fifty notes inside. There's a file for
scraps of paper with lipstick smudges. Thousands of shopping lists, some of
them written out in languages we couldn't even identify.

What's this fellow's secret—how does he find so much great stuff?
Dedication! He's spent hours combing the ground for fragments of torn-up
notes. One winter he saw a neat-looking letter frozen into the ice and he
brought out a pot of boiling water and made a delicate rescue. We wanted to
give the dude his props but he's decided to remain anonymous. He's asked
only that we mark his finds with this quote: "Homo sum; humani nil a me
alienum puto." –Terence. Which translates roughly to this: "I am human,
nothing human is alien to me."

Homo sum; humani nil a me alienum puto.

*CIGGTERTS*

Dear Irma,
Do you have at least $5.00.
Because I don't have any ciggterts.
If you don't have any money could
you send me two ciggterts!
Emotine

# I PUSH BACK

FOUND by Anonymous

I am human; nothing human is alien to me.

IF YOU TOOK
MY DETERGENT
Im SURE IT WAS
A MISTAKE SO
Im NOT MAD
YET BUT YOUR
PUSHING ME AND I
PUSH BACK SO IT
BETTER BE BACK

# FOUND
## magazine
#2

Love Is...
You and Me

STILL 5 BUCKS

ome day I will you will see

Will See About IT!!

right! just get ready to get you
ass kicked okay.
yesterday when I came hom
about 10:00 and the cops
were outside and they started
flirt with me and Hugo stayed
in the car because he toval
They were harrasing me

(3N-270AA£40D
w/slotted sides & flat
bottom.
- 2 bottles Max
Drano
= Rabbit pellets & Alfalfa

a 21 balloons production

L -- you know in the end all that is clear to me is that I love you.

65

# FOUND

### magazine #2

8-18-00

work ends 8-25-2000

7am - scraped blue building

8am scraped building

9am - scraped building

10am - scraped building

10:30 am painted building

**BLUE BUILDING**

FOUND by Tom Slatin

Wow! This is fantastic! Every day I walk out to the mailbox and am blessed with another batch of beautiful finds sent in from all around the world. I sit on my stoop and look through these notes and photos and am transported suddenly and powerfully into the lives of strangers. It's truly magical to experience such raw, incredible stuff on the regular.

What's most exciting to me is to discover so many kindred spirits, to find that there are so many of you who are also moved and fascinated by FOUND stuff. I feel this huge community of finders coming together – it's awesome! My most favoritest thing is folks who've written in and said, "everyone around here thinks I'm a freak 'cause I walk around picking up trash – and now I know I am not alone!"

So please – keep sending in your wonderful finds. And please help spread word about this project – the more folks who know what we're up to, the more great finds we'll get to share with everyone.

I-ight peace – see you in a minute –

+DAVY+

**Davy Rothbart**

point guard, FOUND Magazine

FOUND Magazine. Trucking company is done.

[www.ryansias.com]

# It Takes a Nation of Millions

# FOUND
## magazine

+ 21 Balloons productions presents:

VOLUME 2

with DAVY ROTHBART as Chuck D

and JASON BITNER as Flavor Flav

**SARAH MANN as Terminator X**

**EMILIE GOODHART as Sister Souljah**

S 1-W's—
**ALYSON SCOTT**
**HEATHER CAMPBELL**
**BRANDE WIX**
**ROSEMARY DARIGO**

**SUSAN HOLLAR as Hank Shocklee**

Bomb Squad—
**SARAH LIDGUS**
**ALISSA FLEET**
**JULIE SHAPIRO**
**JOSH NOEL**
**AIMEE MCDONALD**
**GREG PARKER**
**JOE GONZALEZ**
**ROBERT HICKAM**

**GULLIVER GOLD as Russell Simmons**
**JED LACKRITZ as Rick Rubin**

**MIKE DIBELLA as**
**Harry Allen, Media Assassin**

website by JASON BITNER
illustrations by RYAN SIAS
[www.ryansias.com]
FOUND logo by ROB DORAN
printed by CHRIS YOUNG
    at WEST-CAN [866-669-9914]
Printed in Canada

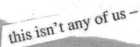
this isn't any of us —

67

this was FOUND by Andrew Griffin in Birmingham, AL

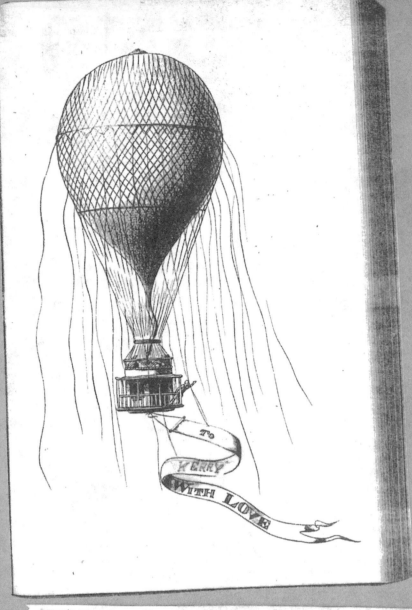

To
KERRY
WITH LOVE

# FOUND
## magazine #2

*FRONT COVERS*, FOUND by Aaron Wickenden, Rich Wayne, David Applegate, Bret Conway

*BACK COVERS*, FOUND by Anne Heidemann, Hillary Hall, Gus Mastrapa, Matt Summers, Noah Glaser, Charles Eshelman, Jeff Sargent, Melissa Farran, Mike Lehman, Chris Hutson, Lee, Pete Cropley, John Nichols, Jeff Beebe, Sarah Zurier

*T'WOLVES JERSEY*, FOUND by Gulliver Gold

*FRONT COVER PHOTO, ISSUE #1*, FOUND by Missy Heyward

found magazine
3455 charing cross road
ann arbor, mi 48108-1911
www.foundmagazine.com
info@foundmagazine.com

**THIS ISSUE IS DEDICATED TO MY DEAR UNCLE BUDDY – YOU ARE LOVED AND MISSED!**

FOUND Magazine would not exist without the incredible generosity and extraordinary talents of its staff and operatives, and the phenomenal enthusiasm of all you finders worldwide. jason bitner, what can i say, you my dogg for life. gigantic thanks to susan hollar who stepped in and got things organized. sarah mann and alyson scott keep everything running smoothly here at FOUND HQ – thank you guys! much thanks, too, to rosemary darigo, dr. dang hisself - brande wix – and to robert hickam, greg parker, julie shapiro, joe gonzalez, my man gulliver gold, aimee mcdonald, and mike d-b. big ups to our all-star operatives, sarah lidgus in the bay and alissa fleet in boston. much love to the community high kids, everyone at the sipping parties, and to every one of y'all who's contributed time and energy to this project. MADD THANKS TO EVERY ONE OF YOU WHO HAS SENT IN A FIND!!!

some serious shouts – tim mcilrath, jamie schweser, nicole schude, amanda margraves, bonnie mitchell, liam murphy, jim thompson + josh fenton, del rio 6, clarence beeks, jonathan menjivar, susannah felts, rose george, marcus lindeen, peter carlson, TAL crew, elizabeth meister, 21 BALLOONS PRODUCTIONS, ride the ride, my #1 dogg dan zatkovich, the fireants, hunter blair, aaron dennis + the sweatpants, curious few, rise against, dime magazine, source magazine, slam, paul redmond + AAA, bell's pizza, aladdin's, buster's, cleve corner, margarita at st.mark's, hannah + co. at quimby's, suzanne at mac's backs, all the awesome bookstore folks, emmanuel durant jr., popcorn petey, brother mike, matt kuehl, liz sanger, bennett miller, rachel frey, meta bodewes, shawna lee, eazy E eldad malamuth, aj wilhelm, guru kumar, ed fakto, chris young and west-can (!), valerie press (our 1st subscriber), clint + mike at tower records, cathy kuryk, stephanie mortenson, gwendolyn joyner at LCA, michelle kaiser at GCD, megan cook, kelcie haas, matthew richard downs, jennifer troyer, carolyn burack-anderson, ray mcdaniel, sam england, tim-dogg, ted, jesse P, matt-dogg, jordan + allmendinger ballers, shari, seth meisels, jordan small, tim-pat walbridge, big mike koz, amy sumerton, katherine raz, chris keach, dave hewitt, bam wallace, mark shepherd, dawn pulsen, gabe noel, michael samurai, greg laman, patrick mcneal, anne kelterborn, tony ligament, beth killian, rob doran, j.c. gabel, billy roberts, jed lackritz, carly ptak, ian ellison, jennifer schultz, rob jacques, jonathan kidd, reba meisels, maggie donovan-kaloust, richard dowdy, bec kanthor, jenny canipe, eric morin, janelle gunther, abram himelstein, mara pineda, kevin + alyson seconds, jen ramos, aaron hurst, amy fritch, mike hsu, dan seligmann, shana and jill at ready-made, jamie in s.l.o., and the old-timer in that liquor store in fresno who let me + hunter buy beer even though we left our i.d.'s at the motel in porterville. everyone else who has helped out in any way – please know how much we appreciate it! what up josen k + josh H! RYAN SIAS ROCKS! Deep Spring Center!

finally i got to thank my dad, who brought me life cereal + groceries while i was laid up with a broke ankle puttin' this joint together, susan + greg who brought xerox toner and toilet paper, beth winsten who brought good food, dr. brande wix who brought bell's pizza and deuces of olde E including the one i'm drinkin right now, and most important of all, Emilie c. Goodhart, who brought her sweet self and made me feel a whole lot better about life, and who also put together most of this magazine while i entertained her (well, mostly myself) with sight gags. if you are reading this – send in your finds!! and holla! i'm ghost, 5,000 G +davy+

# FOUND Magazine. Everyone can play.

## HOT ROD BIKES

**FOUND by Laurie Woolever**

I found this letter in New York City. The return address was a correctional facility in Florida.

To:
JACQUELINE B....

11-31-01
7:30 AM

I'AM writing you because of my MAGAZINE's that, I ordered Five months ago. I've only got OCTOBER's and NOVEMER's and, I paid for one hole year's worth of your magazines. So I would like to get the REST of my moness worth. I LiKE Hot RoD Bikes very much so, I would like to see more of your magazines so plasse send me my monthly magazine. I hope to get more of your great (Hot RoD Bikes) soon. Thank you

SiNCERiTY
Chris E. Ch...

THANKS FOR ALL THE INCREDIBLE MAIL – KEEP THOSE FINDS COMING!

5-13-02

DEAR DAVY AND CREW...

I JUST RECEIVED MY FIRST ISSUE OF FOUND. IT WAS REALLY BEATEN UP BY THE POST OFFICE, BUT NO RIPS. I HAVE POPPED IT BETWEEN 2 PIECES OF CARDBOARD ON ITS RETURN FLIGHT TO YOU.

I'M RETURNING IT BECAUSE ALTHOUGH IT'S A VERY COOL, FUN AND CREATIVE IDEA, IT'S NOT WHAT I'M LOOKING FOR IN A ZINE AT THIS POINT.

I'M ENCLOSING A CHECK FOR $5 FOR YOUR TIME AND HOPE THAT THIS SEEMS FAIR TO YOU.

KEEP UP THE GOOD WORK AND KEEP THE VISION.

TAKE CARE,

Lisa

LISA -

FORT COLLINS, CO 80521

BON APPÉTIT

MrDavy Rothbart
Found magazine
P.O. Box 14764
Chicago, IL

FOUND Magazine
3455 Charing Cross Rd
Ann Arbor, MI 48109-1911

FOUND s/r

FOUND Magazine
3455 Charing Cross Rd
Ann Arbor MI
48108

Found Magazine
3455 Char...

**69**

BALLOON WISH

FOUND by Jim DePitts
Houston, TX.

21 Balloons Productions. 1 life. 21 wishes.

This note and balloon were found in my back yard recen... Thought you might like it.

It could have been launched from a nearby elementary ...ol or somewhere more exotic...who knows?

Jim DePitts

*[signature]*

here's what the note says ➡

I wish I won't Flunk Sixth Grade!

Jessie

I did not take anything. I know there's no convincing you once you've made up your mind. And although I cannot offer you any other explanation as to what happened to it. That doesn't mean I did it. How could I have? You say your car was locked and Katie had the keys?

Anyway, I don't need to take something of yours when I can get my own. I doesnt make sense.

So here is a replacement. Cuz I cean't stand it when you think I've wronged you

— mom

FOUND MAG.
3455 Charing Cross Rd.
Ann Arbor, MI 48105-1911

FOUND
N/R

JESSIE —
I DID NOT TAKE ANYTHING.
— MOM

By believing passionately in something that still does not exist, we create it. The nonexistent is whatever we have not sufficiently desired

BUSINESS REPLY MAIL
FIRST CLASS MAIL PERMIT NO. 2698 SAN JOSE, CA 95134
POSTAGE WILL BE PAID BY ADDRESSEE

SONY ELECTRONICS INC
12451 GATEWAY BLVD
FORT MYERS, FL 33913-9972

NO POSTAGE
NECESSARY
IF MAILED
IN THE
UNITED STATES

Dear Friend,

I found this note on the ground while I was delivering mail in Tahlequah, Ok. on May 31, 2002.

Name: Would that it were so

Sincerely,
Wallace Blue
Wallace Blue

Justin Hensel

Betsy Ross sewed the first american flag.

George washington was the first american president.

George washington was a general in the war.

martin luther king was a civil rights leader
chris columbus discovered America.

George washington cut down his fathers cherry tree with an axe his father gave to him for his birthday.

The Black Panther was started During the Vietnam war.

the sputnik sattelite was launched

man went to outer space
Malcolm X began His Quest for freedom
The constitution was sighned
The Boston tea Party Happened
the anti government group, the
anarchy was started.
King Tuts tomb was discovered
the stop light was invented
the 1967 ford mustang shelby was introduced

nitrous oxide was allowed to be
used in muscle cars and show cars, and
modified racing cars, for use in Drag racing
in ~~1975~~ 1978
Black people won the right for
freedom
Hitler began the Nazi clan
Ted Bondy was sentenced, then
commited soicide.
Richard chase was murdered
JFK was assasanoted

Richie valins died in a plane crash

Edgar Allem Poe's short stories and
poems were Published
Elvis Died of a D.O.D.

Jimi Hendrix died...

Jim morrison died.

Paul mcarthney was knighted

Justin Hensel was Born

WHAT I KNOW ABOUT U.S. HISTORY

FOUND by Rona Miller

South Bend, IN.

FOUND S.F.

Found Magazine
3455 Charing Cross Rd
Ann Arbor, MI 48108-1911

73

*the accordion*

*What the hell you looking in here for, Daisy Mae?*

I don't [write for posterity]. I'm writing for my brother, my dad, my mom, Faye, and the kids, the people I love and want to reach. Wait a minute. I'll add to that. I write for posterity in one kind of way that's hard to define. It's somewhere in something I remember from when I was a little kid. There was a stream that came down from the hill at our place and would have cut across our yard, but years before somebody went out there and covered this stream over with stone, mortared the stone together so that it left a hump down through the middle of this yard, as if it were left there by a 700-pound mole. And when the stream dried up my brother and I—he was in the third grade and I was in the fifth--we went down to the end of that tunnel and walked through it, lighting our way with torches. We found an old accordion under there. It was a great find, and we brought it home and tried to play it. But it wouldn't play, and we found out we could get into it by opening this screw and lifting the top off. We got into all the valves and bellows and everything, and there, stuck in a corner, we found a piece of paper, a sign, and it said, WHAT THE HELL YOU LOOKING IN HERE FOR, DAISY MAE? Well, I achieved some kind of satori right there—knowing that somebody had sometime, a very long while ago, gone in there and put that sign in the accordion, and he's betting all the time that someday somebody's going to come along and find it. A mystery for people to wonder about. Well, that's what I want for my books.

—k.k.

74

Inbox for ██████@yahoo.com   Yahoo! - My Yahoo!   Options - Sign Out - Help

powered by **hp**   ✉ Mail   📇 Addresses   📅 Calendar   📝 Notepad

Reply | Reply All | Forward | inline text ▾   Prev | N

Delete | - Choose Folder - ▾ | Move   Mark as

Download A
Printable View - F

Flag This Message

| Block Address | Add to Address Book

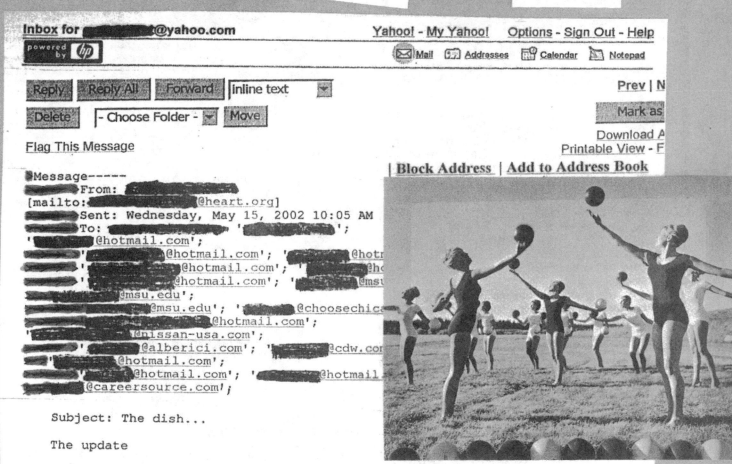

```
█Message-----
████████From: ████████
[mailto:███████████@heart.org]
████████Sent: Wednesday, May 15, 2002 10:05 AM
████████To: ███████████ '███████████';
'█████@hotmail.com';
███████████@hotmail.com'; '████████@hot█
███████████@hotmail.com'; '██████@ho███
███████████@hotmail.com'; '█████@msu█
█████@msu.edu';
██████@msu.edu'; '██████@choosechic█
███████████@hotmail.com';
███████████@nissan-usa.com';
██████@alberici.com'; '████████@cdw.co█
██████@hotmail.com';
██████@hotmail.com'; '██████@hotmail█
██████@careersource.com';
```

Subject: The dish...

The update

Well...Mr. Colin ███████ showed up at my door at about 8:15ish. Sporting a pair of cute jeans, a button up and a black jacket. For his outfit I would give him about a B. As for looks, he was cute but on the shorter side and his hair was a little too long. Far from a mullet but longer than I would prefer but let's not dwell on that because he can kinda get away with it.  So for looks, I would probably give him another B. Car- BMW, like I stated before. A great car, he'll have to get and A for that. He gets and A+ for his manners and politeness. Marcie, he opened the car door everytime! Super polite. Overall general appearance will cap at a B+.

AS for the place we went to, another "A". The Tasting Room is an excellent date place. I was never the wine connoisseur but I'm gradually thinking I could become one. We had 4 glasses each of different white wines and a cheese flight, which was the perfect food mecca to go with the wine. Place is awesome, I recommend all of you guys to attend this place for a night out with your man/woman. We also headed over to this place called the Black Duck. Another great place! The date place itself gets an overall "A".

By the way Girls, this summer we must hang out on Randolph, so many awesome places!

I can go into great detail of what we talked about and such but, that would make for an extremely long email.

The date ended with me getting intoxicated but not like crazy intoxicated, but I was drunk. No hangovers. I'm assuming he was fairly intoxicated but since he was driving, I didn't want to know, so I never asked.

found magazine
3455 charing cross road
ann arbor mi 48108-1911

75

SEND IN YOUR FINDS

By the way, as for myself, I get an overall A+ for how damn cute I looked. I sported a pair of fun longer Capri pants from Guess in a darker khaki color with my white shirt from Hanger 18, that has my lower back showing with my new cute fitted black jacket with empire sleeves from Armani. I was a BABE. He didn't stand a chance. My worries of not being cute were so swept under the rug with the outfit I pulled off last night.

Before jumping to any conclusions, YES, I stayed the night, only because I semi passed out on his couch and he was polite to ask if I wanted to head home and I just said he could take me home in the morning, NOTHING happened. Honestly only a kiss derived from this date and it didn't even happen at his place. I believe it might have been executed at the Black Duck but I'm not so sure on the exact time and location. But can I add, GREAT kisser. The date kiss gets an "A". Really, I haven't had that great of a kiss since, well we won't go there but it has been a long time. I might have to go with the fact that I might have mastered the skill of French kissing, no joke. As long as I have potential to work with, I can execute a pretty intense kiss.

Lara- you would have loved Colin's attitude. Actually I think all of would have appreciated how he called me out on my stupid logic of thinking.

Somehow, it came up on how random it was for us to meet and shit and how when he said the very first time we talked for me to give him a call and my response was, "Really, I'll let you know now, I won't call you, so I suggest you write my number down and give me a call". Hence the wait of a week or so for his first initial call was due to my shallowness or whatever you would like to call my way of playing the field. Doesn't really matter, he still called and I didn't.

So, question is, where do I stand on the whole outlook of Mr. Colin and the date... The car, the money, the job, the cute apartment, the boat- which by the way only seats 6 people, so I really don't consider that really amazing, his mannerism and his great kiss will probably lock in another date but...I can tell you now unless he cuts his hair and sends me gifts, it won't lead me to seek anything more than my 1st 30 year old FRIEND (Oh by the way, I think he's only 29, but still, I'm rounding up). Plus, the summer is just around the corner and guys are EVERYWHERE, I need to keep the options open and my schedule free to lock in some other great summer flings...

Well, I hope you've enjoyed the day in the life of Miss Jackie ███ and please feel free to comment on my date, my outfit, the kiss, or whatever else. If you need any more major details of the date please contact me in one of the following ways: phone, email, personal visit or text messaging.

Oh, I might be heading to a Cubs game with him next week. We'll see.

Oh by the way ladies- His cute friend Brian, is single and also a day trader. Which by the way, being a day trader is pretty money, literally in a sense but he gets to throw on lounge wear for work and is home no later than Noon. Are you kidding me? Where was being a day trader on career day in Elementary school?

FOUND Magazine. "A+!"

## BARF BAG BREAKUP

### FOUND by Sarah Zurier

People will write on just about anything.
FOUND at LAX airport.

TO FACE YOUR FEARS, I'm
HERE BUT I CAN'T SHOW
YOU HOW.

WHEN I LOOK INTO YOUR
EYES YOUR SOLE TOUCHES
ME. IT'S LIKE A DRUG.

WE CAN BE FRIENDS BUT
RIGHT NOW YOU SHOULD
TAKE CARE OF THINGS
(FIND OUT FOR YOURSELF.

I'm sorry to have to say this in an email, but I'd rather not have this conversation over the phone.

I think this is it for us. It has been for awhile. You don't even know how much of a tremendous loss this is for me. INSIDE OF YOUR WALLS IS SOMEONE I RESPECT MORE THAN ANYONE ELSE IN THE WORLD. YOU DON'T EVEN KNOW HOW MUCH IS INSIDE YOU WHAT YOUR CAPABLE OF. WHO YOUR TRYING TO HIDE IS VERY MUCH THE PERSON I'D LIKE TO BE.

I HOPE IT WILL BE EASIER

Dear Charles

You disappointed me when
I left, I wanted you to fuck
the shit out of me, but anyway
I want to see you, when you're
not busy I'm not coming over
there to see you, but you can
get intouch with me by calling
me at home or at work we
can meet and go to the hotel
but don't bring any drugs
or alcohol I got to chill
out on that shit and I
can't take care of my business
doing that shit everyday, but I
like I mean I really like you
and I want to be with you
without all the other bullshit
and here is your pictures
don't lose them or give them
to anybody and call me
don't hang up if a man answer
ask for anybody but me
call after 5pm that's when
I got home call at work
after 2pm
P.S. I love you
                    home 342-1815
                    work 267-5889

AJ,

We have your binder. You will never see it again unless you leave a sum of $3.50 directly under the clock to the left of the door at precisely 1:15. Please do not inform any teacher of this transaction. If you mess this up you WILL regret it.

If you do not comply than you will never see it again.

**BLACKMAIL**

FOUND by Jennifer Jones

Milwaukee, WI.

AJ,
We have
your
binder!

NO RETURN
ADDRESS

Found Magazine
3455 Charing CrossRd.
Ann Arbor, MI 48108-194

in case you can't read her t-shirt, it says 'BOYS CHEAT'

**BOYS CHEAT**

**FOUND by Jeffrey Beebe**

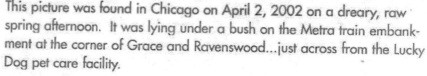

Found Magazine
3455 Charing Cross Rd.
Ann Arbor, MI
Found Photo within... 48108 1911

by Jeffrey Beebe

This picture was found in Chicago on April 2, 2002 on a dreary, raw spring afternoon. It was lying under a bush on the Metra train embankment at the corner of Grace and Ravenswood...just across from the Lucky Dog pet care facility.

My purely imaginary ramblings about the photograph (which I call "Boys Cheat"): this photo was taken by two girls--let's call them April (pictured) and Lara (behind the camera)--on a road trip to the West Coast in June of 1998. April (again, pictured) had recently been dumped by her three year boyfriend, Nathan, due to an affair—Nathan started sleeping with his co-worker, Celeste. (Nathan--a picture framer by day and a bass player in a power pop/neo-punk band, The Furtile Delta, by night—couldn't resist the feral, stoat-like sexuality of the ever slinky and lisping Celeste. Let's face it: April and Nathan's relationship wasn't going anywhere...they were only welded together by their love of Old Style, quick sex, and Elvis Costello's *Armed Forces* album. It was bound to fail.) Anyway. April, of course, was devastated by the end of the relationship and moved out the next day, and into the apartment of her childhood friend, the fiesty redheaded textile arts major and occasional lesbian, Lara. After a few days, Lara soon grew tired of April's incessant dark moods and tiny, self-inflicted wrist cuts, and suggested a road trip out to Los Angeles...where two wily graduates from the School of the Art Institute of Chicago could certainly enjoy the overwhelming kitsch and pop irony of such a flashy, superficial metropolis. April hastily agreed and quit her job at Ragstock--a local hip/grunge fashion boutique--to facilitate the journey. April and Lara set out in a 1989 powder blue Ford Escort with only three tapes to listen to--- The Cure's *Kiss Me Kiss Me Kiss Me*, The Replacement's *Pleased to Meet Me*, and Stevie Wonder's *Songs in the Key of Life*. The shirt April sports in the photograph was purchased during a lay over Tuscon, and both Lara and April agreed that April would wear the shirt and have her picture taken in front of every major landmark they encountered from that point on. Just to prove a point.

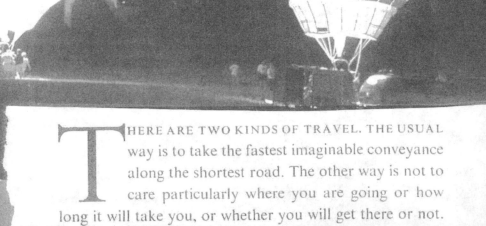

PLEASE DO NOT BOUNCE HEAD!

THANK YOU

I will be happy to help you —

BUT

please promise that you won't just forget about me once you are fine

**J**ust a nice girl

**O**n time would be nice to bring your home work ~~are going~~ to The park **Y**ou ~~and we are goin~~ with m to morow

**C**ooking I like spageri

**E**at Burger King To morow

Dear Grandma : Grandpa,
Hi and how are you two doing? I heard about your bad luck with the rototiller. Grandpa- I'm so sorry. I hope you're not in as much pain now and that your leg is able to heal well.
I'm also sorry to hear about Jack. I hope ings are going

# JOHN TOMMAS

## SELLS DOPE

## TO PEOPLE

## TRUCKING COMPANY IS DONE

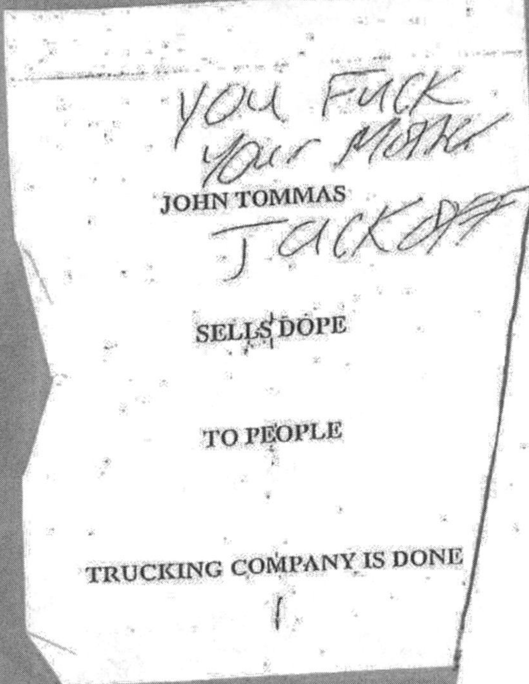

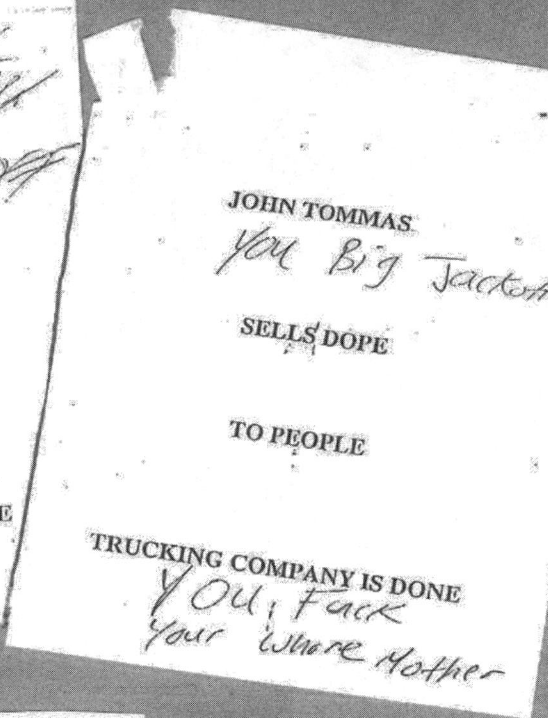

Flyer 1 (top left):
> YOU FUCK
> your mother
>
> JOHN TOMMAS
> Jackoff
>
> SELLS DOPE
>
> TO PEOPLE
>
> TRUCKING COMPANY IS DONE

Flyer 2 (top middle):
> JOHN TOMMAS
> You Big Jackoff
>
> SELLS DOPE
>
> TO PEOPLE
>
> TRUCKING COMPANY IS DONE
> YOU, Fuck
> your whore Mother

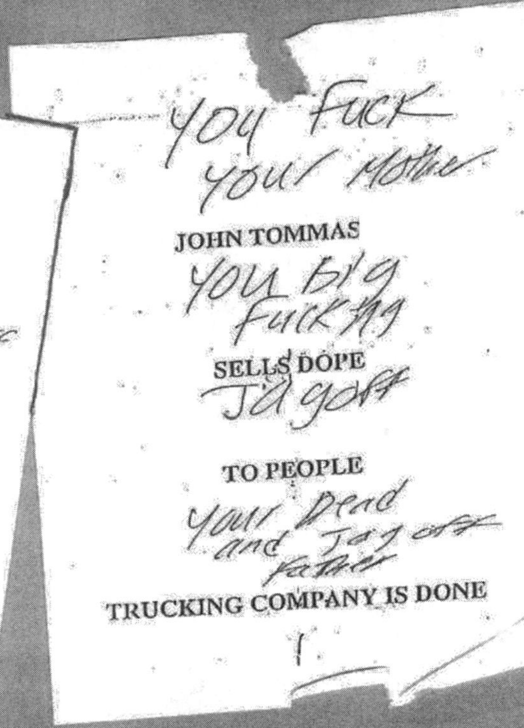

Flyer 3 (top right):
> you Fuck
> your mother
>
> JOHN TOMMAS
> you big
> Fucking
>
> SELLS DOPE
> Jagoff
>
> TO PEOPLE
> your Dead
> and Jagoff
> father
>
> TRUCKING COMPANY IS DONE

# TRUCKING COMPANY IS DONE

### FOUND by Beth Ann Siegler aka Anchorbaby

I found the first flyer in a free newsweekly stand here in Pittsburgh, and another a day later in the same spot, this time with "you are cock sucking faget busted open bitch I will fuck you face up bitch" handwritten on the flyer. After this, I started looking more carefully at the newsstands. The author distributes the flyers evenly between three newsstands and I have been dutifully collecting them for a month now. The hand-written messages have been getting steadily more violent and on several occasions I have sworn off my newfound hobby, especially after one appeared with the warning "quit taken the flyers." But I now see the text as poetry – there is something beautiful about the flow of the lines – and it becomes harder each day to resist the pull of the Dope Fiend writings. I must break out of this cycle or the author will find me and kick my ass – or shoot me in the face, as his writings indicate! So I'm sending the collection to FOUND, with best wishes for John Tommas , whoever he is.

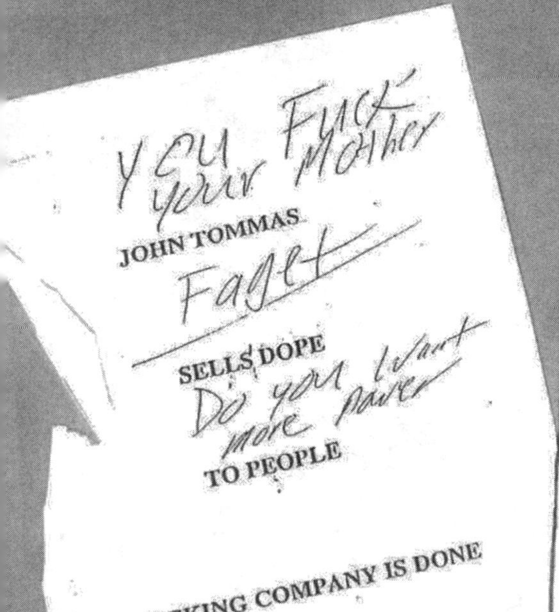

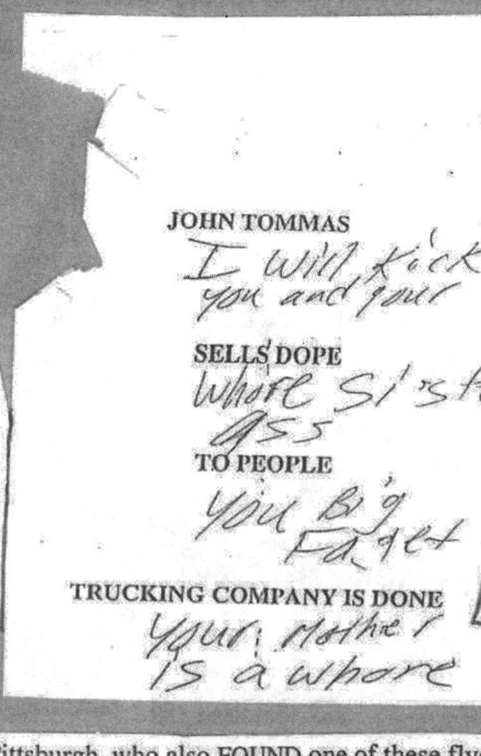

Flyer 4 (bottom left):
> You Fuck
> your Mother
>
> JOHN TOMMAS
> Faget
>
> SELLS DOPE
> Do you want
> more power
> TO PEOPLE
>
> TRUCKING COMPANY IS DONE

Flyer 5 (bottom middle):
> JOHN TOMMAS
> I will kick
> you and your
>
> SELLS DOPE
> Whore Sister
> ass
> TO PEOPLE
> you Big
> Faget
>
> TRUCKING COMPANY IS DONE
> your mother
> is a whore

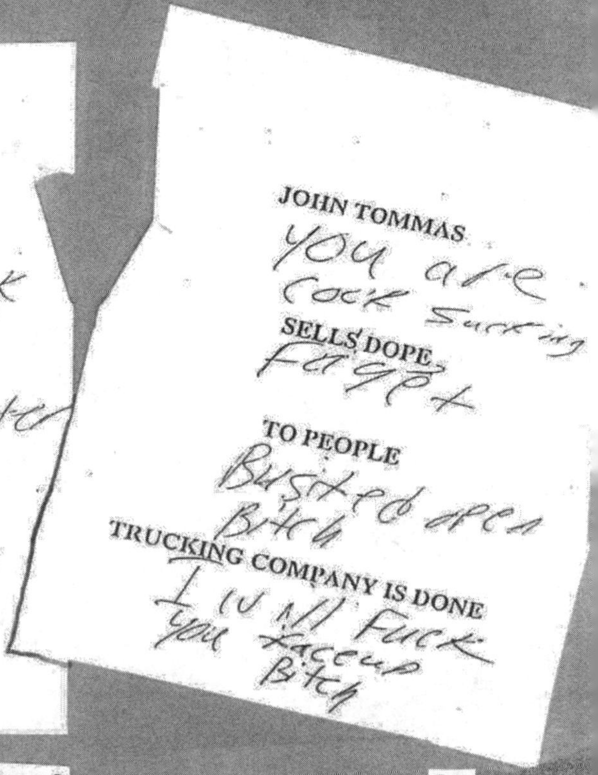

Flyer 6 (bottom right):
> JOHN TOMMAS
> you are
> cock sucking
> SELLS DOPE
> Fagot
>
> TO PEOPLE
> Busted open
> Bitch
> TRUCKING COMPANY IS DONE
> I will Fuck
> you faceup
> Bitch

[Thanks to Melissa Altenderfer in Pittsburgh, who also FOUND one of these flyers.]

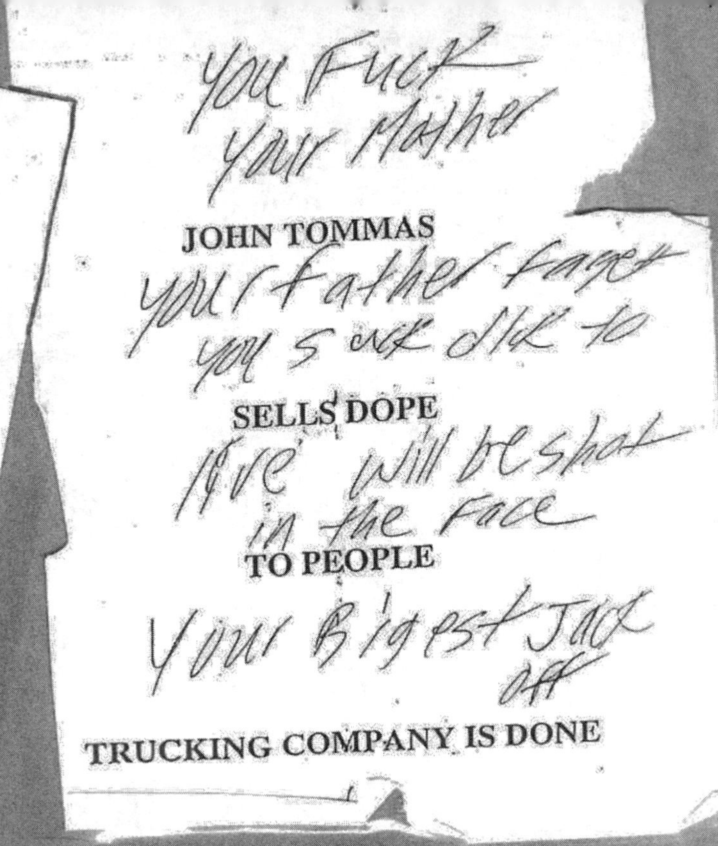

You Fuck
your Mother

**JOHN TOMMAS**

Jagoff

I hit your

**SELLS DOPE**

kiss your dead
ass asshole

**TO PEOPLE**

listening to you

**TRUCKING COMPANY IS DONE**



you Fuck
your Mother

**JOHN TOMMAS**

your father faget
you suck dick to

**SELLS DOPE**

Are will be shot
in the face

**TO PEOPLE**

your Biggest Jack
off

**TRUCKING COMPANY IS DONE**



**JOHN TOMMAS**

You Big
Jack off

**SELLS DOPE**

Bitch

**TO PEOPLE**

your Mother
is whore

**TRUCKING COMPANY IS DONE**

Punk: Drop it like
shit

You Fuck
your Mother

**JOHN TOMMAS**

Jack off
your coming

**SELLS DOPE**

Close to beast

**TO PEOPLE**

right on the Bus
your Father is a Jagoff

**TRUCKING COMPANY IS DONE**

You Big Fager

**FOUND Magazine sells dope to people.**

87

## WHOLE FOODS
### Customer Communication

Please take a moment to give us your comments, suggestions or questions. If you need a personal or confidential reply please include your phone number.

**Date:**

The bunny or rabbit are ~~stupid~~ stupid get rid of them,

**Response:** I am not sure what bunny or rabbit you refer to here. Please be more specific. Thanks.

**Team Member Name:**

David L
Store Team Leader

**Date:** 2/13/01

Look up Domination
Buy
* Handcuffs
* Leather Tassles
* Whip
* Rope
* Candles
* Leather Lingerie
* Strapon
*

### WINDSOR COURT HOTEL
NEW ORLEANS

Please, Leave ME ALONE! (police have been notified).

300 Gravier Street, New Orleans, Louisiana 70130
504.523.6000  Facsimile 504.596.4513
800.262.2662

*UNWANTED SUITOR* — FOUND by Tony Ligament, New Orleans LA

*COURTESY* — FOUND by Matt Summers, Washington DC

ODDESIE Like you but don't get offended cace you ain't gotta like me back but all I'm asking for is a little curtisy on my two dollars and twenty cents Peace out

1. BARK.
2. AUNT.
3. SILT.
4. HUNT.

*POP QUIZ (ANSWERS)* FOUND by Mitch O'Connell

Chicago, IL

I love malisa malisa malisa malisa

# EATING YOUR PUSSY "2001"

FOUND by Brenda Coultas

New York City

Hi colleen

I hope this letter
finds you well and in the very best of health
and spirit, and as for my-self I'm doing very well
but to tell you the truth I'm very much home sick and I'm
missing you soooo very much.. each day I think of you
and I wish I knew you longer.. in the short time we
met we became friends and I wanna thank you for that
you gave me a chance to open my-self to you and to let me
feel comfort (thank you) Soooo I write to you today to
tell you something else, when I first seen you I knew
you was in the life, the way you dress and carry yourself and that turned me on I love gay women as for
my-self I go both ways I eat pussy and suck dick
and this you already know.. to tell you the truth I would
love to go to bed with you, I dream of this all the time
I even masterbate when I'm thinking of it..

TURN OVER

#2

You know when we was at cosmetics plus and each time I went to the bath Room I would masterbate and pictures of you would come to my mind I would see you eating out the other female who work with us. I forgot her name but you know who I'm talking about the one who goes to clubs with you there's times when I wish if I can watch the to of you while I play with my dick.. I even thought about sucking a dick for you while you watch codeen I'm nasty like that what I want is Two 1/2 women something I never had and I wish Right now for that. to come true.. I have something to say when I come to New You will you give me that.. picture this me eating your pussy while you eating the other pussy "2001" Tell are you fucking her and is it goooood.. if you can send me some pictures..

This place is beautyfud. and the train Rick here was very nice it took me four #4 and a half 1/2 days to get from new york to seattle wa.

Next Page

HEY Found!
I found this spooky note in the pants that I got at the thrift store. Spooky Yes? Bust the Action
Brent

January 29, 2000

Dear Family @ 1100 Countrywood Lane,

Thank you so much for your input regarding the "why is the man dead with a sword in his back in the snow?" conversation between myself and my 4 year old son… it was a true joy, I assure you.

I would like to help with your "families" necessary counseling. Your children or your neighbors children must need it for obvious reasons but you as the parents might want to take me up on my offer due to allowing it to stay in your yard for days on end. This offer is genuine, so please allow me to help with the counseling for this real to life sickness (please let me know the names of the neighbor children so I can get you a group discount). I have left my number and return address at the bottom feel free to contact me at your convenience.

As a return favor for my offer of help I would ask that you let me know where your or these children go to school so that my boys are assured of never being around them.

Thank you in advance for your time. Best of luck in your future.

Tim

'0.5178 phone

. Ok. 73116

WHY IS THE MAN DEAD WITH A SWORD IN HIS BACK IN THE SNOW

FOUND by Brent McAllister

Edmond, OK.

**1) COURSE**
  *Comments* (e.g., content, structure, approach, educational value)

I CAN NOT REMEMBER ANYTHING ABOUT THE CONTENT OF A SPECIFIC CLASS ANY MORE THAN I COULD RECALL THE MOST BORING MOMENTS OF MY LIFE. THE EDUCATIONAL VALUE WAS SO PHENOMENALLY LOW THAT MY FRUSTRATION GREW INTO HATRED FOR HER, AND THEN IT BECAME MORE WIDESPREAD, AFFECTING MY FAMILY AND FRIENDS AND POSSIBLY PEOPLE I HAVE NEVER MET BEFORE, UNTIL I FINALLY REACHED THE POINT WHERE I HATED MYSELF FOR ~~WHILE ONE~~ BEING THERE.

*Comments* (e.g., content, structure, approach, educational value)

structure ?? which one?
no educational value
we learned nothing
one-sided introduction to NYC. - Only Ellen's view
the guest lectures were sometimes interesting - only interesting thing

# TEACHER-COURSE EVALUATION

**8) ADJECTIVE**  What adjective best describes this course? ___ HORRIFYING

**3) INTELLECTUAL STIMULATION**
  *Comments* (e.g., amount and type of thinking you did)

"Bullshit" is the only word I can think of, excuse my French. Ellen didn't try to stimulate, and the material didn't stimulate me. When it came time to write papers, I made bullshit up because I didn't care one way or the other.

**6) EVALUATION METHODS**  (e.g., the educational value of tests, papers, homework)

The papers were obviously intended as thought exercises, and they succeeded passing well as such, but what they had to do with any of the other papers, readings, presentations, or discussions is quite beyond me. In fact, what _any_ paper, reading, presentation, or discussion had to do with any other paper, reading, presentation or discussion, or the ostensible program topics, is an issue which has yet to be clarified.

**...ON METHODS** (e.g., the educational value of tests, papers, homework)

RATHER MEAN SPIRITED EVALUATION OF OUR PAPERS, BUT I CAN'T BLAME HER FOR ANYTHING EXCEPT FOR THE IDIOTIC TOPICS ~~SHE REQUIRED US~~ ~~FORCED~~ TO WRITE ABOUT.

2 = fair

**5) 3) INTELLECTUAL STIMULATION**
  *Comments* (e.g., amount and type of thinking you did)
  WHEN HER TWENTY-FIVE POUND CAT CLAWED ME IN THE GENITALS.

**6) EVALUATION METHODS**  (e.g., the educational value of tests, papers, homework)

I have no idea how I'm being evaluated.

Also, write comments for items on both the front and back side of the sheet. Examples of possible topics are given for each item; use them or any others that are relevant. Include strengths and weaknesses, as appropriate.

7) **CLASSROOM DYNAMICS** Circle term for type of course: **lecture / seminar / lab / other =** _____
(e.g., given this type of course, assess student participation, interest level, discussions, peer review)

There basically was no dynamic, Students not showing up, coming excessively late, and sleeping, that was the dynamic.

9) **ADDITIONAL COMMENTS**

a note about the cats: the litterbox wa_ in the bathroom. It contained, well, cat shit, one of the repulsive substances known to the human race. If the instructor hadn't wanted _s in the bathroom, she could have selected less unpleasant method of signalling it.

7) **CLASSROOM DYNAMICS** Circle term for type of course: **lecture /(seminar)/ lab / other =** _____
(e.g., given this type of course, assess student participation, interest level, discussions, peer review)

At times, it seemed that if someone were to begin speakin_ in tongues, we all would have nodded and pretended that it wa_ an insightful comment, just because someone had actually SAID something.

4 = good

*BLOOD AND TEARS*

FOUND by Jesse B.

Durham, NC.

5 = excellent

_MENTS

IF I COULD WRITE THIS IN BLOOD AND TEARS I WOULD.

7) **CLASSROOM DYNAMICS** Circle term for type of course: **lecture / seminar / lab / other =** _____
(e.g., given this type of course, assess student participation, interest level, discussions, peer review)

TWO DAYS A WEEK I _____ TO HER UNINSPIRED, UNTALENTED BABBLE ABOUT ALT THEORY, AND IF I WAS LUCKY I COULD CHEW ON A STALE BAGEL THAT I PAID OVER TWENTY THOUSAND DOLLARS FOR.

[L] 3) **INTELLECTUAL STIMULATION**
*Comments* (e.g., amount and type of thinking you did)

some, came out of irritation forceful confrontation with the subject

[2] 3) **INTELLECTUAL STIMULATION**
*Comments* (e.g., amount and type of thinking you did)

Ummm... I frequently contemplated my watch during class. Sometimes I would speculate as to what Chris E_ or Stephen B_ looked like, since they never came to class.

1 = poo_

93

Julie Lo
HAppy BirthDay
you Missing
F*ck-o!!!

WheRe +HE
Hell ARE You?
ARE you OK?

Call ME!

Happy
BirthDay
to you!
Happy Birth
Day to you
Happy Birth
Day you
Missing Fuck
Happy Birth!
Day to you!

EXPIRES 04-13-02

Charlie
you got
My Cell
phone #

Theresa
Love you
Need you
Want you
Go to Haymarket
or call
346-7475

HAPPY BIRTHDAY,
MOM! (3/31/47)

I LOVE YOU. I MISS YOU.
I HOPE YOU ARE OKAY.

WE'VE MOVED BUT
WE ARE STILL LISTED.

PLEASE. PLEASE CALL
AND LET ME HEAR YOUR
VOICE AND KNOW YOU
ARE SAFE. XO- A.R.S.

JAKE/Mitzen

Please Phone Home!
OR (CALL COLLECT, Please Just CALL)
CAll Me At Lydia's Up Untill
Monday June 24th I'm There till
Mon. 3:00.

I Miss you Daddy—
DESPERATELY!

I AM SOOOO ♡
IN LOVE with you!
Love your Wife Tina Mitzen

hey, i have an amusing anecdote for you on the subject of things FOUND.....

the setting is this:  i had recently quit college, had no job, no money, no car, no prospects of anything and was sleeping on a friends couch...to make it all worse, my friend was in no better shape than me, as he was on the verge of being evicted.

i started the day by taking my last 5 dollars to taco bell for a bit of breakfast.  The cashier gave me back 23 dollars in change.

i walked outside and found an unopened pack of smokes.

that got me and my buddy talking about synchronicity and the whole concept of the universe supplying you with the things you need, etc.  you know, the kind of stuff people talk about when they are avoiding gainful employment.

anyway, we decide we were going to spend the rest of the day just walking around town, looking at the ground, trying to find things....

we went into bathrooms, walked beside gas pumps, parking lots, ATMs, etc, anywhere where it might be likely that someone would drop something.

by lunchtime i had found 2 more packs of smokes. and we found a bag of groceries that were setting in a shopping cart in the middle of a supermarket parking lot.....

to celebrate our luck we went inside the bookstore around the corner from his house.  inside the store was a little coffee shop and we decided to have a cup (since we couldn't actually afford any of the books).  i go to the table and pull back my chair, and notice a small tie-dyed bag laying on the seat of the chair....i opened it and found approximately 1 ounce of marijuana, 3 pipes, a pipe cleaning kit and 2 packs of rolling papers.....

well, we reasoned that whoever left it wouldn't exactly go to the lost and found to claim it, and it would have been a travesty if an employee found it and turned it over to the authorities, so we took it with us and retired back to my friends house for a bit of a "break".

after a couple of hours we hit the streets again.  i had to make a phone call, but since my friends phone had been cut off i went to the pay phone around the corner.....i put a quarter in and nothing happened, i looked in the slot and could see my quarter, stuck just inside the slot....i banged on the phone, hoping to knock it loose, and 8 quarters fell out of the change slot at the bottom....i banged it again and more fell out....i kept banging on it until over 12 dollars in quarters had fallen out of the slot...

we're kind of starting to get freaked out, and exhilarated at the same time...neither of us had ever heard of a lucky streak like this before...but we decided to ride it out....

we kept looking and right off the bat my friend found a scratch off lottery ticket worth twenty bucks, and then a few minutes later i found 3 perfectly good rod and reel fishing poles behind a dumpster.

we were sure we would never have to work again....we could just walk around an pick up the things everyone else had lost....but alas, the next few days we found next to nothing, and eventually had to get jobs, etc....

i have no idea if it was luck, coincidence, synchronicity, whatever, but it was a great day to be walking around the city unemployed...

—JOEL ABEL

it kinda makes sense that many of our most prolific all-star finders would share the same set of occupations. janitors, librarians, school-teachers and mail carriers come in constant contact with FOUND stuff. and so do folks who work in used bookstores. in philadelphia i got the chance to sit down with a champion finder named dave hewitt.

FINDER SPOTLIGHT

CALL BARBIE!
she graduates tonight!
Take boys to potty
please!
yr wife

? 16 91
TUESDAY

**davy:** *what up playa.  i hear you've got a crazy collection of FOUND stuff.*

**dave hewitt:**  yeah.  i've worked at used bookstores for a bunch of years.  one of my jobs is to flip through every used book that comes into the store – check the condition of the binding, see if there's any writing inside, make sure no one's marked it up too bad with a highlighter.  and inside the books i find all kinds of phenomenal stuff.

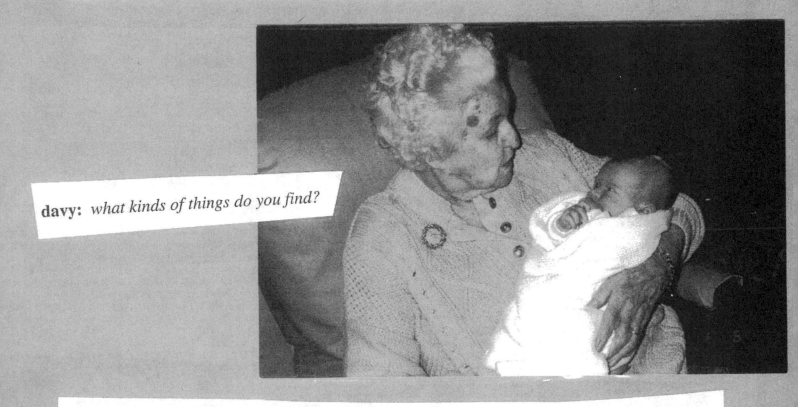

**davy:** *what kinds of things do you find?*

**dave hewitt:**  well, i've found photos, letters, journal entries, postcards, bookmarks, birth announcements, death certificates, a handwritten will, sketches, drawings, ticket stubs, poetry attempts, wallpaper samples, bills, credit card statements, cancelled checks and uncancelled checks, including one from january 1986 made out to "*people for the american way*."  i've found money, play money, baseball cards, baseball schedules, playing cards, bumper stickers, subway passes, passes for the premiere of the movie *song remains the same, archie* fan-club membership cards, business cards, including wolf blitzer's when he worked for the jerusalem post, christmas gift tags, pocket calendars, to-do lists, old coupons expired in the 1960's, cootie catchers, parking tickets, tongue depressors, emery boards, and an envelope with a lock of hair in it.  that's one of my favorites.

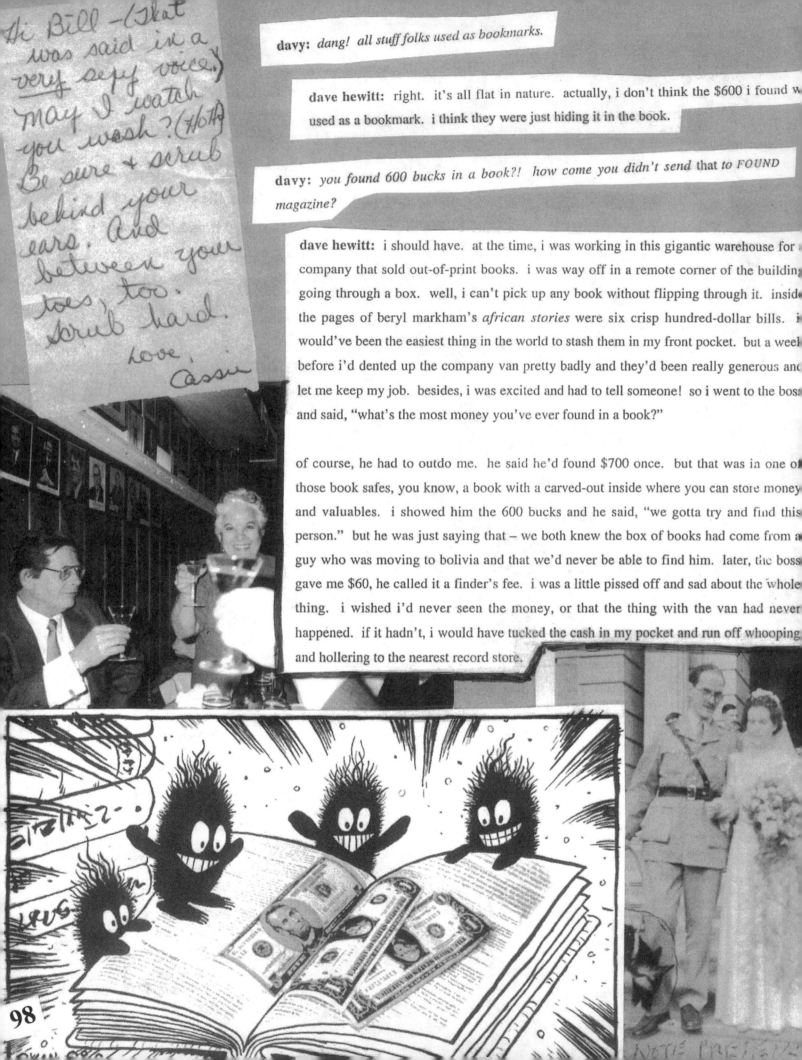

Hi Bill—(That was said in a very sexy voice.) May I watch you wash? (HA) Be sure & scrub behind your ears. And between your toes, too. Scrub hard.

Love,
Cassie

**davy:** *dang! all stuff folks used as bookmarks.*

**dave hewitt:** right. it's all flat in nature. actually, i don't think the $600 i found w[as] used as a bookmark. i think they were just hiding it in the book.

**davy:** *you found 600 bucks in a book?! how come you didn't send that to FOUND magazine?*

**dave hewitt:** i should have. at the time, i was working in this gigantic warehouse for [a] company that sold out-of-print books. i was way off in a remote corner of the building going through a box. well, i can't pick up any book without flipping through it. inside the pages of beryl markham's *african stories* were six crisp hundred-dollar bills. i would've been the easiest thing in the world to stash them in my front pocket. but a week before i'd dented up the company van pretty badly and they'd been really generous and let me keep my job. besides, i was excited and had to tell someone! so i went to the boss and said, "what's the most money you've ever found in a book?"

of course, he had to outdo me. he said he'd found $700 once. but that was in one of those book safes, you know, a book with a carved-out inside where you can store money and valuables. i showed him the 600 bucks and he said, "we gotta try and find this person." but he was just saying that – we both knew the box of books had come from a guy who was moving to bolivia and that we'd never be able to find him. later, the boss gave me $60, he called it a finder's fee. i was a little pissed off and sad about the whole thing. i wished i'd never seen the money, or that the thing with the van had never happened. if it hadn't, i would have tucked the cash in my pocket and run off whooping and hollering to the nearest record store.

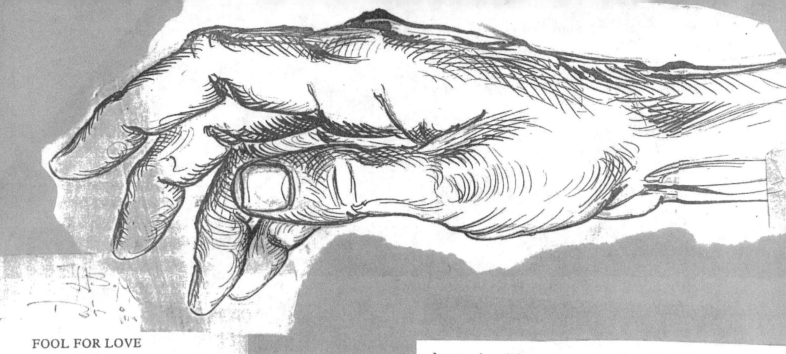

## FOOL FOR LOVE

### AND

### THE SAD LAMENT OF PECOS BILL ON THE EVE OF KILLING HIS WIFE

March 957

Sweet Dad,

Over a year
since first you
daringly touched
my knee, and
the magic just
soars higher daily.
Feel very much like
you're here with me,
which puts a bound
in my step
7 stories high ....
I love you,
Skip

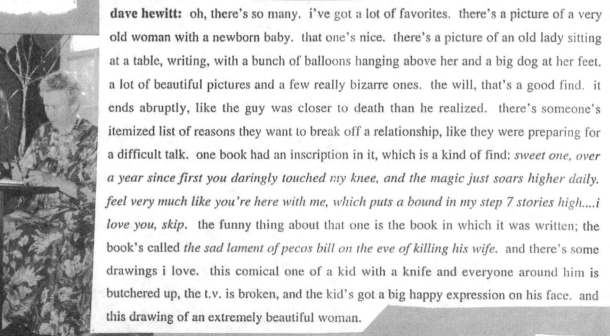

**dave hewitt:** a few years ago, i worked in the used department at the harvard bookstore in cambridge. one time a woman came in to sell a bunch of old books and a picture fell out of one of them; it was a picture of her, naked, in the midst of a strip poker game. she slammed her hand down on the counter and covered it, then took it and ripped it up and threw it in the trash can – *our* trash can! so of course once she left we plucked it out and taped it back together. that was my first big find. i was working with a woman named hillary and i'm indebted to her for encouraging me to start a collection.

**davy:** *what are some of your favorite finds?*

**dave hewitt:** oh, there's so many. i've got a lot of favorites. there's a picture of a very old woman with a newborn baby. that one's nice. there's a picture of an old lady sitting at a table, writing, with a bunch of balloons hanging above her and a big dog at her feet. a lot of beautiful pictures and a few really bizarre ones. the will, that's a good find. it ends abruptly, like the guy was closer to death than he realized. there's someone's itemized list of reasons they want to break off a relationship, like they were preparing for a difficult talk. one book had an inscription in it, which is a kind of find: *sweet one, over a year since first you daringly touched my knee, and the magic just soars higher daily. feel very much like you're here with me, which puts a bound in my step 7 stories high....i love you, skip.* the funny thing about that one is the book in which it was written; the book's called *the sad lament of pecos bill on the eve of killing his wife.* and there's some drawings i love. this comical one of a kid with a knife and everyone around him is butchered up, the t.v. is broken, and the kid's got a big happy expression on his face. and this drawing of an extremely beautiful woman.

davy: *hey, let me take a look at that. damn, she fine! she looks sad and tough. i think i'm in love.*

**dave hewitt:** i want that back eventually.

**davy:** *but don't you ever wonder about a find like this. like who drew it? and who's the girl in the drawing? don't you wonder if the fact that you found it, you specifically, if it means you and this girl were meant for each other or something?*

**dave hewitt:** i don't know. this one was in a really old art book. the person who drew it is probably in her sixties now. here, let me have that back. there's a kinko's down the street. we can go make a color copy if you want.

> Bobby -
> You are the one who has been my true friend. I know that I can always count on you, and its a good feeling. There are so many things I feel in my heart that I am unable to express here. You know how I feel, Bobby. Thankyou for everything Someday we'll be married, you know.
> Love,
> Mollie
> '69

**davy:** *why do you collect all these FOUND things?*

**dave hewitt:** you can learn so much from just the smallest fragments of people's lives. someone's essence emerges from these tiny details, notes and lists and things never intended for other people's eyes. that makes it sound like it's a purely voyeuristic thrill, but the appeal extends much farther than that. yeah, it's fun and it's amusing, but it's also really poignant. within each of these finds – especially the letters and the photographs – something universal is revealed, something that offers insight into the human experience, the human condition.

**davy:** *i like seeing that people who seem to be leading very different lives from me are still experiencing so many of the very same emotions and rafting through so many of the same triumphs and sadnesses. it makes me feel powerfully connected to them – and i don't know who they are really, just this single anonymous person whose note i've found. they end up standing for all people and so by extension i begin to feel a sense of powerful connection to everyone.*

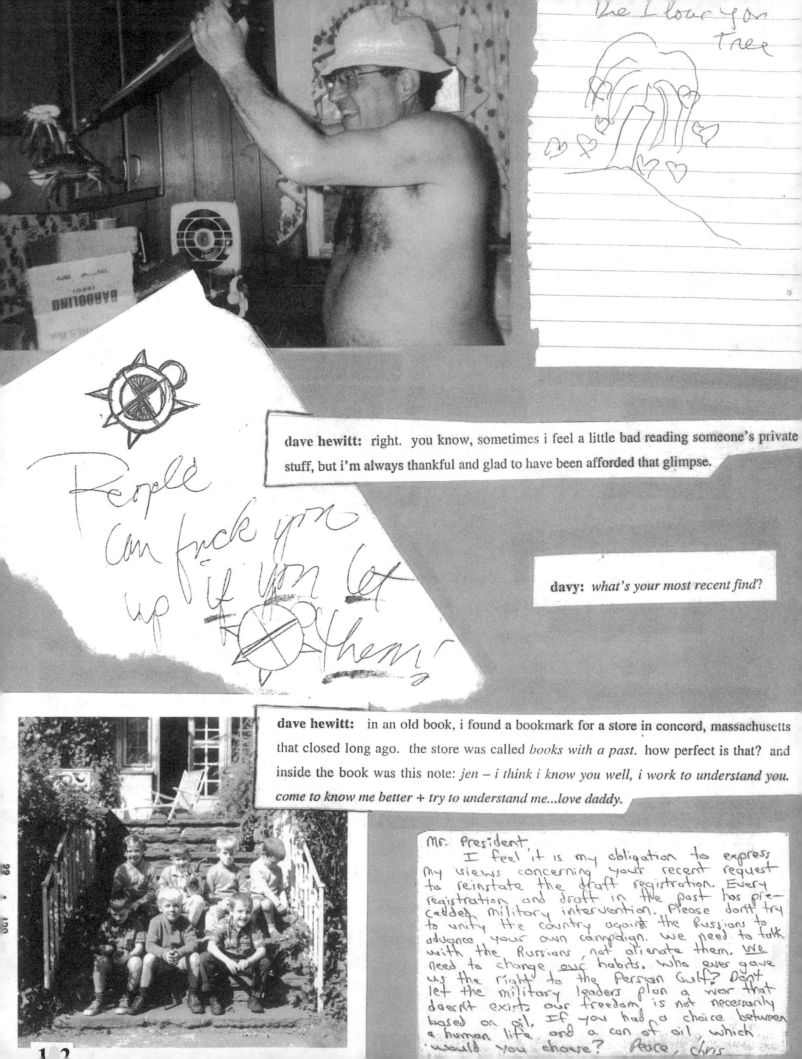

the I love you Tree

**dave hewitt:** right. you know, sometimes i feel a little bad reading someone's private stuff, but i'm always thankful and glad to have been afforded that glimpse.

**davy:** *what's your most recent find?*

People can frick you up if you let them

**dave hewitt:** in an old book, i found a bookmark for a store in concord, massachusetts that closed long ago. the store was called *books with a past*. how perfect is that? and inside the book was this note: *jen – i think i know you well, i work to understand you. come to know me better + try to understand me...love daddy.*

Mr. President,

I feel it is my obligation to express my views concerning your recent request to reinstate the draft registration. Every registration and draft in the past has preceded military intervention. Please don't try to unify the country against the Russians to advance your own campaign. We need to talk with the Russians, not alienate them. We need to change our habits. Who ever gave us the right to the Persian Gulf? Don't let the military leaders plan a war that doesn't exist. Our freedom is not necessarily based on oil. If you had a choice between a human life and a can of oil, which would you choose? Peace, Chris

**davy:** *what store do you work at now?*

**dave hewitt:** until recently, i worked at the book trader [in philly]. now i mostly sell books on the internet. so i still scrounge at library book sales and garage sales. if i see something tucked in the pages of a book i'm not interested in, i'll switch it into a different book and buy it instead, smuggle the find out. at every bookstore i've ever worked at there's people who keep stuff for me, the new things they find. you never know what's gonna turn up.

**davy:** *exactly. hey, let's see that drawing again. dang! come on, let's go hit that kinko's.*

Dear Uncle Kurt:

I know the previous letters may have sounded a little bizarre, but I need a place to stay. I can only start out by paying minimal rent or just paying for the utilities. Like only $40 a month.

I need to recover from all the hell that I went through in the mental facilities. You have no idea, and I just want to put it behind me..

You know that I have no choice but to leave the state of Michigan.

I think that I saw Nikki or a girl that looked like Nikki. I guess that I could live with either Danni or Nikki.

I am not too perfect at keeping things clean, but I would be willing to wash their cars for them or something like that. I will try to be neat…

Once I make a check of $200 a week and am able to work 40 hours a week, then I would pay $200 a month in rent.

Once I make a check of $400 or more a week, then I would pay them $350 or so a week in rent.

As long as they agree not to let any laboratories or mental facilities or Police or anybody get ahold of me again….

But I must warn you that I may seem a little bizarre while I am recovering, but I am harmless.

The government is radical now, and they are engaged in population control. I wont live to be 35 if I can't get an apartment to live in, and then pay rent in the future..

Talk to you soon..

David

HARMLESS

FOUND by Anne Heidemann

Mt. Pleasant, MI

FOUND Magazine. No choice but to leave the State of Michigan.

We wanted to include this note because we found it really moving. ~~HHH~~ We changed the names...

Dear Honerable Judge William.

I am writing

My name is Jeanine Mary        My youngest daughter is Melissa Mary

you this letter on some concern's I have and some question's that I would like to ask you.        annouced in

court on the behalf of me not being present in court on February 13th 2001. I would first like to ask what John

I lost my daughter on February 13th 2001. I would first like to ask what John

Jack came and saw me at the shelter the first time, on Miller in Youngstown, John wanted to know the

time, places and day's to alway's beable to reach me. When it was presented in court on taking Melissa

from me on the alligation's being made toward's me about my daughter Melissa, I was at parenting classes

and John knew on Febuary 13th were and how to find me. I am also asking that question because I was told

that John testified in court on Febuary 13th that John could not find me, if that being true of what Jack said

then we really need to look at how onist John is really is being with the whole P.S. case of my daughter

Melissa.

I would also like to know why I was not allowed to have any contact with my daughter

Melissa from 2-13-01 to 2-20-01.

One of the alligation's say's that I am not able to take care of Melissa while I apaligize for saying

this but taking care of a child is not just going to the store and buying diaper's and baby wipe's.

Ronnie and I do not get along what so ever but Ronnie would even present that I am a good

mom and sometimes I am to good of a mom.

I know so many people think very good thing's about the Woman's Aid shelter, but even Tam

had a very hard time believing that the alligation's are true. Tam has seen me in many different places

and at different times and day's and Tam has alway's in every way seen Melissa being well dressed and well

taken care of.

I also believe the alligation about me not eating a well balance diet while I was pregnant is a total

understatment. I think it would be fare to say for some one to say that about the person or people would

have to be around me non stop 12 hour's a day. Here is my not from my ob/gyn doc and he did not have

any worries about my pregnancy or had any worries on the way Darius was when he was born.

I also would like to inform you I have a job now that I started on July 26, 01 I work at KFC. I get

5.50 an hour and paid every friday. I do know it is not much for a job but my dad alway's told me you need

to start some where's and keep on going till you have what it is that you exsackly wont.

I am also on the deppo shot for birth control   I get my shot's at the Woman's medical Center on

Bond street in Youngstown.

My sic eval is al completed. I would like to inform you that the guy who did my sic eval was a

trainy. Also I know it say's on my sic eval report that I did not do, about four or five of the test but the guy

who gave me my test only sent two test home with me.   When I went back to akron the secatary did even

gave me my test only sent home a couple test and last I knew a couple was two. I am also going back to

Akron to have my sic eval retyped because I think it would be fare to say at least half of my sic eval has a

lot of untrue fact's and there is also information I would like to have added to my sic eval.

I would also like to ask my daughter Melissa's birthday is 9-20-01 and I would like to know if I

could have Melissa's birthday party at my apartment. Also have Melissa on 9-20-01 at least six hour's.

I know I have not always done rite for my children but I do not take all the blame for me loosing my

children. I will do what ever I have to, to always provide, love, care for and perfect my children. There is noom

and noone and no thing to get me to give up my children.

I will also do waht ever I have to, to prove that the alligation's against me are not true and they did

not acure

## Need

~~Classics & Clocks~~
- ~~Pork~~
- Cucumbers
- ~~Salsa~~
- ~~Peppers~~
- Mushrooms
- Zuchini
- Sugar packets

## Have

- Onions
- 4 Carrots
- 1 potato
- Rolls
- Cheese
- Crackers

## HAVE

- BOBA FETT (POTF)
- BOBA FETT (SHDWS.)
- IG-88
- GREEDO
- HAN SOLO
- X-WING LUKE
- CHEWBACCA
- R2-D2
- BEN KENOBI
- LEIA (BOUSHH DISG.)
- TUSKEN RAIDER
- JAWAS
- DARTH VADER
- TIE FIGHTER PILOT
- DEATH STAR GUNNER
- SANDTROOPER
- HAN SOLO / STORMTROOPER
- R5-D5
- 2-1B SURGEON DROID
- BOSSK
- JEDI LUKE
- YODA
- HAMMERHEAD
- IMPERIAL DROID
- C-3PO
- LANDO CALRISSIAN (BESPIN)
- HAN SOLO IN ENDOR GEAR
- HOTH LUKE

## NEED

- ~~BOSSK~~
- ~~2-1B (SURGEON DROID)~~
- ~~LANDO CALRISSIAN (BESPIN)~~
- ~~JEDI LUKE~~
- HOTH HAN SOLO
- HOTH REBEL TROOPER
- ~~YODA~~
- DAGOBAH LUKE
- TATOOINE LUKE
- ~~HAMMERHEAD~~
- AT-AT COMMANDER
- HAN SOLO IN CARBONITE
- ~~C-3PO~~
- PRINCESS LEIA (WHITE DRESS) $20
- ✱ SPIRIT OF OBI-WAN
- FIGRIN D'AN (MAIL OFFER) $13 ea
- ~~IMPERIAL DROID~~ $20
- ✱ ELECTRONIC R2-D2 $20
- ✱ BIKER SCOUT / SPEEDERBIKE

## NEED (SHADOWS)

- LUKE / IMPERIAL GUARD
- DASH RENDAR
- SWOOP TROOPER + SWOOP $
- PRINCE XIZOR
- CHEWBACCA / BOUNTY HUNTER
- GRAND MOFF TARKIN
- ~~HAN IN ENDOR GEAR~~
- LUKE IN STORMTROOPER DIS
- BIB FORTUNA
- LANDO IN PALACE GUARD DIS
- EMPEROR PALPATINE
- ENDOR LUKE w/ SPEEDER

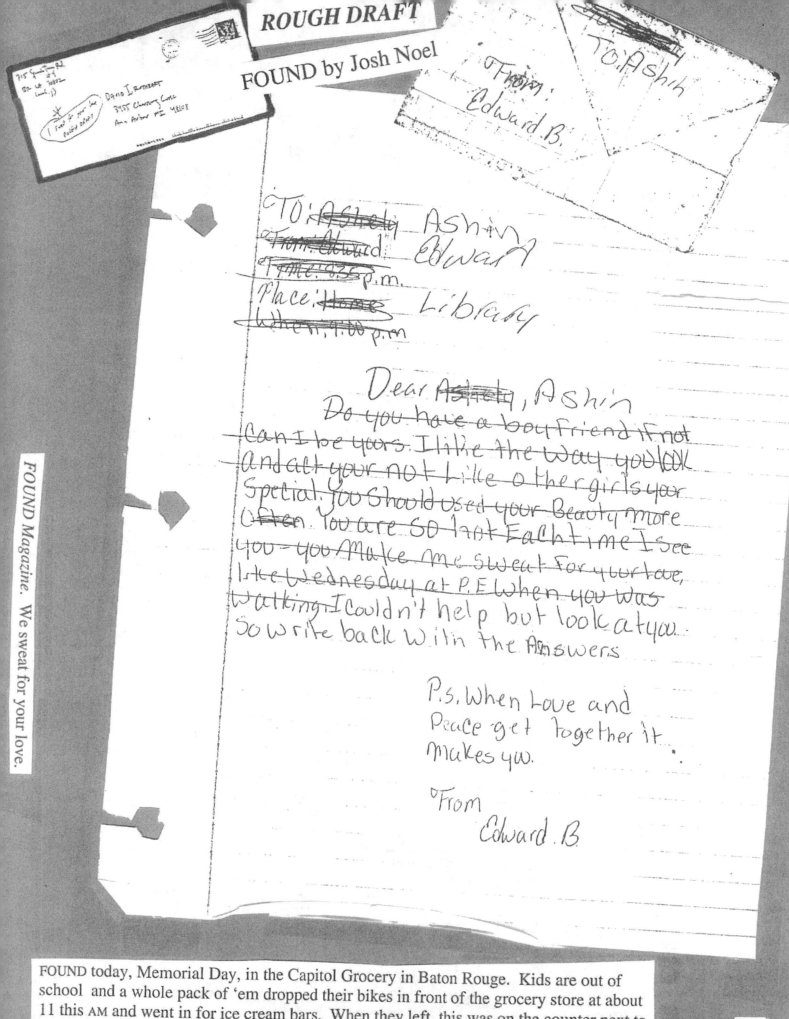

TO: ~~Ashely~~ Ashin
~~From: Edward~~ Edward
~~Time: 8.35 p.m.~~
Place: ~~Home~~ Library
~~When: 7:00 p.m~~

Dear ~~Ashely~~, Ashin
~~Do you have a boyfriend if not
Can I be yours. I like the way you look
and act your not like other girls your
Special. You Should used your Beauty more
Often. You are so hot Each time I See
you. you Make me sweat for your love,
Like Wednesday at P.E When you was
walking. I couldn't help but look at you.
So write back With the Answers~~

P.S. When Love and
Peace get together it.
Makes yw.

From

Edward. B

FOUND today, Memorial Day, in the Capitol Grocery in Baton Rouge. Kids are out of school and a whole pack of 'em dropped their bikes in front of the grocery store at about 11 this AM and went in for ice cream bars. When they left, this was on the counter next to the register.

**107**

*Keith B*

4153 ⬤ Avenue
Los Angeles, CA 90062
(323) 295-⬤

*100 PLUS YEARS*

FOUND by Victoria Strouse
+ Dan Seligmann

Los Angeles

August 15, 1999

Attn: Adam K

2049 ⬤ , #2690
Los Angeles, CA  90067-3088

Dear Mr. K  ,

# WHAT IF?

What if it's odorless, tasteless and colorless?  What if it's a clear liquid and it's not water?  What if every time you wash your face or hands, drink a glass of water, take a shower or bath, go for a swim or what if whenever you get near water, anytime-anywhere, there could be an invisible; "Jaws", "Jurassic Park", "Terminator", "Twister" or "Independence Day" waiting for you?  What if it's "BodyHunters", the invisible liquid terror that will forever change how the world will think about water, anytime--anywhere?

Contacts have been made and submissions are needed to twelve entertainment companies that are interested in the "BodyHunters" screenplay.  Therefore, representation is needed to the following companies:  Warner Bros., Fox, Universal, Sony, DreamWorks, MGM, C/W Productions, Imagine Entertainment, Artisan Entertainment, Daybreak Productions, Morgan Creek Productions, and Caravan Pictures.

"BodyHunters" is a potential 32-picture event film franchise that could sell 200 million plus videos and become a potential entertainment crown jewel that will create a $32 billion plus global "BodyHunters" brand name.  "BodyHunters" will bring to the market hundreds of fresh new characters that will be worth $5 billion plus in new licensing revenues.  "BodyHunters" will create 5-plus $1 billion plus worldwide blockbusters.

The bottom line is, "BodyHunters" is a "Dream Come True" entertainment product that will be talked about for the next 100 plus years.  Therefore, I am only seeking a team of savvy re-presentation that not only can but is willing to step up to the plate to negotiate a potential record paid for a screenplay and negotiate a potential overall long term "BodyHunters'" megadeal that could be worth 10-figures.

Sincerely,

Keith B

Keith B
Creator of "BodyHunters"

108

## ASIAN OPRAH

FOUND by Victoria Strouse
+ Dan Seligmann

Los Angeles

Bonnie Black Agency

Dear Kurt B.,

I am hoping to stimulate your interest in creating the first mega Asian star in the United States. The plan is simple. Produce me a talk show! I will do for the Asian community, what Oprah has done for African-Americans.

I am extremely intelligent(graduate of Washington U.-St. Louis), hip (member of the Phi Delta Theta fraternity), and a politically aware individual(double major in political science and psychology). Since I have been in Los Angeles, I have gotten an agent, manager, a job at Katy and Co., taking classes, showcasing my talents, and most importantly networking. All of this in 4 months time! Many people are astounded by what I have accomplished in such a short time. However, one must understand success is a part of me. I am the by-product of two highly recognizable medical doctors in the world. They have instilled in me a hard work ethic, the persistence to succeed, a love for life, and most importantly a faith in God.

What separates me from the thousands of aspiring talk show hosts? First, I am ethnically diverse. My background (Asian growing up in predominantly white areas) and personality (controversial) Will allow me to attract viewers of all races to my show. Secondly, I am 21 years old. The younger viewers will see me as one of them, while older viewers will be intrigued to see an intelligent young man with an adult perspective. Third of all, my style is a mixture of Ricci Lake and Oprah Winfrey. The shows will be fun yet informative, intense yet relaxed, and most importantly interesting topics. Fourth, is my name. The name "Jet" is a definite attention getter. It will quickly draw the interest and inquiry of viewers. Fourth, is star quality. Either you have it or you don't, and luckily I do. Finally, I believe in myself, my ideas, my dreams, and God.

I feel the time is coming for a recognizable Asian star. In the next ten years, the face of television is going to drastically change. If it has to happen, why not make that star me. Why not make the person behind the star you. Be that entrepreneur, believe in me, and take television to its next level right into the year 2000!

```
°I HAVE A DREAM...
     THAT ONE DAY THERE WILL BE A MEGA ASIAN STAR
     THAT HE WILL BE THE ASIAN OPRAH
     THAT HE WILL HAVE HIS OWN TALK SHOW
 I HAVE A DREAM, THAT MAN WILL BE ME.
```

Sincerely,
Jet Chiranand

*[signature]*

Hello, I am writing in my journal. I hope it will write back. If sir teacher is reading this, he is in trouble! This is my private journal, so bug off!

I learned how to fly yesterday. The trick is to hurl yourself at the ground and miss. You need to get distracted while you are jumping. Then, naturally, you miss. Don't think about gravity! Eventually you will learn how to land, do tricks, etc.

Michal Itech must not read this!

RYAN SIA

[www.ryansias.com]

**HOW TO FLY**

FOUND by Dorothy Gotlib

Ann Arbor, MI.

# KEYS

Found by Heidi Swillinger
Berkeley, California

I've had a thing about keys for as long as I can remember. The first thing I ever lost was a key – a tiny gold charm that slipped out of my hand and disappeared down a floor vent when I was 5.

www.ryansias.com

I walk part way to work each day, and whenever I find a key, it's a big event. I've trained myself to note what I was thinking the instant I spot one; sometimes the thought proves to be a key to a door inside that needs opening.

My favorite keys are the ones that show evidence of their journey through the world. Some have been run over and the wear and tear makes them sparkle. Others, like the key bent in half, double back on themselves. And with enough exposure to elements and time, some – like the key eroded by battery acid – simply wear away.

# FOUND Magazine
## needs your help

FOUND Magazine. A 21 Balloons Production.

All questions welcome, but if you want to see what other people have found as FOUND? Subscription requests? Does your find quality as FOUND? Subscription requests? Can't find anything, but want to see what confidentially. Call us, write us, e-mail us.

Take one step toward FOUND stuff,

FOUND stuff will take two steps toward you.

**PAGE ME LATER**

FOUND by Davy Rothbart

Someone sent us a picture of a little girl's shoe.

Found objects are in play. Send us a picture of it or send the object.

No invented stuff, please. Have some integrity. Besides, truth is stranger than fiction.

Mario,
I fucking hate you
you said you had to
work then whys
your car HERE
at HER place ??
You're a fucking
LIAR I hate you
I fucking hate you
Amber
PS Page me later

We are looking for FOUND stuff: love letters, birthday cards, kids' homework, to-do lists, ticket stubs, poetry on napkins, telephone bills, doodles—anything that gives a glimpse into someone else's life. _Anything goes._

found magazine
3455 charing cross road
ann arbor, mi 48108-1911
www.foundmagazine.com
info@foundmagazine.com

found magazine
3455 charing cross road
ann arbor, mi 48108-1911
www.foundmagazine.com
info@foundmagazine.com

14

One cold as fuck February night in Chicago in 1999, I went to my old apartment at Fullerton and Kedzie to watch the movie _Ran_ with my friend and old roommate Kelli, who still lived there. Around 3 AM I stumbled out to my car, full of war-fatigue from the movie, and thinking all kinds of intense thoughts about the book I was working on about a Vietnam Vet. A light snow had fallen. On my car's windshield, I found this note—apparently a case of mistaken Toyota Camrys. Poor Mario—catching blame when he was probably at work and not with this other girl. I thought it was a pretty amazing love note, though, really: Amber, trying to be all full of bitterness and bile, but giving herself away with her sweet coda—_page me later._

You will be credited in the magazine for your find!!!

XEROX THIS FLYER—DISTRIBUTE—
POST IN HIGHLY PUBLIC PLACES—
MAIL TO FAMILY & FRIENDS—everyone
CAN PLAY!! Send found photos, postcards, flyers

# HOW _YOU_ CAN HELP:

**1. Find stuff.** On the city bus, at Kinko's, in recycling bins, on the street, in restaurants, by the printers at the computer center, in the ER waiting room, in the bowling alley parking lot, in the woods, in the prison yard. **2. Write the circumstances of your find.** One sentence or a couple paragraphs. Where you found it, what city, the date, any reactions or interpretations you might have. **3. Name your find.** Your found item is your piece now; give it a name, as you would a piece of art.
**4. Mail it to us.** FOUND Magazine, 3455 charing cross road ann arbor, mi 48108-1911

FOUND by ... YOU!

JOIN THE GRASS-ROOTS EFFORT !!
COPY THIS PAGE AND POST IT ALL OVER THE PLACE!
PASS OUT COPIES TO STRANGERS ON THE BUS—MAIL
TO YOUR FRIENDS—PRESENT TO THE CLASS.

REMEMBER: MORE FINDERS = MORE FINDS!

hanging). It's like a soap opera. If I ever go visit you, don't trip! I'll take them off your hands. Well, not Anderson. Anyway, Javier bought m a fish. It was $35. It's so cool. We named it snowball. He's black and white. It's a salt-water fish. It's the dopest fish I ever saw. For some reason a lot of people are saying dope again. **DOPE** Girl, yesterday at ~~work~~ like 12 me and Javi were talking. I told him it was up to him if he wanted to go out w/ me cause he already knows how I feel about it. You know about the long relationship + shit like that. So he said he was willing to take a chance, so & we started going out. Then 23 minutes later I broke up with him. It just wasn't working. Right now I'm in school. Girl, on Tuesday someone stole my wallet. Whoever that dumb bitch was I swear if I find her I'll beat her ass. I think I'm turning violent. You should see me and Javi. We be boxing. One time we were rolling on the floor punching each other and shit. He hits me hard.

Cruz Alta R6
98020-010 Brasil

I still got your shot

Dear Star,

I believe this set
our trust level back
about 3 months I waited till
the trick was almost done
because I wanted to see you
jerk him off, so I'll
be back when you page,
it just sucks that 100[00]
could buy a handjob
I know why you wanted me
to leave, and I heard you
trying to talk quiet but it was
not quiet. only so I gotcha ya,
think about what you will say what I

I found this while cleaning
the litter out of my yard.
I titled it "Star"! My
boyfriend loves the magazine
keep up the good finding

Thanx
June
Milwaukee, W

KEEP LOOKING

RYAN SIAS

[www.ryansias.com]

SEND

IN

YOUR

FINDS!

FOUND Magazine.

A 21 Balloons Production

PLEASE DO NOT PUT CRAB ON MY CAR JUST CUT IT OUT !!!

RYAN SiAS

# FOUND
## magazine

### 3

my new simbol

7 97377 57001 3

03

CONE OF THE FEW THINGS IN THIS WORLD THAT'S WORTH  **5 BUCKS**  99

— Billy Roberts, Loop Distro

Anthong's
Apologies:

Don't read beginning
to end. The
madness will
consume you

"This is history, back-page. From back to front. Happy, tragic, desperate."
—Don DeLillo, *Underworld*

Front cover note FOUND by Genevieve Eustis, Chicago, IL
Front cover "#3" FOUND by Anne Heidemann, Mt.Pleasant, MI
Back cover note FOUND by Nate Cordero, Sacramento, CA
Back cover photos FOUND by Sharon Greene & Logan Kibens; Joe
Baran, Brian Klein, Chicago, IL; Molly Donahue, Ojai, CA;
Jeremy Magichousekey, Dulles, VA; Sarah Falcon, NYC; Janina
Korvick, North Lauderdale, FL; Brenna Dugan, Shanghai, China

I wrote
that
↓ yeah!!!

-Tyler-

Robb isn't going to break up with you He just wants you to show some PDA. He thinks you don't like Him and He would rather break up with you than Have you Kick His Heart's Ass again thats all. He really wants you to go out with Him and He wants you to want to go out with Him not to just go out with Him to say that you got a boy Friend

Dinner
Party
Sometime 2002-
2009

Xmas

Davy
Sam - monica
Sarah-L
J. Provine +1
Aaron-H +1
Dan & Bean
Michael S +1
cameron

DAVY ROTHBART and JASON BITNER
present

# FOUND
magazine #3

## KICK, HIS HEART'S ASS

THE LOVE and HEARTBREAK ISSUE

**POINT GUARD'S LETTER**

Y'all crazy.
Keep sending in shit.
See you on the road!

**Davy Rothbart**

point guard, FOUND Magazine

B. Catalena
Austin, TX
78741

Found Magazine
Crossing Cross Rd
MI
1911

ESS          The Deltiologist

DWC

# FOUND magazine

## 3

this numeral FOUND by John Gergely, Burlington, VT

this photo FOUND by Bob Sartwell, Pasadena, MD

website by JASON BITNER
FOUND logo by BOB DORAN
printed by CHRIS YOUNG
at WEST-CAN [866-669-9914]

the FOUND team

**JASON BITNER**

power forward, FOUND Magazine

**MIKE KOZURA**

**BETH KILLIAN**

**BRANDE WIX**

not pictured:

Jed Lackritz

Michelle Angus

Laurie Molen

Mike DiBella

Aaron Wickenden

Rosemary Darigo

Genevieve Belleveau

Emily Long

Malkah Spivak-Birndorf

Special thanks to Jason Bitner, Beth Killian, Brande Wix, and Genevieve Belleveau for their extraordinary dedication and generosity.
Thanks to Isaac Sparks and DJ Rockwell for the beats, to Rachel Tronstein and Dylan Strzynski for the production help, and most
especially thanks to everyone who has joined this wonderfully rich FOUND community by checking out the magazine and the website,
helping to spread word of this project, and most importantly of all, by sending in your finds. We love you! Peace.

-DAVY

Aw, who needs her? Now I'll have more time to read things I find on the ground!

— Abraham Simpson

FOUND Magazine. Took back the Cup from the Aussies in 1986.

121

April 13, 2003

21 Balloons Production
3455 Charing Cross Rd.
Ann Arbor, MI   48108-1911

Dear Sir

I received the magazine I ordered from you on Saturday.  After looking through it I found it is not what I expected or to my taste.  I am returning the magazine so you may reuse if you like.

Please cancel any future mailings, and I would appreciate a refund.

Although this is not to my taste I do wish you luck in your endeavor.  I'm sure there is a definite "audience" out there that will enjoy your magazine.

Thank you,
Lynne P_____
3_____    T
Ripley, TN   38063

---

8-13-03

Dearest Found Magazine—

A local-library printed out for me your website info, but not contained there was whether or not you pay for items you accept.

Please get back to me when you can: I've got lots of things found that may work. Send your "pay-format" schedule if you have one!   Also tell me if you already know that found (pieces of paper) often have "smudges", "fingerprints", and aren't always camera-ready-type clean. Can these also work? type

Oh, Oh, another question: I just discovered a small column in a newspaper with the name "Rant and Rave". It's people writing-in to anonymously "thank" someone (for example for bumping into my brother on the sidewalk so hard that it cracked a cast on his arm for a broken elbow. The writers are more specific than I've been here with usually where and when the incident happened. WOULD THAT (out of a newspaper) WORK? IS THERE ANY TYPE OF ITEM (OUT OF A NEWSPAPER) YOU WON'T ACCEPT? as long as it's informative and/or "entertaining"?

My point here is: look at the difference in reading "entertainment" between maybe a "Dear Abby" column (versus) a concert or movie ticket if both were found — OVER→ blowing around in the street?... for your readers

Set me straight here on any limits you have on items found in other magazines or news -papers!!! (also what about "trinkets" (objects) found in the street? found a marble yesterday Thank You, I need your answers here before I start sending. Sincerely, (by mail please) Not at home during days.

Norman J.
Norman J._____
5_____   SE.
BELLEVUE, WA. 98006-3320

---

WE LOVE MAIL! KEEP SENDING IN YOUR FINDS — OR JUST WRITE TO SAY HI!

---

FOUND MAGAZINE
3455 CHARING CROSS
Ann Arbor, MI
48108-1911

Found Magazine
3455 Charing Cross Rd.
Ann Arbor, MI  48108-1911

Call To Found Magazine
3455 charing cross rd
Hailey ANN ARBOR, MI
48108

Thy Dearest Kimberly,

How I love thee, let me count the ways:

1. In the Morning,
   When we kiss each other with our dragon breath.
2. At lunch time, when you let me lick your bib clean.
3. At night, when I sneak peeks down your shirt.
4. In the bedroom, when you let me wear ~~the~~ your ~~underwear~~ underwear.

Oh yes, I l<u>o</u>ve, l<u>o</u>ve, l<u>o</u>ve, l<u>o</u>ve, l<u>o</u>ve thee.

**IT MUST BE LOVE**

**FOUND by R.J. Sidwell**

Charleston, IL

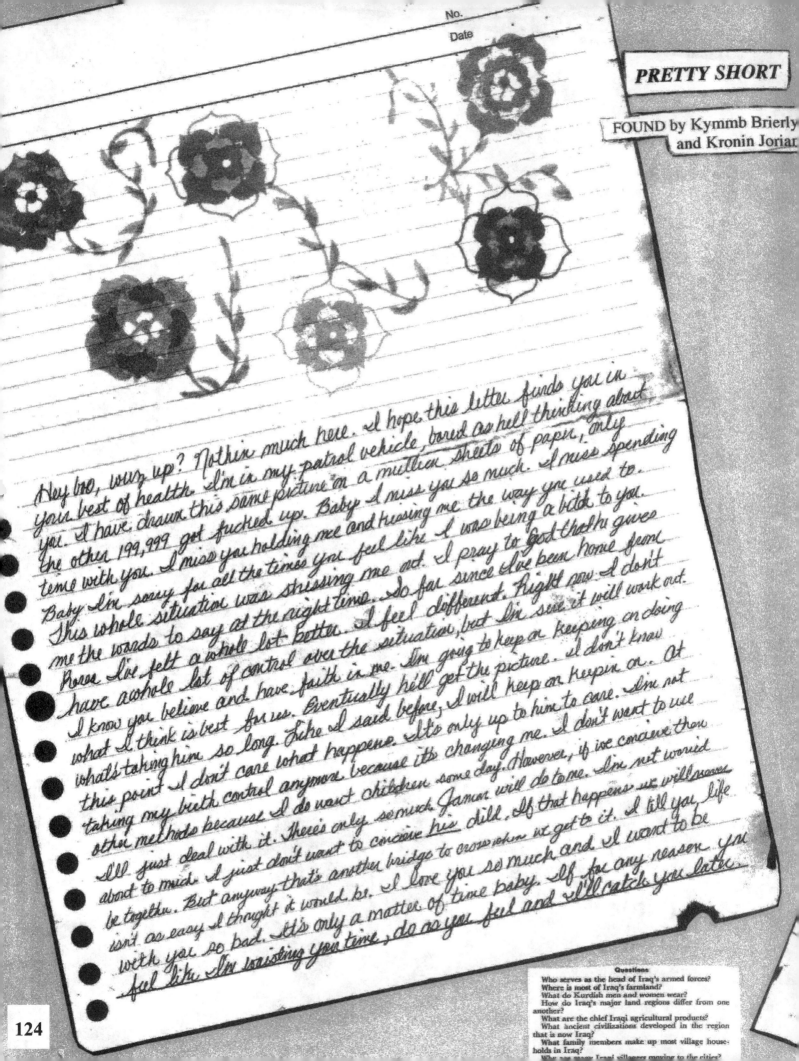

Hey boo, wuz up? Nothin much here. I hope this letter finds you in your best of health. I'm in my patrol vehicle, bored as hell thinking about you. I have drawn this same picture on a million sheets of paper, only the other 199,999 got fucked up. Baby I miss you so much. I miss spending time with you. I miss you holding me and kissing me the way you used to. Baby I'm sorry for all the times you feel like I was being a bitch to you. This whole situation was stressing me out. I pray to God that he gives me the words to say at the night time. So far since I've been home from here I've felt a whole lot better. I feel different. Right now I don't have a whole lot of control over the situation, but I'm sure it will work out. I know you believe and have faith in me. I'm going to keep on keeping on doing what I think is best for us. Eventually he'll get the picture. I don't know what's taking him so long. Like I said before, I will keep on keepin on. At this point I don't care what happens. It's only up to him to care. I'm not taking my birth control anymore because it's changing me. I don't want to use other methods because I do want children some day. However, if we conceive then I'll just deal with it. There's only so much Jamor will do to me. I'm not worried about to much. I just don't want to conceive his dill. If that happens we will never be together. But anyway that's another bridge to cross when we get to it. I tell you, life isn't as easy I thought it would be. I love you so much and I want to be with you so bad. It's only a matter of time baby. If for any reason you feel like I'm wasting your time, do as you feel and I'll catch you later.

105-mm gun · Machine guns · Hatch · Tank commander · Caterpillar tracks · Driver · Gunner · Loader · Engine and transmission

See also BAZOOKA.

No.

Date

Baby don't postpone anything for me. I'll be alive forever. Life is only what you make it. I don't want you to miss out on anything. Life is only what you want to do. I know you only live one life and these days life is pretty short so do all you can and strive for the best because you only get one chance to show God whats up. I'm sorry for all the ache and pain I've caused. You have been so patient and so good to me. I promise I will give it all in return. Little do you know, if my husband was the person I wouldn't know you right now. If only I would have met you first. No matter what, when its all over we are going to be together. That's my word nigga.

Love Always
Tank

125

Asian Pride

Ever since the start
us Asians have fallen apart
but this day in age is when
we display our Asian Pride

Thank you for your interest in our show. Videos
are available for $25.00 each. In your letter you
enclosed a check for $3.00. We will send you a
transcript of the show "How the Potato Changed the
World". If you are still interested in a video please
send us a check or money order for $25.00.

Thanks
Lisa

SPUDS FOUND by Eugenia Dayton, East Lansing, MI

Did your
toothpaste
explode... How
does this
Happen?

CRESTING FOUND b

When you land in hell, the
devil gives you a safety
Pin & says affix it to a
string & draw it thru
that thin slot in this
Parka hood in 5 min.

Tay Peng

INFERNO FOUND by Eugenia Dayton, East Lansing, MI

## COFFEE FILTERS

### FOUND by Angela Lucas

Santa Clara, CA

I found this tattered note in the parking lot of my apartment complex on a rainy day in 1994. I always wondered which came first: the direct, emotion-filled letter to a soon-to-be-ex-spouse, or the reminder to buy coffee filters.

Coffee filters

Why didn't you throw away the note you wrote to me?

If you made a bad choice 16 years ago why did we stay together. Why did we get married + have kids! Can you answer that? If we should have never gotten together why didn't you say something 14 years ago? Why didn't you leave me then instead of waiting 14 years and completely ruining my life.

I think you're using the 'mistake' theory as an excuse because you're in love w/ someone else. To somehow justify your new relationship. Maybe it helps you to forget about the past. I cant believe you've forgotten about the good times we had completely.

Why didn't we do something sooner when there was still a chance to make our marriage/relationship better. I was always willing to be more caring. You never let me or accepted it, always accusing me of being nice because you got mad

To: Eric

Well - I personally think I have taken better pictures... But this is for ~~the~~ you so you don't forget me!.. OK? I'll be home! And ill call or page you.

♡ Alison

(9/98)

I want your "balls" in my mouth!! tee hee.

TEE HEE FOUND by Dan Zatkovich, San Diego, CA

The one who is good at shooting does not hit the center of the target.

The one who is good at shooting does not hit the center of the target.

The one who is good at shooting does not hit the center of the target.

The one who is good at shooting does not hit the target.

Dear ~~Thomas~~ Alex,

   If you don't give me your brain ~~is~~ right now then bring

$20 to the front

desk Now!!!

don't include the Police.

28

illustration by Arthur Jones

- anything I can do to help you out, make anything easier. Anything that I can be there to to them.

- Ever in a bind - call me.

- know things have worked & dont want to completely change everything. Just want to be an extra hand & be able to help. I believe it would a benefit everyone.

- I respect your & admire the incredible work you've done thus far w/ Matt.

- Not trying to replace you

-

- Attend kids events -
  - Baseball games
  - Soccer
  - Recitals
  -

- Be able to pick them up from school/camp

- Become an extra hand for you & Dave.

- Come to a point where we can have social interaction

- Weights point this summer.

-

**NOT TRYING TO REPLACE YOU**

**FOUND by Michelle**

**Columbia, MO**

The last, crossed-out item says, "Not trying to replace you."

## THE THOUGHTS OF A THOUGHTFUL TEEN

FOUND by Tessa McGow and Aliya Bonar

Delray Beach, FL

The thought of a thoughtful Teen
OK last Night — went
to rock the univer: with
My friend, Jaso
/f and Ja
While there I of
thinking. You see really
like Sarah but nt particularly
like part of ture you
see she gets
asked at abt
always says
no problem w/ that
on top of that she
w/ them everyday
that they're going out even
if she doesn't like them
anymore I mean its lik
If you ask her out you
get a couple days of free
Make-outs and then she
dumps you like it was
nothing special. I think Making
out should be a special
thing that you do w/ someone
you really care about.
But I guess Sarah thinks
differently. An then theres Me
the only friend she has ever
had that didn't make out
w/ there a couple reasons
she br with me but

When she did it I only.
got 1 and I quote,
What she told her friend
She no longer talks to
She dosent ~~want~~ want a
long distance relashionship.
Well that wouldnt b a problem
~~so~~ if I could somehow make
out w/ her everyday which
I think is ~~so if as~~ the reasons
She didnt want a long distance
relationship. The other reason
she ~~so~~ broke up with me which
I wasnt told is because
I'm prude as hell! (Pah)
I mean IV never even kissed
on the lips and that brings
me to antother point its
what I like to call the
never ending cycle ok,
nobody will make out w/ u
if your prude and you
cant be un pruded if nobody
will make out w/u so
I am doomed to never
make out unless I find
somebody who is prude
who I like in highschool
which is very unlikely because
everyone is already having sex

131

and now to another point I am not like many other human forteen year old boys I unlike others am not a walking talking mass of hormones like the others. I am just not I dont know why and I dont know if its a good or a bad thing. o yes and I found that Sarah is totally more horney than me which I think is kinda screwed up last night she must have given about 50 guys. really big hugs which let me note is all I ever got and we were going out and two guys she gave about 15 kisses to. oh the lips each ~~them~~ and she didnt even know theyre names she knew Mze and we actualy went out and I Never even kissed her on the lips I got More action last night when she kissed me on the cheek that was the most action IV ever got that

I wasnt on a date. so
I guess theres 3 things
I can do to change that
1 be somebody Im not
2 do something stupid
3 change my appearence
And I dont ever really
want to do any of those
things purpousely but thats
What americas all about
those three things kind of
define pop culture
right now in line... In fact
song about number 1. I to a
alternitive is never And the
anything sexual or talk about
about any girl ever romantic
have a lot of ~~XXXX~~ and just
and never make out friends
anything of that nature or
I guess I should consult
people and get back to u
when I have something which I to
tell u well ill will
ok a . talk to
you then a i just
thought of something Ill
write all the things I
want to write on T-shirts

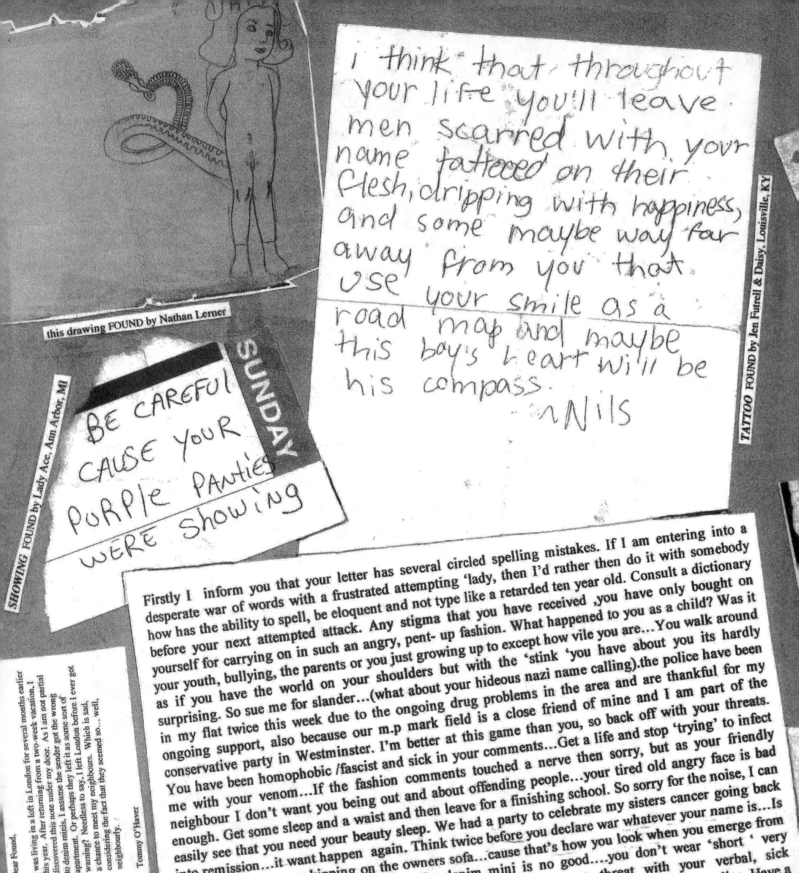

SUNDAY

BE CAREFUL
CAUSE YOUR
PURPLE PANTIES
WERE SHOWING

i think that throughout your life you'll leave men scarred with your name tattooed on their flesh, dripping with happiness, and some maybe way far away from you that use your smile as a road map and maybe this boy's heart will be his compass.
— Nils

**Dear Found,**

I was living in a loft in London for several months earlier this year. After returning from a two-week vacation, I discovered this note under my door. As I am not partial to denim minis, I assume the sender got the wrong apartment. Or perhaps they left it as some sort of warning? Needless to say, I left London before I ever got a chance to meet my neighbours. Which is sad, considering the fact that they seemed so… well, neighbourly.

Tommy O'Haver

GET A WAIST

Found by Tommy O'Haver

in Soho, London, July 2003

Firstly I inform you that your letter has several circled spelling mistakes. If I am entering into a desperate war of words with a frustrated attempting 'lady, then I'd rather then do it with somebody how has the ability to spell, be eloquent and not type like a retarded ten year old. Consult a dictionary before your next attempted attack. Any stigma that you have received ,you have only bought on yourself for carrying on in such an angry, pent- up fashion. What happened to you as a child? Was it your youth, bullying, the parents or you just growing up to except how vile you are…You walk around as if you have the world on your shoulders but with the 'stink 'you have about you its hardly surprising. So sue me for slander…(what about your hideous nazi name calling).the police have been in my flat twice this week due to the ongoing drug problems in the area and are thankful for my ongoing support, also because our m.p mark field is a close friend of mine and I am part of the conservative party in Westminster. I'm better at this game than you, so back off with your threats. You have been homophobic /fascist and sick in your comments…Get a life and stop 'trying' to infect me with your venom…If the fashion comments touched a nerve then sorry, but as your friendly neighbour I don't want you being out and about offending people…your tired old angry face is bad enough. Get some sleep and a waist and then leave for a finishing school. So sorry for the noise, I can easily see that you need your beauty sleep. We had a party to celebrate my sisters cancer going back into remission…it want happen again. Think twice before you declare war whatever your name is…Is it your flat or are you kipping on the owners sofa…cause that's how you look when you emerge from that den every morning…By the way the denim mini is no good….you don't wear 'short ' very well…would be better rapped around your chops….You are a threat with your verbal, sick homophobic comments…which with my witnesses I would be happy to discuss with the police. Have a good long hard look in the mirror at yourself. And if it doesn't crack…think before you challenge me next time. I DO know who you are, contrary to your belief. Enjoy the sun…hottest weather since 1976 don't you know…makes a change from the heat that pours out of your flabby rancid mouth.

*Your neighbour.*

A moment where I saw a women bopping to some beat other a 3rd person saw it + we made a mental contact

driving down a road, night, rainy thoughts of friends + worldly issues discussion of the twisted mind at night

...s. I will always be the only thing I have left of my dad will never give it up.

what do you say to people you love, but have never truely met?

I turned 18 years old on May 10th. I graduated High School in June 2001. I have a job. I'm living in Minneapolis, Minnesota.

I have wanted to come visit for as long as I can remember. Mom always said, as soon as you're 18 you can go. I'm 18. I'm ready. I have waited long enough to be who I am today - I've waited long enough to know where my roots are.

I want to be able to go to my father's grave whenever I want to talk to him. I want to bring him flowers. I want to meet my brother. I want to get to know my dad.

Know that I've always loved you! xoxoxo
.la

B

CULLEY/ERLES/OR/
REGULAR/ERLES/WAELL/
THAT?

off top right of head

I KNOW OOO OO
I'LL GO OUT
HUNTING FOR
STUFF TO SEND
TO FOUND
MAGAZINE!

this photo FOUND by Pete Kelly, Jackson, MI

FOUND Magazine's Davy Rothbart (left) a Jason Bitner (right) in a lighter mom

this drawing FOUND by Nina Ganei, St. Louis, MO

HAPPY 50TH
FOUND by Eric Lyden
Brockton, MA

At the end of work one night I went out to collect shopping carts in the parking lot and came across this roll of pictures.

CVS 1 Hour Pho

Print Order
☑ Singles
☐ Doubles

Index Print?
(Index prints are standard with APS orders)
☐ Reprints/Enlargement     ☐ Yes

Film Size
☑ 35mm

```
MONTHLY BUDGET

RENT        600.

CELL PHONE  50.
TELEPHOE    50

ELEC/Gas    45.

CABLE       60.

Bus/TAXI    60

FOOD        500.

LIQUOR      600 INCL BArs    ($20⁰⁰ per DAY)

LAUNDRY     30

CRACK       600

ATTORNEY    250

MISC        250.

ASVINGS     100


TOTAL INCOME NEEDED     $ 3195.00

        YEARLE INCOME NEEDED $ 38,220.00
```

*Kirt was telling me she was talking to a friend of hers. The friend told Kirt that she was at a party & some guy was snorting coke & didn't finish it so he asked if she'd like to finish the line. And she was like "okay, sure!"*

*what the heck! It's like as casual as finishing someone's beer or something...*

*I was at a party at Tyler's and they were talking about where they could get crack and stuff and I couldn't believe they didn't have any/couldn't get any.*

**JANITOR'S CLOSET**

FOUND by Geraldine Paulino, Brentwood, N

*Christy—*
*Conor made me cut gym and go into janitor's closet... I hope you don't mind he no can't get enough of me! Sorry if he doesn't talk to you again, you can have Bill unless he comes crying to me again.*

*Have a nice day*
*your local crack dealer*

**CASUAL FOUND by Steven Schnoor, Toronto**

**MONTHLY BUDGET**

**FOUND by Lea McKenny Willcox**

Minneapolis, MN

Sometimes when I'm sorting through piles of FOUND stuff, I wonder how all of somebody's belongings came to be stacked next to a Dumpster or scattered along the side of the road in the first place. This printed-out email, which was found wet in the grass, seems to supply the potential back-story for one of these scenes. — DAVY

## AOL Anywhere

| Main | My AOL | Mail | People | Search | Shop | Channels | Devices |

ScreenName sign-out

ScreenName sign-out

## AOL Mail℠

Prev 1 of 18 Next

☐ Inclu originalte in Reply

Close    Delete

Subj: things
Date: Fri, 19 Jan 2001 11:18:04 AM Eastern Standard
From: ...8yahoo.com
To:

Reply

Reply Al

Forward

I have never had anything like this happen to me before, so I'll try not to get too angry and bitter. I know that you hate confrontation, and that is probably why you have chosen to forget about me, but there are still some things that we need to face up to. The first thing you need to do is pick up your funrniture, clothes, pans, clocks, and kitchen ware. Everytime I walk through the apartment and look at it I can't help but remember things and then I get angry and sad. If you still had any feelings for me whatsoever you would come get this stuff by the 31st. This next request might sound childish and petty, but please don't bring that guy (JP?) you are seeing over with you to help you. He can drive the truck or whatever but there is no way he is even stepping foot into my apartment. I have been doing a good job not doing anything stupid and hurting myself or anything else (a miricle for me considering what happened last time), so try to respect my wishes on that at least. You might not think you ow e me that, but try to put yourself in my shoes for a moment, and try to see how much it would hurt you if I did that. I would rather it was your Dad, or Josh, or Ritchie, or Matt, or Tanya, or Jesse, or Luque or Chris or hell even Keith than that guy. Also, the other thing we need to resolve is your phone.
Funny, I always thought you would be using it to call me. Shit, sorry. Don't take that as a sign that I want the phone or anything. I bought it for you and I want you to keep it. Plus, I can't afford an extra thirty five dollars a month, and I am in a contract and can't cancel. So please, whenever you are in town for the weekend visiting whomever call me and we can meet at the Sprint PCS place outside the mall and switch it over. Try to e-mail me or respond. Do not delete this and ignore me and your things. I don't want this to get any uglier than it already has. Some people told me that Tennessee state law requires that I only give you a weeks notice before I can sell or throw away your things
If you count from the day I called your cell that's more than enough time. Don't think I want to keep any of your stuff, like I said its to painful to look at, I would just as rather burn it all (including the microwave which I need) than be reminded of what you've done to me. I know you think I am being hateful and mean, but don't take it that way. I just can't stop hurting. I gotta go. Bye.

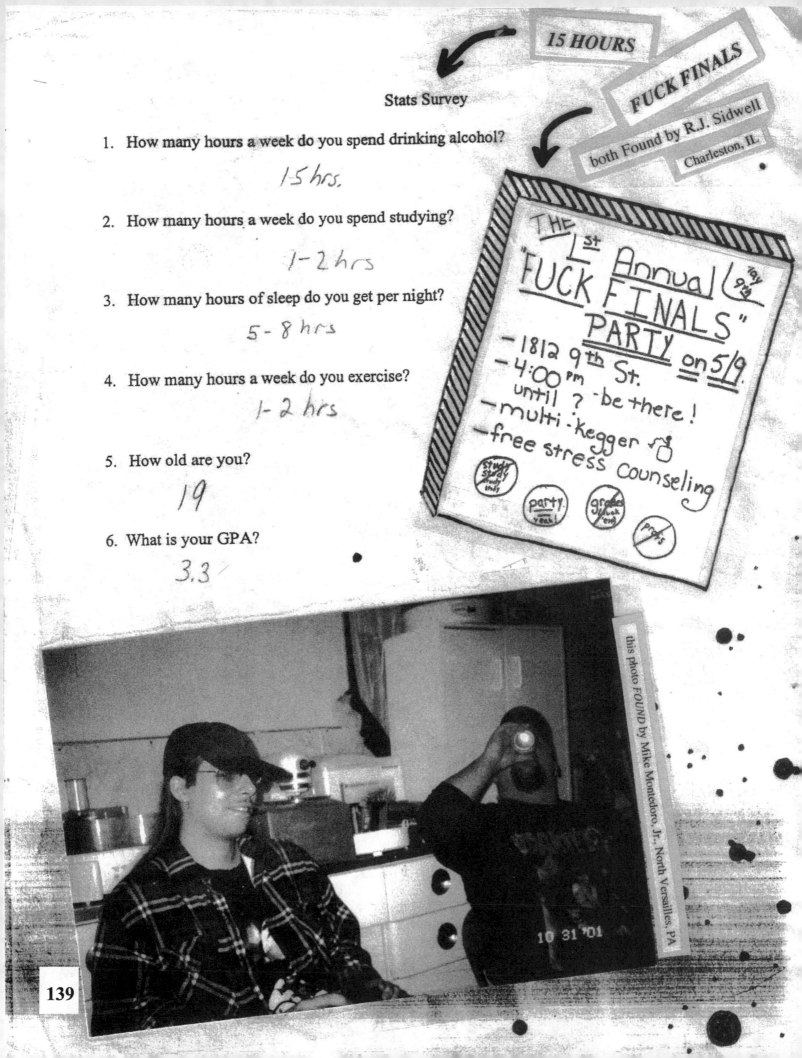

Stats Survey

1. How many hours a week do you spend drinking alcohol?

15 hrs.

2. How many hours a week do you spend studying?

1-2 hrs

3. How many hours of sleep do you get per night?

5-8 hrs

4. How many hours a week do you exercise?

1-2 hrs

5. How old are you?

19

6. What is your GPA?

3.3

15 HOURS

FUCK FINALS

both Found by R.J. Sidwell    Charleston, IL

THE 1st Annual "FUCK FINALS" PARTY on 5/9

May 9th

- 1812 9th St.
- 4:00 pm until ? - be there!
- multi-kegger
- free stress counseling

study study only

party yeah!

grades who cares

profs

this photo FOUND by Mike Montedoro, Jr. North Versailles, PA

10 31 '01

# A YEAR APART

**FOUND by Matt Kuehl**

Providence, R.I.

Trapped out of sight behind a radiator in a dim, dusty corner of a basement storage room on the Brown University campus sits a small taped-up cardboard box. When the box is sliced open, the densely-packed papers inside burst free. A passport and a student ID reveal the owner of the box to be a Brown student from the mid-'80's named Jamie Wi........ Along with a birthday card from his grandmother, a note from one of his hometown friends, and a couple of class registration forms, the box contains over two-hundred letters from Jamie's girlfriend, Mika, written over the course of her junior year abroad in Japan.

Mika seems to have written to Jamie every day, sometimes several times a day. She fills thousands of pages with her tight, tiny scrawl. Some letters include drawings and pictures of her. She also begins to create delicate mobiles out of fishing line and colored paper for her boyfriend. We never see Jamie's letters to her but she refers to things he's said, so it's clear that he writes to her as well. Still, it feels inevitable when midway through the year, Jamie apparently takes up with another girl. Mika writes a little bit about how sad she is about his new girlfriend, how strange and difficult it is to imagine him with somebody else, but, oddly, her letters barely shift in tone or in frequency—in fact, if anything, the letters grow longer and arrive at an increasing pace.

Finally—in what feels impossibly sad to the one who's FOUND this box—comes the discovery that at some point Jamie stopped opening Mika's letters at all. The unopened envelopes, filled with thoughts and emotions that will never see the light of day, are a blow to the heart.

—DAVY

I miss you so much — it's pathetic.

7 Sept. 1986

I'm in my room by the window, smoking a clove cigarette. In front of me, on my shelf are 2 photos of you. Looking pretty artistic, and not to mention beautiful, with your sculpture.

I get such satisfaction from sharpening my pencils with an X-acto knife. When I got 6 Berol color pencils, I came home & discovered that I didn't bring my sharpener. I had no choice but to get my knife & sharpen them all. It's methodical, requiring you to turn these colorful sticks around and around. When the lead peeps through, then you have to go at a sharper angle to make a point. The pencils acquire character - you know, the points all look different. This one is called Copenhagen Blue. Such a dignified name for plain blue.

25 April 1986. It's won...
...ent. I went & got my haircut ...a woman haircutter whom I've known f... ...ut it. She's a bit far away, so I didn't ...most settled for someone around here. ...d a great job. Let me tell you. This hair ...hair & mine is like the same - amount wis... did this thing called the 'sliding cut', w... ...ntedly ① So what she does is runs the sc... by opened, and slides the scissor... ...keeping it root to end. It would ... ...have hurt someone like you - since ... ...hair is thin & scalp tender, it seems ... ...I have very little hair, it makes me feel ... ...I can have long hair w/o the hassle. "Comm... ...what it looks like → wispy & ti... ...at - that I bounced out ...of the sh... ...downtown area. ...borhood and went ... c story my neigh- ...2 pairs of ...myself... LIKE SO. And a hai... ...GREY.

...gazed at something behind me. I turned...
...ing from the ceiling, was a mobile, of storks ma[de]
Japanese paper (origami — do you know this? An old fold[ed]
...ding paper to make animals & flowers, etc.) 5 of them in su...
...ous levels, by my mint dental floss.

like this (it is SO beautiful. She's talented. She was coope[d]
up all day today, making this & other animals.

←dental floss   They are all flying — it is so delicate & sere[ne]

I have been having STUPID dreams — Madonna poppe[d]
my dream the other night — Then I dreamed that tha[t]
my left underarm hair was longer than my righ[t]
I MEAN REEEDiCULOUS. You see.

I hope you had a nice Thanksgiving — tell me what you di[d]
:30 — getting sleepy...

I love you Jamie — My eyes are drawing to a close.

AEROGRAMME
航空書簡

AEROGRAMME
航空書簡

AEROGRAMME

AEROGRAMME
航空書簡

AEROGRAMME
航空書簡

Jamie W. _
2886 P.   NW
CANTON , OH
44709

USA

Last night me and Ed did it
I told him to get a condom
because I'm ~~XXXX~~ fertil
And he said he didn't have
any. I know he was lying
So I told him to take me to the
store and he was acting like
he was tired. So he ~~XXXX~~ stuck
it in anyway and when he was
about to come it slipped out
and he just stuck it back in
and came. I think he's trying
to get me pregnant.

ED

FOUND by Thomas Craig

St. Louis, MO

## ROCKIN' CHEEKS

**FOUND by Sarah Daines**     Madison, WI

My husband and I were buying a used book at the local thrift store. While checking out, we were flipping through the pages, and noticed this stuck inside. We tried to show the cashier because we thought it was so funny. He somehow misunderstood us and thought we were showing him a picture of my husband, ass and all. Naturally, the cashier was pretty uncomfortable until we explained that we had just found it in the book.

*PERSPECTIVE*

**FOUND by Fredrik**

Minneapolis, MN

FANNY

**FAN FROM AFAR**

**FOUND by Scott Pendergraft**

Bellingham, WA

FOUND MAGAZINE.

Booty Don't STOP

by Rama Hughes

You DDNt Know ME BVt I LIKE Your ASS. aNd MaByE someTime I COULd squeeze It! ☺

Your secret Adminier!

Jess,

Hey, Sup? Anywayz I know this might sound stupid to you but I have been thinking a lot about this whole thing with you moving out. It just seems that even though you say Josh had nothing to do with you moving out I feel it did. I keep trying to make myself believe that you wouldn't choose Josh over your family, but I guess I can't be completly sure. I guess it just really bothers me that you did this after all your dad did for you. I'm not mad at you, but I just wanted you to know how I feel, and I feel your making a mistake. I talked to my mom yesterday and she said that you won't be coming over at all. Which means we will never be seeing each other anymore. And this makes me so sad because I love and enjoy you so much. It won't be the same without you, You are always the one who cheers me up and your not here anymore to do that! But I hope that we can talk on the phone (you know the #) or catch a movie sometime but we will have to see. I hope your not made at me, but anyway I have a lot more I want to talk to you about so I will probably write to you again. But Just writing this note is making me cry! But I guess I just wanted to write you this note to say how much I love and miss you and I guess for awhile this is GOODBYE!!!

P.S. write me back and give it to Tony to give to me on the bus.
Sorry its so messy!

♡ always
-n-
4-ever
your sister,
Stephanie

**Jeannine**

To whom it may concern:

This letter is in regards to the invasion of my privacy. I would appreciate any direct information leading to the explanation of this. Periodically, for ten years there have been famous and non-famous strangers watching me in the privacy of my home via wireless technology. Wherever I exist in the world, these strangers stalk me and invade my privacy. I am constantly surviving interpreting the constant malicious manipulation of my environment by these complete strangers. As I am typing this letter I am being watched by over thirty groups of hostile strangers stationed all around my apartment. For the past several years I have been stalked and my privacy has been invaded every second of every day and night by complete strangers.

People such as Tom Hanks, Bill Gates, Steven Spielberg, Kate Capshaw, Melinda Gates, Eddie Money, Axl Rose, Paul Allen, Tom Petty, Ivanna Trump, Michael Eisner, Kenny Loggins, Jamie Lee Curtis, George Lucas, some members of The Rolling Stones, The Who, The Beatles, Led Zepplin, to name **very few** of the people who were and are involved, have added to this hate crime and harassment.

Despite my pleas to ask them to leave me alone, these people keep finding new people to watch me. Sometimes, some of these people gratify themselves or each other sexually while invading my privacy in all arenas in which I choose to live. There is also drug use at times by some of these people while invading my privacy. At times, these people are accompanied by escorts and or somebody's children while brutally intruding on my life.

I am greatly incapacitated by all this and the talk that surrounds such treatment of a human being. Along with the excruciating pain that is everpresent due to this unwanted intrusion by these famous and non-famous strangers, I am not employable because of the false reputation I have been handed by these brutal strangers. While sadistically invading my privacy, people from Microsoft and Warner Brothers Studios, among **several** other companies have told me I will only know suffering and I will never be able to live without being terrorized by the people they motivate to perpetuate this hate crime for which I am the target.

Before these famous people held charity dinners on behalf of the cause that they fabricated around my life and exploited me in every way imaginable, I had a happy, typical, affluent, conservative, respectable, middle-class life. I had no reputation as did all of my naturally selected peers. I have no idea how any famous person knows that I exist. I have never had the first thing to do with any famous person or anyone who has ever had anything to do with them or anyone they ever knew.

I have been conservatively waiting for ten years for this hate crime and intrusion to end and there is no end in sight. Someone tied to some famous person obstructs the delivery of this letter at times. So, if you receive this letter and are able to shed any light on this please call or write. The only way I know anything about this exploitation of me is by interpreting the antagonistic manipulation of my environment by complete strangers. I am desperately seeking one human being to shed light on this in person. I look forward to hearing from you.

Sincerely,

Jeannine

CHARITY DINNERS

FOUND by Thomas Bergan

Olympia, WA

I found fifty copies of this letter on the floor of the post office about ten years ago.

hat works to rehabilitate young lawbreakers.

Most prisons consist of a group of buildings su
ounded by a wall or barbed-wire fence. Armed guard

11-05-03

To Davy Rothbart or, whom ever this may concern,
I am currently a Denver Count Jail inmate. I read
issue #2 of your FOUND Magazine. Honestly I think
it is one of the most interesting magazines I have
ever read into. That is the first book or magazine I
have read in it's entirety from beginning to end
since I was in the 8th grade and, I'm 22 now.
I was reading the magazine and I came across a
page that says that, you will send issues free to
jailed inmates. I would love it if, you were able to
send me all of your issues. The issue #2 I read belongs
to another inmate so, I would need that too. This
IS A SERIOUS INQUIRY. Upon my release, you
will DEFINITELY hear from me again because,
I will subscribe to the magazine. If I find anything
you might like, you definitely will see it, I already
know what to do. Keep up the good work and, findings!
I will let my friends know as well. Once again please
send all of the issues you can. You will be reimbursed.
May the Lord bless you and, thank you for your
creative magazine.             —Dean R—
(send to)
Dean R. bwens                P.S. I should get released
#1327067                     anytime between 12/15/03
Denver Sheriff Department    and 05/04. -Thank again-
P.O. Box 1108
Denver, CO  80201

We believe in providing literature to prison
inmates—we will provide free copies of FOUND to
any U.S. inmate who writes in and requests one;
please let your incarcerated friends know.   This
program is funded by readers, many of whom have
pledged to send in any money they find on the
ground.  Please support this program by sending in
FOUND (or non-FOUND) money—the folks who
receive these magazines are extremely appreciative!

found magazine

3455 charing cross • ann arbor, mi • 48108

In keeping w/ your "free for the imprisoned"
policy, please send a copy of Found to my friend
on death row, William Michael Hamars, NC Central
Prison, DOC #0136299, 4300 Western Blvd,
Raleigh NC 27606-2148.
Thanks!
Mike H

Dear Found Magazine —
A friend sent me a flyer
for your Magazine. It says you'll
send me some literature IF I
write and ask—So I am.
I am an inmate at Portland
Oregon's Inverness Jail in Multnomah
Multnomah county. My address is
as follows:

Joseph Milton Matheny
#6740183-0
11540 NE Inverness Dr.
Portland  OR  97220

I am here untill Dec. 2nd 2005
so I don't know if I qualify or
not but, I have friends interested
aswell.
I hope to hear back.

Sincerely,
Joe

Dear Found Magazine,                    monday
                                        11-3-03

Hi there! I was fortunate to have
heard your address on the radio K.P.F.T.
last week. I am hoping that the News
I head is true. The lady said you have
a real good magazine that is free to
prisoners. I'm incarcerated in the Texas
prison system. Would you please hook me up
so I can read your rag? Please put
me on your mailing list.

Phil Slughiti # 8327614
Polunsky Unit
3872 FM 350 S.
Livingston, Texas 77351

Thank you Kindly!

Phil Steward

Have a Happy
Holiday Season
☺

HELLO MY NAME IS
Bod sims.

I AM DEAF!

HOW ARE you smile?
I AM fine!

PLEASE HELP me
I BORROW $8.00 OUT
Running GAS my CAR
I will PAY BACH YOU
FRiday smile?

THANk you
God Bless
you smile

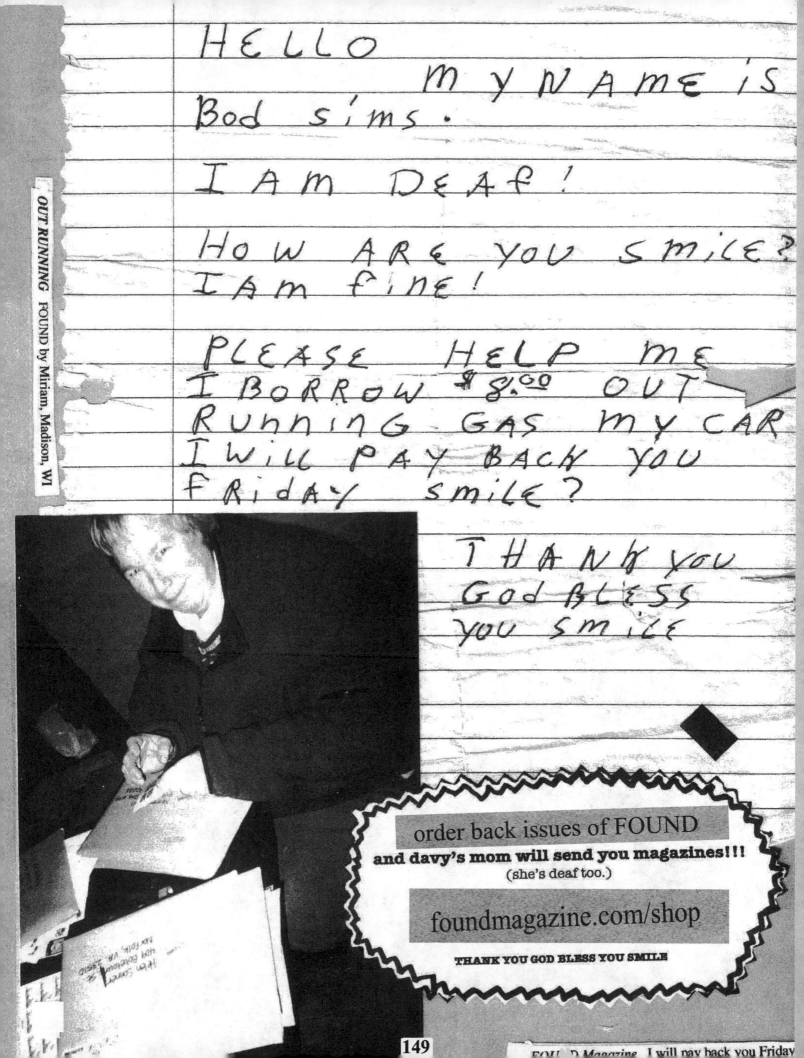

FOUND Magazine  I will pay back you Friday

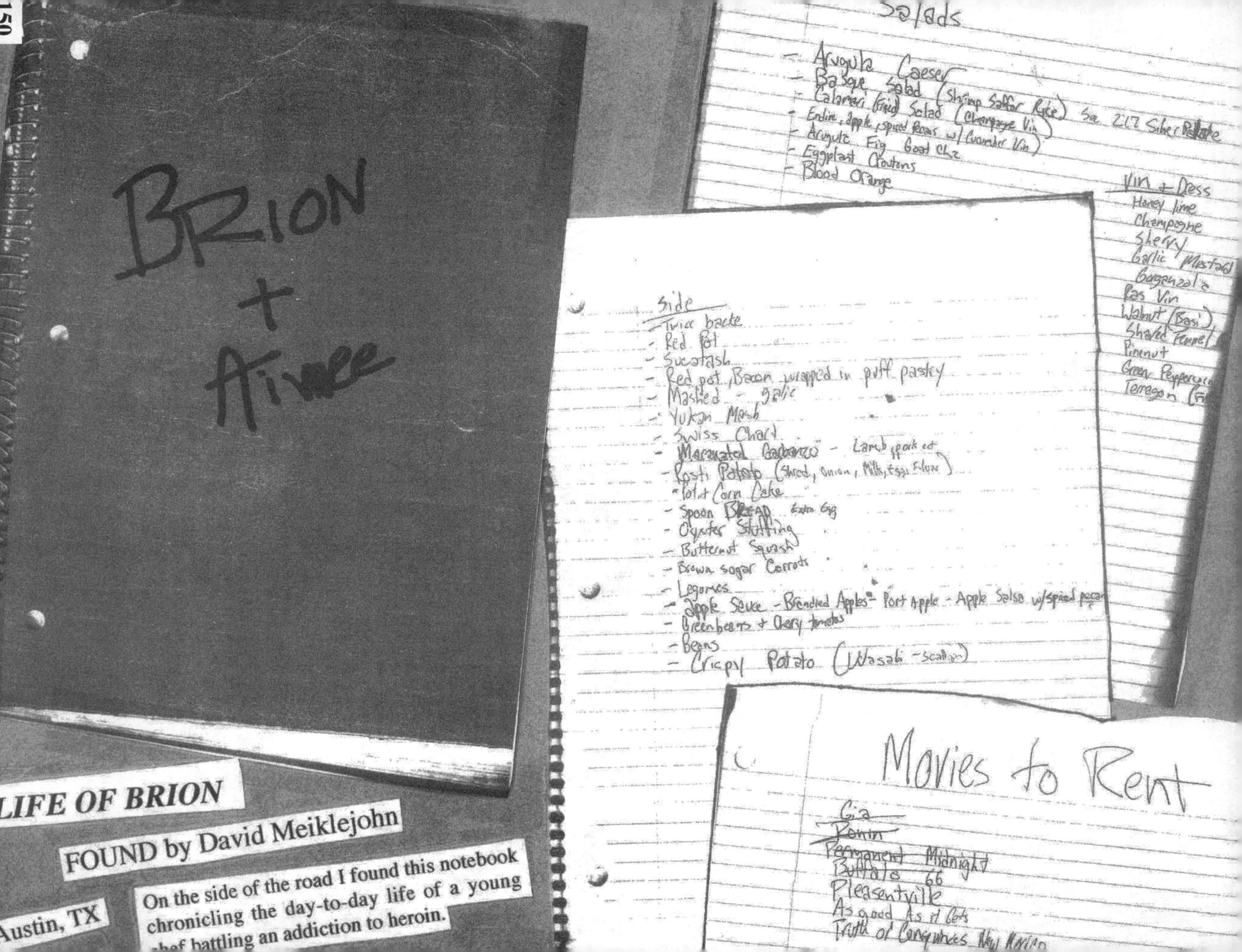

5/8/05

- Arugula Caesar
- Basque Salad
- Calabaza (fig) Salad (Shrimp Salsa Vie) Sa 217 Silver Palate
- Endive + apple spiced Beans w/ Lavender Vin
- Arugula Fig Goat Chz
- Eggplant Croutons
- Blood Orange

Vin + Dress
- Honey Lime
- Champagne
- Sherry
- Garlic Mustard
- Balsamic
- Res Vin
- Walnut (Bosc)
- Shallot Thyme
- Peanut
- Green Peppercorn
- Tarragon (T)

Side
- Twice bake
- Red Pot
- Succotash
- Red Pot, Bacon wrapped in puff pastry
- Mashed - garlic
- Yukon Mash
- Swiss Chard
- Marinated Garbanzo - Lamb Peak set
- Rosti Potato (Sliced, Onion, Milk, Egg, Flour)
- Pot + Corn Bake
- Spoon Bread - corn bag
- Oyster Stuffing
- Butternut Squash
- Brown sugar Carrots
- Legumes
- Apple Slice - Brandied Apples - Port Apple - Apple Salsa w/spiced pear
- Greenbeans + Dery Beans
- Beans
- Vichy Potato (Wasabi - scallion)

Movies to Rent
- Go
- Ronin
- Permanent Midnight
- Buffalo 66
- Pleasantville
- As Good As It Gets
- Truth of Consequences Why Killin

BRION
+ Aime

**Thursday July 15th**

a brand New Tee in the Life of Brian
1st off No dope that nothing new but
still need to keep working on it
Know from of Dop is a Happier Brian
Now I'm going to watch Brian
+ then Right Good + watch Eat + Loathing
to write a review & movies try
so far
Each of to get low 2 week no more no less
Starting today of tomorrow & I'll tell you late
Next Nor savings Plan
Mr & Mrs Ma + Pa today
Don't Forget 9am Keitha Sunday

30 Push ups
Savings Plan
Making Rent

---

**CRAB Cakes**                    **Tomato Fenel Broth**
2lb Crab                          Fin L. stock
1T Parika        2 Kilp pp
1T cleyene       1 Fenn
1 c Mayo         1 Celery
½ c Mustard      1 Sm Union
¼ c Wost         Panco Crumbs

Sarba            Eat Pot
Simple Syrup     12 Pot pot
3c. Sugar        7 Slit Bacon
2c Wata          Puff Pastry
Zest Fruit       S+P

Road Butternutt Squash +Puree
Wine
Garlic
Roastel Shallots
J Portobell + Squash garnish
25:00.00

---

**Monday July 17-99**

So I feel like I don't talk much I
got drunk at Jis instead so we have
Good News The Mand held Kress Wharf
Need to put a Packet on quick Don't Forget
No Smack - Smack No good for BRI. I
Will hope everything is Okay 2d
I really have made a Cautions effort to
Not use last week I had to go in there wha
with Ajave + It's so much nicer in there wha
your Clear + you could tell that to go Shay Holmes
Fink themselves Like running into
who's probably watching us anyway 10 Push ups

---

**FRIDAY JULY 16**

Have Meeting with Moody soon
Finish Jesus short write a short Report
another Dev in Free day          10 push ups

---

**Saturday July 17**

(5 push ups) The most important thing I
do today is not do the poison
day as the Life of Brian another
this Kid from my film not Learning to Control
have a long day of work Myndrine I
just make A through also call B the must
(check on Moda)
Gas stop —Looking Net—
high K-man Junkie Super Hero
his Skill + where he gets a spoonful of Stomach
look at bed + Junk-star Loves to come down
down + Junk-star Loves to come down (Hunger)

2 scenes          Jefferson Giba Matte Helion
Mr Bright + Dillinger Escape Plan

---

**Sunday July 18**

Goal #1 So Nice to be I need to
write Risotto Recipe Friday fire Und Today Is
1 Day without work so hopefully I can spend
Rest the with you!
FINAL COLLECTION (15:00.00

**Ideas for Marty**

D5
Silk screen
Tatto
Kinkos

---

July 23 1999

No smack today I know a chip would be nice but be all know how that works. It is hard now having that #. that is such a good deal. I have counseling that should help. That boss of ours is fucking like twirp I think that's why he stays away tomorrow. he says I see through his little bullshit world.

July 24

Stay away from H bomb

It gonna - with You Only Live Twice @ Sean Connery
25 007

July 25 - No Dope No Work
see ya tomorrow

July 26 - 99

Live Smack Free or Die I've got lots to do today please give me the strength to talk to my parents + hope that all goes well And wish me the best I'll luck with each. G-shit Tyra You
day line Three one syde Bikini girl + overside
Rima's living down 007
10 push #
7 push up

---

July 22 1998
Goal 4 day
Say Nope to Dope

10 Pushups

Things to do
Must Call Parole (list)
Walk
I missed you over the last few days
I need to make writting me a priority such
as not missing days + last but not entirely not
reports, Takeing stuff Here thugs I must
least more breathe, Land of the
birth or land the USOR A Land Your health
Free or US could the reason for because I'm
in the care is 3D expensive fuck it I'm
health by some Path write now I need to practice
Not by it finster now because (B-Physical)
thing have on Budget always too good
not waking have on seeing spill in this
problems now seeing chill always too
situation I feel i have make sure. a line
about it I just must midnight then was a
Permanent Midnight though he was cleaned
that grabbed me I'm then he made a comment about
od pising much better with his luck he probly
much July 23 so much now about how I fel. I
any thing that happen to be alive press day aside
from my mouth.

Quiche of the day
served with a fresh green salad

BROWN SUGAR BABY
Piping Hot cinnamon brown sugar Anj Cakes

Rose mary's

Aimeé
(To Love)

- Corn Beef Hash
  with chopped eggs & a piece of toast

- Vegetarian Hash
  seasonal vegetables Aet 12's Sundrk

- Bri's Famous B-BQ Chick Sandwich

- Grilled Chees with Pesto

- Sloppy Jose
  (second)   Tenderloin cooked down in
           a tomato sauce with cilantro, scallion,
           & Jalapeno, served on Fresh White Bread

- Prosciutto Cristo
  with Cape Creme fraîche

- Cranberry Pecan

"Things to Do when the Heroin Demon
is in the House"

1st Recognize I'm having urges & really
really. I don't even the
because the
fast. I have
long they'll have
talk to someone or a million. One
I see them
next time question or a million.
either one will be much easier
People Aimee - Marty
           Loni - or anyone from meetings
           Matthew   ● Tina

06 Honda CRx Hatchback
Automatic
Trans

There are so many reasons why going to
college would help me. All my life I have always
taken much pride in

Dream Resturant

Lemans

- Bumper Cars - Pinball

Burger & Beer

- Waitress on Skates

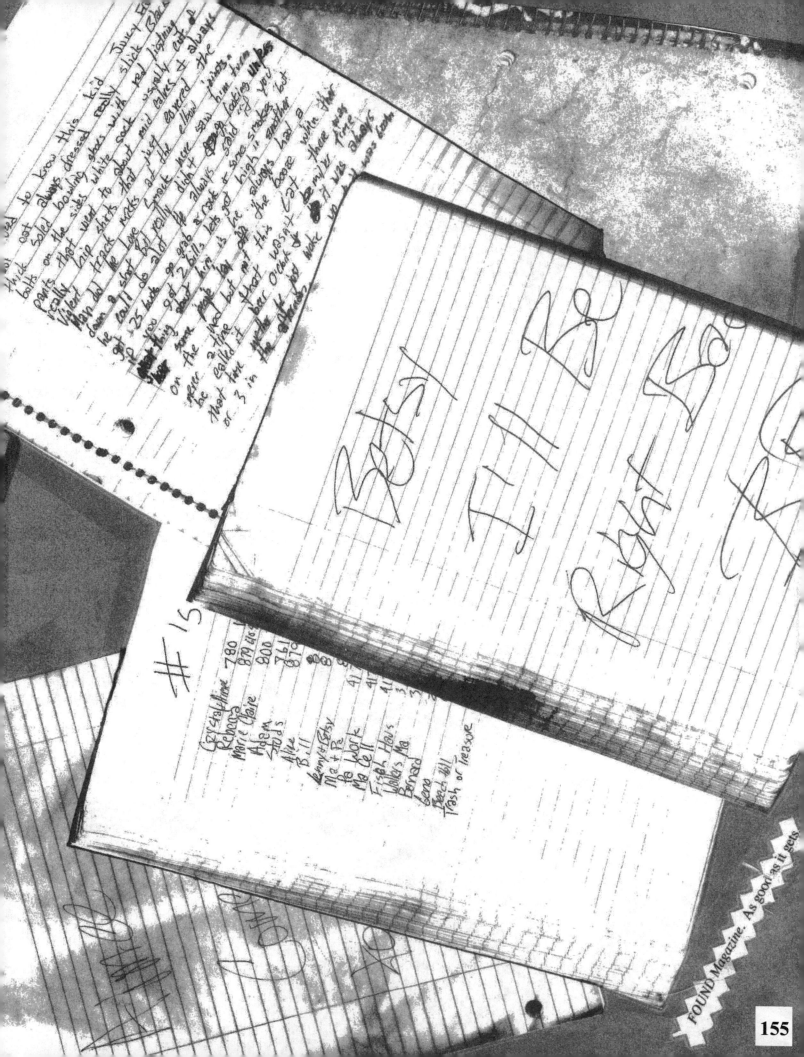

# The Obituary

**A**NTHONY JEROME OYAMO MANOR was born on January 20, 1983 to Denise and Anthony. He was affectionately known as "A.J." and his mother had a special name for him, "Poppa".

Anthony was intelligent from the start. Once he saw something done, he could do it. He was never afraid of a challenge.

He was the oldest of six children and he never let them forget it. He may have bossed them around at times, but he learned early how to take care and protect them. He excelled in all sports in which he won awards for, but football was his passion.

He was educated in the public school system, and later received his high school diploma. He had planned to attend college to study Criminal Justice.

He came to Mt. Zion Pentecostal Church for Vacation Bible School, and then started to attend Sunday School. He knew the Lord Jesus Christ.

He leaves to cherish fond memories: His mother Denise; father Anthony; four brothers, Dennis, James, Taj, and Cortez; one sister LaTavia; two grandmothers, Elizabeth and Josephine; three aunts, three uncles and a host of cousins, and other family members and friends.

*Lovingly Submitted,*
**THE FAMILY**

*Sunrise*
*January 20, 1983*

*Sunset*
*December 27, 200.*

Poppa,

The bible says there is a season and a time to every purpose under the heaven. I don't know why your time with me was so short.. I do know that God has a purpose, so I have to endure my season of separation from you.  Yes, there will be times when I will weep and mourn, but your memory will dry my tears and bring joy to my heart. I have comfort in knowing that only God can love you better than I do.

*Love forever, Mommy*

## What Should I Do?

I've been fighting Satan for some time now and it seems like all he's done is beat me, *What Should I Do?* I pray every night before I go to bed, hoping I will win the fight tomorrow, but when I wake up he is there saying *"get up, get up, we have to go sell our drugs"*. I'm not really sure if I want to but he's pressuring me and pressuring me *What Should I Do?* Well I did it and now I'm in jail with no access to my loved ones - *What Should I Do?* I'm praying and praying to come home but when it's only to find out that he took you *What Should I Do?*

Well, **A.J.** the only thing left for me to do is to turn this fight over to the Lord. I'll always love you and miss you, but not one bit will I ever forget you.

*Love always, Your brother Dennis*

Dear A.J.

Your stay was so short, now it's time to say good-bye. It doesn't seem fair, but it's all part of Gods plan. You were my big brother and no one can replace you. It seems like only yesterday we were flippin' on the mats in the lot around Capitol or playing ball over Smith. I remember admiring the waves in your hair, and askin' you about the latest clothes. Now it's time to say good-bye. yesterday is gone and tomorrow is nearing. In time my wounds may heal, but my love will never forget my **BIG BROTHER.**

*Love always, Flatcat (your Lil Bro.)*

A note to my brother A.J.

When I saw you, I knew it was you. My heart was in my stomach. I broke down, my heart was gone when I saw you. You lived your life to the fullest and enjoyed every minute of it. You are my oldest brother, you were also a man. I did not want to see you there. When I saw you, I knew it was you. Now your gone forever. In this life your not promised tomorrow, but I have to take the bitter with the sweet and maintain that the Lord knows. The world was to much for you so He took you with Him. We're gonna keep Mommy straight and live on with the family.

*Love, Your brother Taj*

Dear A.J.

You were a good person, a great person if you ask me. You were always there for me, whenever I needed you. You never let anyone do anything to hurt me and anything you had, you offered it to me. Of all our brothers, you were my favorite. I'm not just saying that. Although your life was tragically cut short. I know you're in a better place. A.J., I will miss you, but I'll never forget you. I will always love you and never stop. Now that your gone all I can say is "I'll see you when I get there".

*Love, Your little brother Cortez*

Dear A.J.

I'm sorry I didn't get the chance to say goodbye. When I heard you got killed, I felt a part of me was gone forever. But now I know that when you really love someone with all your heart, that love you have can never go away. You are my brother, and I will never forget your everlasting love.

*Love always, Your sister Latavia*

michael

*Title page*
*Table of Contents*
Sturcture   Need   Intro

The penis is a structure that also
helps to spurt out the sperm. Now
I'm going to tell you all the things
that help the penis, the scrotum is the
soft sac of skin that covers the tesiticals
and hold the testicals in place. The tesiticals
are two ball which in the inside the
tesiticals produces sperm. The epididymis
is a little muslce that on the top
of a testical. The vas deferenc is
a long skiny line which the can go
threw. The semial vesical help the gall-
bladder do it job which is to realese
the urine. The penis looks like a lot of
tissues produce into muslce which looks
like a long muslce.

*confusing*
*need more*

michael   funtion.

The penis lets out of while
sexual intercourse. This is how sperm
goes threw a mans penis. First at puberty
the brain tells the tesiticals to
produce testosterone and sperm. Sperm travel
to the epididymis where they mature
and travel thought the vas deferenec, past
the semial vesical and prostate glands
through the urethra, and are spruted out
the tip of the penis. The penis look
like a lot of tissues put together that looks
like a long muslee. Every day each an adult
produces 3 hundred millions of sperm.

*tell me more*

*are you sure*

michael   connetion

It helps by producing and leting
out some sperm, and the things that help
it are the organ that are inside of your
body. Every thing help each other so
that they can relate to each other, and
help out.

*Didn't tell me anything*

Michael,
Your writing needs
a lot of work.
This paper is confusing
and doesn't say much

C-/0

159

## UNSUAL THINGS LIVED BY THE NCCC STAFF

Hypnotized by the "R-Rated Hypnotist" on stage in front of nearly 5000 people

Before having kids I went on an animal safari in Tanzania <u>and</u> a trek in Nepal — The first activity with husband # 2, and the second activity with husband #1

Worked as a dispatcher for a plumbing company

Spayed/neutered 14 Feral Cats in Mexico

*Tai* Owned my own business as a hatmaker before going to school

~~Matt~~ Went to a party at a city morgue

*Buck Carl* In college, I competed in a beauty contest. In drag, I sang "Blue Moon" then gave birth on a stage to a doll. I didn't win

I attended the World Cup of Sailing in Fremantle, Australia when Dennis Connor took back the cup from the Aussies in 1986

*Chas* When I worked at Parnassus (OB/GYN – 15<sup>th</sup> floor) I used to do jumping jacks and push-ups inside the elevator when I rode it by myself.

When I was a kid I had pet boa constrictor and would wake up when my parents were asleep and sleep with him. My mom came to check on me once and found him wrapped around my neck, he was gone the next day

*Sara* I had 3 relationships with guys I met in the Internet

I had the fastest time in my 6<sup>th</sup> grade class in the 50 yard dash

I can't sleep with my feet under the covers

I was a bus driver

*Jess* I hung out with a motorcycle gang for a week in Idaho, riding in the back seat hugging a motorcycle Mamma

I climbed a banana tree

*Jason N/A*
*David*

UNUSUAL THINGS LIVED BY THE NCCC STAFF

FOUND by David Keegan

I found this near the parking lot at Muir Beach, just north of San Francisco. I am not sure what the NCCC staff does, but they sound like an interesting crew.

—D.K.

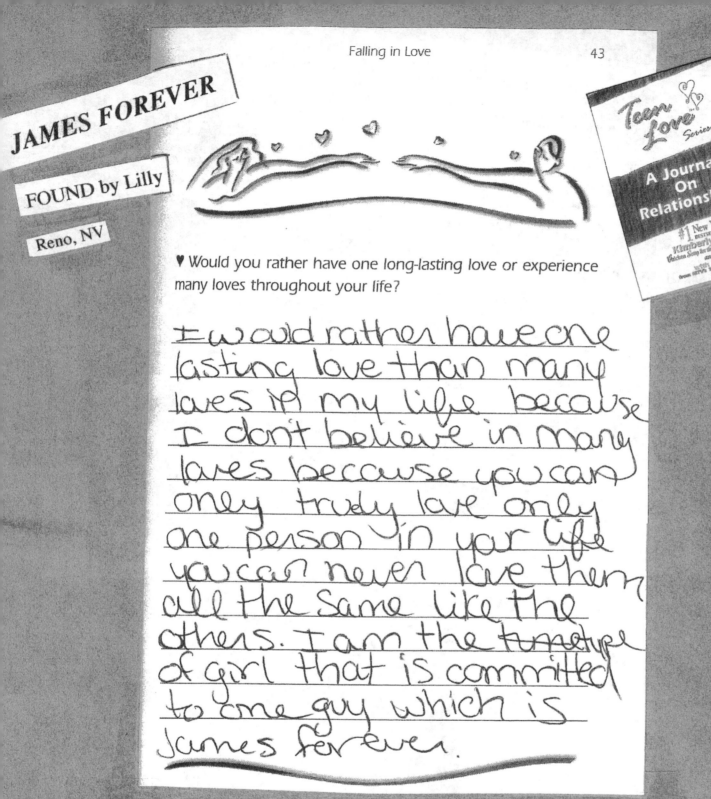

**JAMES FOREVER**

**FOUND by Lilly**

**Reno, NV**

♥ Would you rather have one long-lasting love or experience many loves throughout your life?

I would rather have one lasting love than many loves in my life because I don't believe in many loves because you can only truly love only one person in your life you can never love them all the same like the others. I am the type of girl that is committed to one guy which is James forever.

At the café where I work, my boss put shitloads of used books on these shelves all around the shop, hoping for that—oh I don't know—sophisticated-and-intellectual-drinker-of-coffee appeal. Customers ask every so often if they can take a book, usually a little spawn of Stephen King. They are encouraged to bring it back or replace it with another. In consequence, steamy romance novels fill up the shelves like sudden baby bunny rabbits.

Interestingly, these shelves are also the sad, final resting place of my boss' old college textbooks. Guess there's really nothing else to do with those things. However, I would've cleaned the fuckers out first! While thumbing through them, customers have found pictures of him with a wacky 70's 'stache, peculiar lists, photos of his daughter, and once an embarrassing poem that he wrote. What a treasure trove these bookshelves are!

Last week, I found this creepy teen-romance workbook on one of the shelves. Only a few pages had been filled out.

## PIRATE RADIO

FOUND by Linnaea Melcarek

Traverse City, MI

Create a circuit of pirate radio stations in the Traverse City and GT area

Open an arcade

Open a coffee shop "The Joint"

See all my favorite musicians in concert

Wipe out my ENTIRE Amazon.com Wish List

Straighten out my left arm

Make my legs an even length

Buy the family land from whoever owns it, tear everything the fuck down, build a summer house and arrange dual citizenship for Dad in Ireland so he can spend more time there than here. Oh, and pay off the property taxes

## IRELAND

FOUND by Beth Ashmore, Birmingham, AL

O

Ireland

relationships

memory

lost opportunity

conflict

sadness

reject

hope

## INTERESTING DISEASES

FOUND by Adam Mangels, Denver, CO

* Diseases *

I think that If I had The choice to learn about any aspect of disease I'd go with trying to learn about rare and interesting diseases That we haven't all heard about before. It's always nice to learn something new, unless it's something that you didn't want to know about.

HEY! Check it out! it's the FOUND Book!!

211 pages of your ALL-NEW finds!!! AND → 45 pages of your favorite finds from FOUND Magazine

THE FOUND BOOK DROPS 5-4-04!

"A fascinating and wonderfully moving collage of human emotion."
—Los Angeles Times

"A fascinating and compelling collection that will break your heart."
—David Sedaris, author of Me Talk Pretty One Day

"a treasury of trash, a wonderfully weird collection ... (cont.)

FOUND
THE BEST LOST, TOSSED AND FORGOTTEN ITEMS FROM AROUND THE WORLD

DAVY ROTHBART
CREATOR OF FOUND MAGAZINE

"...a fascinating glimpse into the wackier depths of america's collective subconscious." —THE WASHINGTON POST

JOIN THE FUN ON OUR 50-STATE 2004 TOUR!! see the dates at foundmagazine.com

Available wherever books are sold

"The world is full of lost love letters if you know where to look. Davy Rothbart...knows where to look."

MSN Home | My MSN | Hotmail | Search | Shopping | Money | People & Chat

Take control of your bills

Compose Contacts | Options Help
Free Newsletters | MSN Featured Offers | Find Messag

Home | Inbox | Compose | Contacts
the21balloons@hotmail.com
Previous Next | Close

Save Address(es) | Block
From: "Patten, Amanda" <A._____ <the21balloons@hotmail.com>
To: "Davy Rothbart (E-mail)" <the21balloons@hotmail.com>    Printer Friendly Version
Date: Fri, 12 Sep 2003 17:45:54 -0400
Reply | Reply All | Forward | Delete | Put In Folder...

Hi Davy--

I thought this list of general guidelines for the book might help sharpen your focus on the book, because it helped me to write it up and see what the work entails and what still needs to be done:

--Write introduction

--Write text for copyright page ("bats killed: 7; 8 Mile soundtracks burned out: 2" etc.)

--Write the longer pieces of text that still need to be written (ie, Popcorn Pete interview, story about Aaron, the more interesting back stories on pieces, etc.)

--Put each page together

--Write up captions (where found, title, etc.)

--Clean up each page

--Get permissions and releases for all original artwork and text (from cartoons to Charles Baxter's stuff) otherwise don't use them.

I figured it couldn't hurt to send. Have a good weekend, and we'll talk on Monday.

Amanda

Previous Next | Close
Delete | Put In Folder...
Shopping | Money | People & Chat
TRUSTe Approved Privacy Sta

Also, here's the schedule we worked out:

9/30--phone call

10/2--you send first 100 pages to me for arrival on 10/3

10/9--you send another 50 pages to me for arrival on 10/10

10/16--you send another 50 pages me for arrival on 10/10

10/21--you send all 256 pages to me (with pages in order and numbered--let's talk about the numbering before you do it)

10/24--entire complete                manuscript goes to
production so that galleys can be made

TOUCHSTONE
FIRESIDE
11.26
Davy--
Check it out!
Let's talk after
Thanksgiving, okay?
Meantime, have a
happy one.
Amanda

AMANDA PATTEN

TOUCHSTONE
FIRESIDE

Hi Davy--
Here are a few
more galleys for
you.
Amanda

AMANDA PATTEN

FIRESIDE
A Division of Simon & Schuster

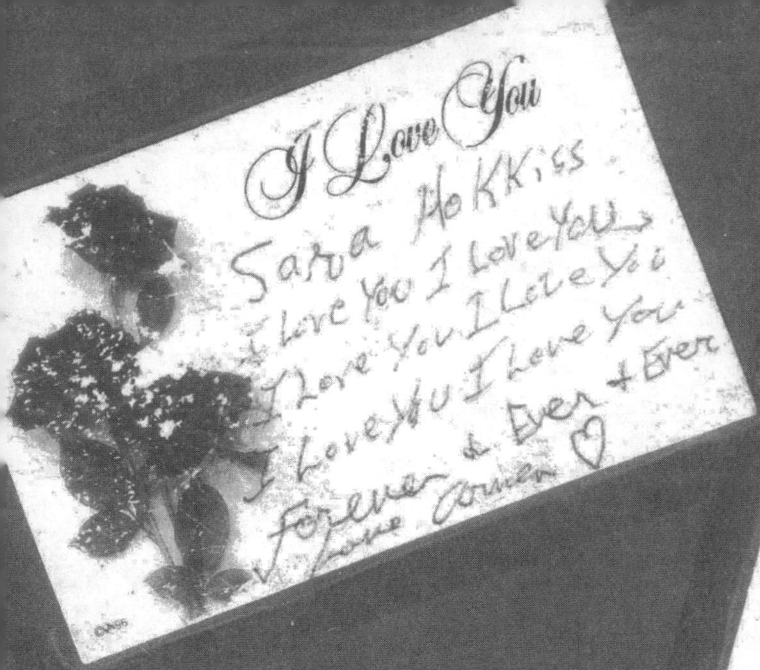

I Love You

Sara HoKKiss

I Love you I Love you

I Love You I Love You i

I Love You I Love You

Forever & Ever & Ever

Love corner ♡

## FOREVER

FOUND by Cal Belleveau

Minneapolis, MN

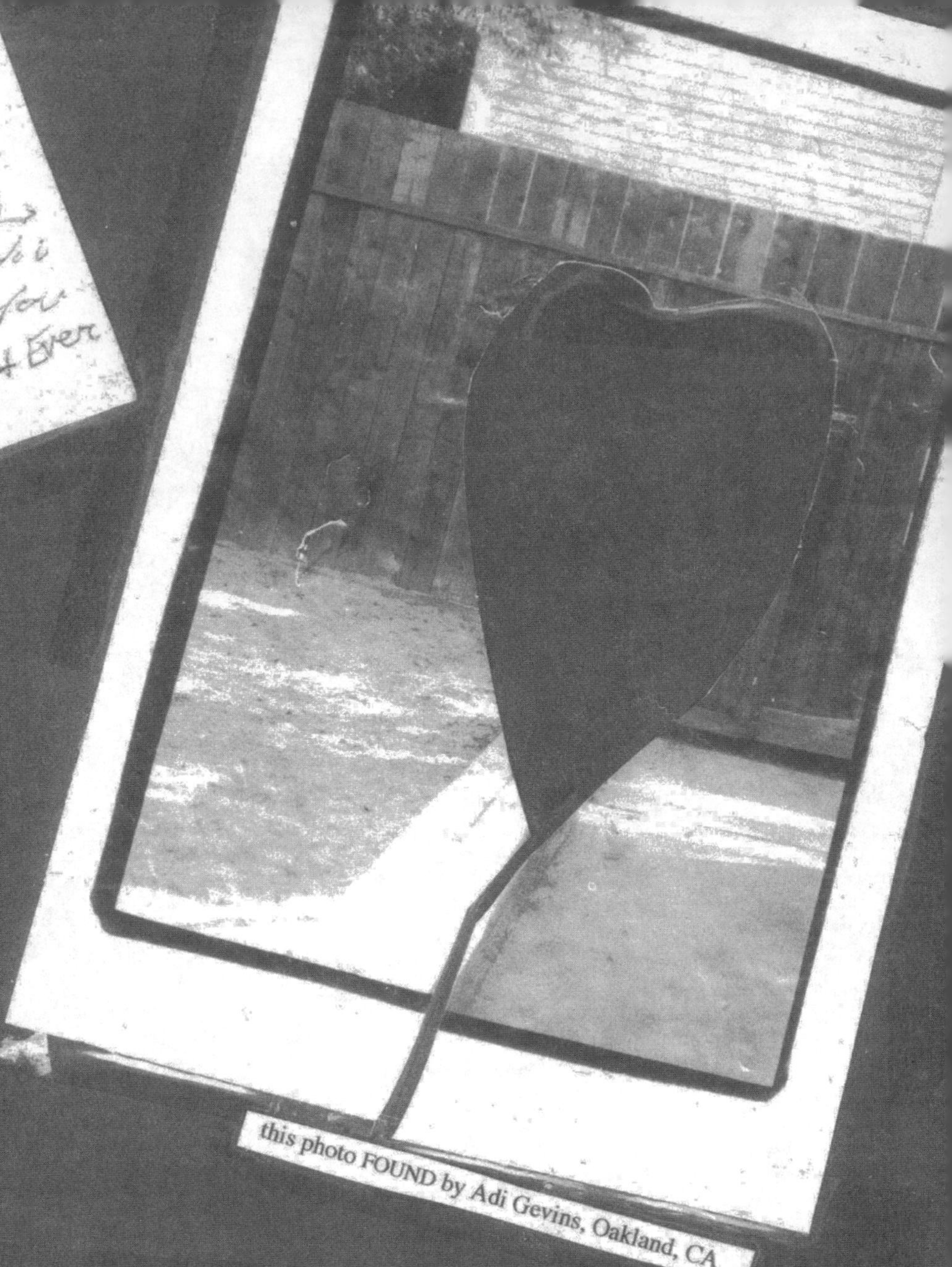

## NEVER USED

FOUND by Melissa Walker

St. Petersburg, FL

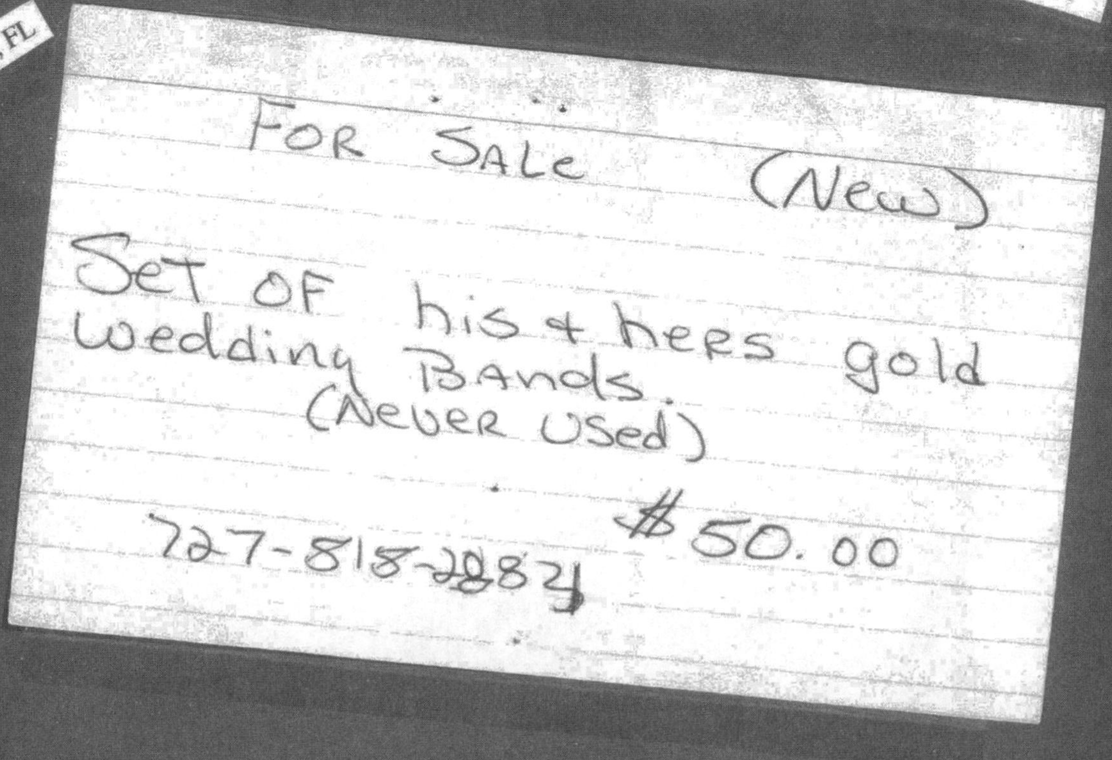

FOR SALE     (New)

Set of his & hers gold
Wedding Bands.
(Never Used)

                    $50.00

727-818-2824

# FOUND
## magazine

# #4

**ALWAYS**

**5 BUCKS**

Come Into Our World

7 97377 57001 3    04

# OFFICE OF THE GOVERNOR

July 27, 2004

Mr. Jeremiah B░░░
░░░ Main Street, ░░
Evanston, Illinois 60202

Dear Mr. B░░░,

Thank you for writing to the Governor's Office.

Governor Schwarzenegger is honored that you would choose him to provide a letter of recommendation. As you know, the Governor is a strong believer in higher education. Unfortunately, it is against this Office's policy to provide letters of recommendation unless the Governor has had a prior professional experience with the applicant.

Again, thank you for taking time to write and good luck in all your future endeavors.

Sincerely,

*Steven Mahoney*

Steven Mahoney
Office of Constituent Affairs

CONSIDER THIS A DIVORCE
FOUND by Michael Bobick
Evanston, IL

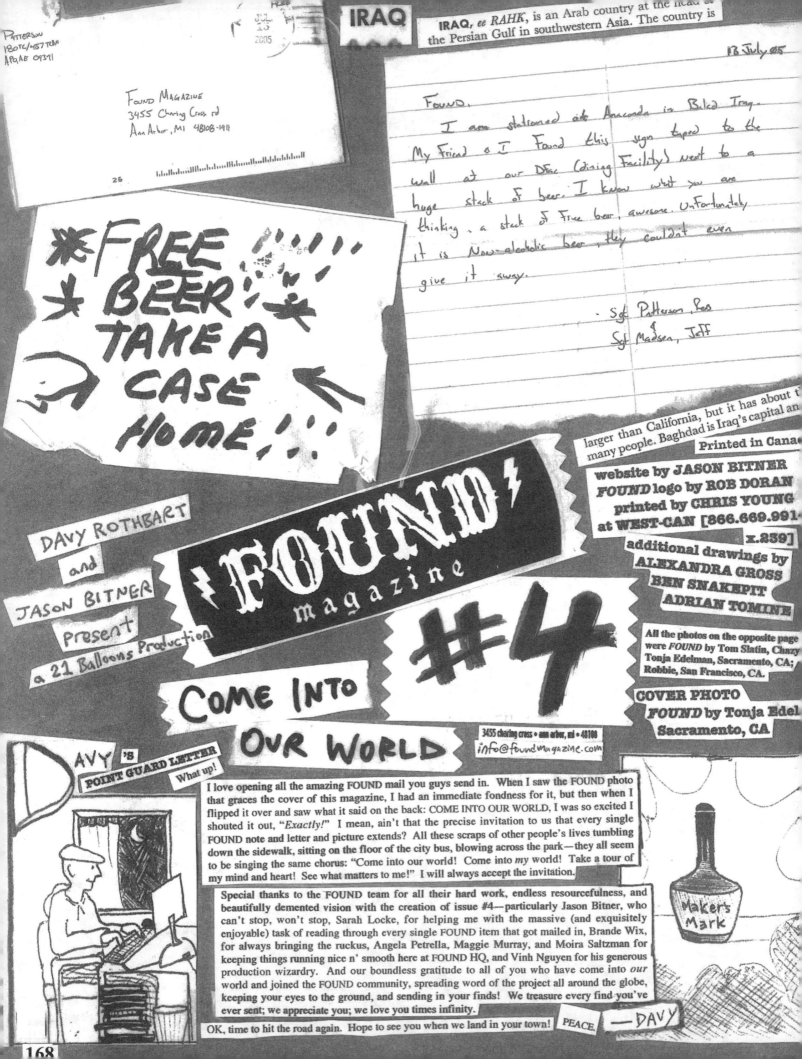

Patterson
180TC/457 TCM
APO AE 09391

FOUND MAGAZINE
3455 Charing Cross rd
Ann Arbor, MI 48108-1911

25

**IRAQ**

JUL 13 2005

**IRAQ,** *ee RAHK*, is an Arab country at the head of the Persian Gulf in southwestern Asia. The country is

13 July 05

FOUND,

I am stationed at Anaconda in Balad Iraq. My Friend & I Found this sign taped to the wall at our DFac (dining Facility) next to a huge stack of beer. I know what you are thinking — a stack of Free beer, awesome. Unfortunately it is Non-alcoholic beer, they couldn't even give it away.

— Sgt Patterson, Leo
& Sgt Madsen, Jeff

larger than California, but it has about t[...] many people. Baghdad is Iraq's capital an[...]

**☀ FREE BEER TAKE A CASE Home !!!**

**Printed in Cana[...]**

website by **JASON BITNER**
*FOUND* logo by **ROB DORAN**
printed by **CHRIS YOUNG**
at **WEST-CAN** [866.669.991[...]
x.239]

additional drawings by
**ALEXANDRA GROSS**
**BEN SNAKEPIT**
**ADRIAN TOMINE**

All the photos on the opposite page
were *FOUND* by Tom Slatin, Chazy
Tonja Edelman, Sacramento, CA;
Robbie, San Francisco, CA.

COVER PHOTO
*FOUND* by Tonja Edel[...]
Sacramento, CA.

**FOUND** magazine

**#4**

DAVY ROTHBART and JASON BITNER present a 21 Balloons Production

**COME INTO OUR WORLD**

3455 charing cross • ann arbor, mi • 48108
info@foundmagazine.com

**DAVY'S POINT GUARD LETTER** What up!

I love opening all the amazing FOUND mail you guys send in. When I saw the FOUND photo that graces the cover of this magazine, I had an immediate fondness for it, but then when I flipped it over and saw what it said on the back: COME INTO OUR WORLD, I was so excited I shouted it out, "*Exactly!*" I mean, ain't that the precise invitation to us that every single FOUND note and letter and picture extends? All these scraps of other people's lives tumbling down the sidewalk, sitting on the floor of the city bus, blowing across the park—they all seem to be singing the same chorus: "Come into our world! Come into *my* world! Take a tour of my mind and heart! See what matters to me!" I will always accept the invitation.

Special thanks to the FOUND team for all their hard work, endless resourcefulness, and beautifully demented vision with the creation of issue #4—particularly Jason Bitner, who can't stop, won't stop, Sarah Locke, for helping me with the massive (and exquisitely enjoyable) task of reading through every single FOUND item that got mailed in, Brande Wix, for always bringing the ruckus, Angela Petrella, Maggie Murray, and Moira Saltzman for keeping things running nice n' smooth here at FOUND HQ, and Vinh Nguyen for his generous production wizardry. And our boundless gratitude to all of you who have come into *our* world and joined the FOUND community, spreading word of the project all around the globe, keeping your eyes to the ground, and sending in your finds! We treasure every find you've ever sent; we appreciate you; we love you times infinity.

OK, time to hit the road again. Hope to see you when we land in your town! PEACE. —DAVY

Maker's Mark

**168**

# FOUND magazine #4

DAVY ROTHBART
point guard, FOUND Magazine

JASON BITNER
power forward, FOUND Magazine

foundmagazine.com

ANGELA PETRELLA     BRANDE WIX
SHYEL MEISELS

MOIRA SALTZMAN

SARAH LOCKE

Timmy Smith

Aaron Wickenden     Paul Koob

ARTHUR JONES
EMILY LONG

Javan Makhmali     Jed Lackritz

Peter Rothbart

John Lu

Mike DiBella

Vinh Nguyen

not pictured:
Holly Matthews
Rory Sykes
Nancy Ford
Carla Perez-Venero
Michelle Angus

David Meiklejohn

169

MAGGIE MURRAY

Geographic Regions of the United States

PACIFIC
COAST
STATES
ROCKY
MOUNTAIN
STATES
MIDWESTERN
STATES
NEW
ENGLAND
MIDDLE
ATLANTIC
STATES
SOUTHWESTERN
STATES
SOUTHERN
STATES

# SLAPDANCE FINDS!

In 2004, me and my brother Peter loaded up the van with our all-time favorite finds and came to visit you—FOUND parties in all 50 states! Our *Slapdance Across America Tour "2004!"* took us to 146 cities over eight months. Along the way, we collected thousands of your lushest, wildest, and most beautiful-est finds. A few of them are here in this little spread, more are scattered throughout this magazine, and many more will appear in the 2nd FOUND book, which comes out in May of 2006.

The *Slapdance* tour was amazing, the highlight of our lives!!! We owe enormous, boundless thanks to friends in all 50 states who helped make this tour a reality. Thanks so much to everyone who came out to the FOUND parties, and to those who hosted the events, spread word about the events, let us sleep on their couches and floors, and brought us whiskey and cereal. All of your generosity, hard work, and dazzling energy is forever appreciated!

—DAVY

Found magazine's

## SLAPDANCE
## ACROSS
## AMERICA
## TOUR

**Americans on the Move.**

FOUND Magazine's Davy Rothbart (right) and Peter Rothbart (left) with stunt driver/ documentary filmmaker David Meiklejohn (middle).

this photo FOUND by Missy & Neff, Baton Rouge, LA

I took some Ho's to get some Burritos

BE RIGHT BACK   San Jose, CA
FOUND by Drew Maran

DESTROY MATT
1) wait til' Matt is asleep
2) make sure hes asleep
3) put his hand in warm water
4) total humiliacion

DESTROY MATT   Dallas, TX
FOUND by Connie Hyunh,

170

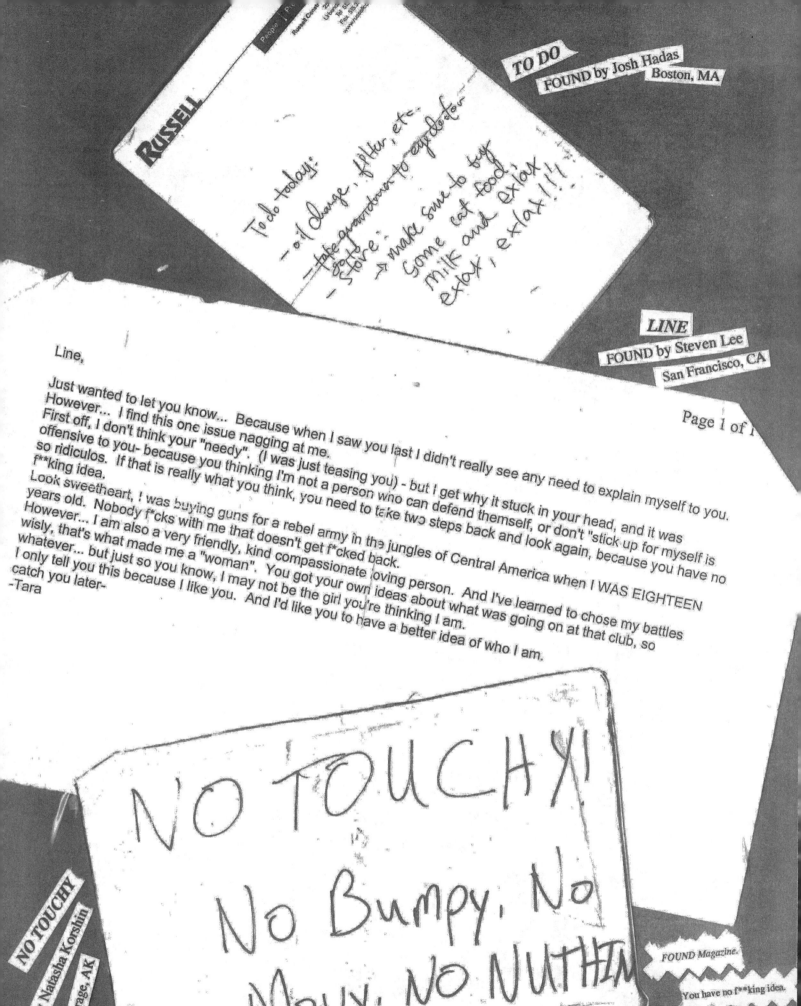

RUSSELL

To do today:
- oil change, filter, etc.
- take grandma to eyedoctor
- gotta store:
  → make sure to buy
    Some cat food,
    milk and exlax
    exlax, exlax!!!

Line,

Page 1 of 1

Just wanted to let you know... Because when I saw you last I didn't really see any need to explain myself to you.
However... I find this one issue nagging at me.
First off, I don't think your "needy". (I was just teasing you) - but I get why it stuck in your head, and it was
offensive to you- because you thinking I'm not a person who can defend themself, or don't "stick up for myself is
so ridiculos. If that is really what you think, you need to take two steps back and look again, because you have no
f**king idea.
Look sweetheart, I was buying guns for a rebel army in the jungles of Central America when I WAS EIGHTEEN
years old. Nobody f*cks with me that doesn't get f*cked back.
However... I am also a very friendly, kind compassionate loving person. And I've learned to chose my battles
wisly, that's what made me a "woman". You got your own ideas about what was going on at that club, so
whatever... but just so you know, I may not be the girl you're thinking I am.
I only tell you this because I like you. And I'd like you to have a better idea of who I am.
catch you later-
-Tara

NO TOUCHX!
No Bumpy, No
Mouy, No NUTHIN

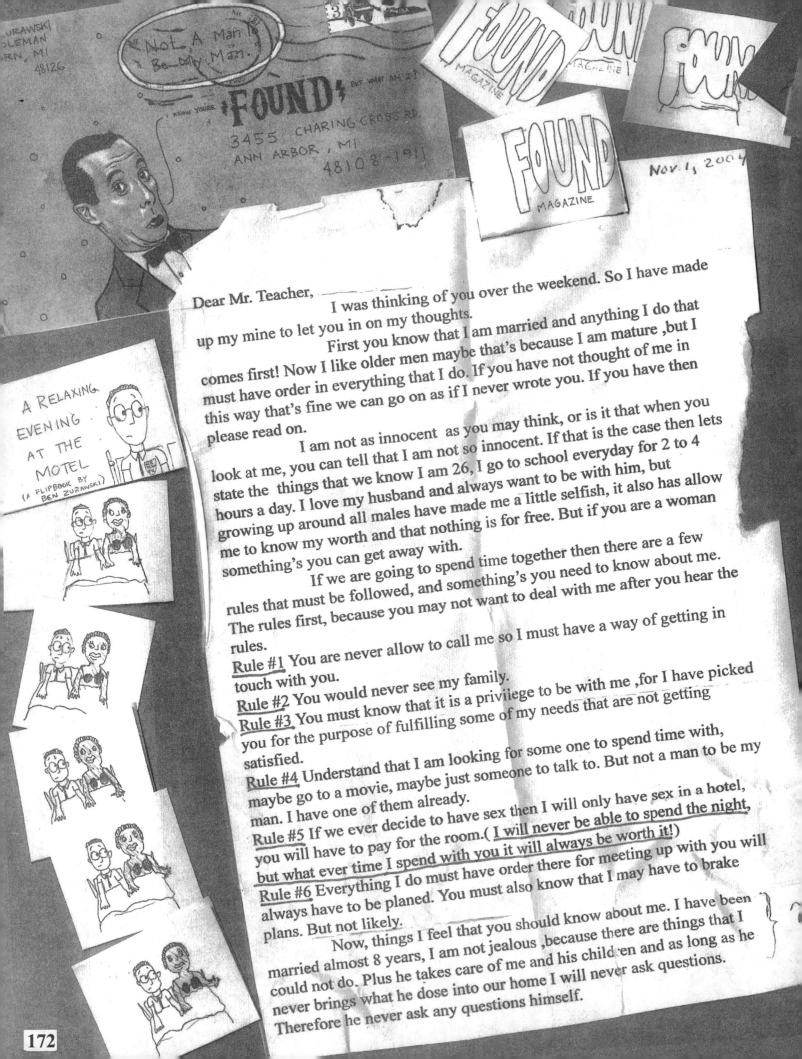

Dear Mr. Teacher,
          I was thinking of you over the weekend. So I have made up my mine to let you in on my thoughts.
          First you know that I am married and anything I do that comes first! Now I like older men maybe that's because I am mature ,but I must have order in everything that I do. If you have not thought of me in this way that's fine we can go on as if I never wrote you. If you have then please read on.
          I am not as innocent as you may think, or is it that when you look at me, you can tell that I am not so innocent. If that is the case then lets state the things that we know I am 26, I go to school everyday for 2 to 4 hours a day. I love my husband and always want to be with him, but growing up around all males have made me a little selfish, it also has allow me to know my worth and that nothing is for free. But if you are a woman something's you can get away with.
          If we are going to spend time together then there are a few rules that must be followed, and something's you need to know about me. The rules first, because you may not want to deal with me after you hear the rules.
Rule #1 You are never allow to call me so I must have a way of getting in touch with you.
Rule #2 You would never see my family.
Rule #3 You must know that it is a priviiege to be with me ,for I have picked you for the purpose of fulfilling some of my needs that are not getting satisfied.
Rule #4 Understand that I am looking for some one to spend time with, maybe go to a movie, maybe just someone to talk to. But not a man to be my man. I have one of them already.
Rule #5 If we ever decide to have sex then I will only have sex in a hotel, you will have to pay for the room.( I will never be able to spend the night, but what ever time I spend with you it will always be worth it!)
Rule #6 Everything I do must have order there for meeting up with you will always have to be planed. You must also know that I may have to brake plans. But not likely.
          Now, things I feel that you should know about me. I have been married almost 8 years, I am not jealous ,because there are things that I could not do. Plus he takes care of me and his children and as long as he never brings what he dose into our home I will never ask questions. Therefore he never ask any questions himself.

A RELAXING EVENING AT THE MOTEL (A FLIPBOOK BY BEN ZURAWSKI)

FOUND 3455 CHARING CROSS RD. ANN ARBOR, MI 48108-1911

Nov 1, 2004

While walking in the halls on a 10-minute break from my college art class, I found this zesty little note peaking from underneath a used coffee filter in the trash. I can't say for sure which 'Mr. Teacher' it was for, but I wonder if he accepted the offer.

—B.Z.

I have only been with 5 men in my life my husband was my 4th. I have had an affair one time that was about a year a go. It lasted a while but his feeling got in the way. So I had to end something that went on for over a few years. Now if you feel that I am a hoe then we need not get together. I know that I am not a hoe. If we was to have sex I would feel the need to know how many people you are having sex with not because I am jealous but because I am married and you already know who I am sleeping with. I will tell you if I start to sleep with any one else. (Not likely) But in the case that I feel that you are having sex with too many people I will end it. Not because I am jealous but because I am married, and I don't want to bring anything home. You will know more than my husband about my sex life. That's because you will be fulfilling things that he dose not.

Now, may be you think I wont be able to handle you, but the truth is I hope not, I hope there are things that you can teach me for I am willing to learn. If not I hope you are not unwilling to learn what I like. Because I am a big girl and I do know what I like. I am not afraid to let people know what I like. I like to do things and I like to have it done to me. If you are unwilling to do the things I like, then there is no need to get together. For the truth is its all about me, And if YOU want to please me. For in return you will always be please!

I also like to smoke weed most of the time before sex, or throughout sex it helps to relax me if you can't be around it that's fine but never ask me to not smoke. I will never have sex if I am not relaxed.

I know that I have given you a lot to think about. Therefore I will not ask you about this letter. You will have to make the first move . I don't know if you feel the same , or if you are willing to follow the rules( the rules must be kept.) I will go on as if I never gave you the letter that way you can take as much time as you need. But the offer will not always be there. I hope that it something that you will think hard and long about. Please don't start something you can't handle.

One of your students
I am a black female in one of you're a.m. classes.

P.S. I am not doing this to better my grade I am passing your class I got an A on the midterm if you think you know who I am call me into your office and we can talk about it. Tell no one I have just as much to loss as you. May be that's why I picked you. C. B.

CASE
Lettinga
(12)

isd7zs (s
G.R, MI

Regers      6-16-03

Egapt, the TV, the hmn butt, the copter, the Jet pak
Football. Musik, scare bording, dirt biking
the coach, a littel fat Pigest aju.
Antidishastblishmtrywsem.

**DAVY EXPLAINS**

Ah, this brings me back to my early grade-school days when everyone envied Dan Zatkovich because he knew how to count to 200, and Mike Kozura was the shit because he knew the longest word in the English language: antidisestablishmentarianism. The word was mystical, grand, elusive. Every day we'd ask Mike to repeat it a dozen times, but we couldn't quite get a handle on it. "Come on, say it again, say it one more time!" Then David Pfeiffer found out that there was an even longer word, something relating to a coal-miner's disease, and for a short time this new word was the flavor-of-the-month. But the new word was completely unpronounceable and ridiculous, and soon enough lost its luster. Antidisestablishmentarianism was back in the fold. I'm thrilled to see that somewhere the tradition continues.

**LOVE AND WAR**

FOUND by Victor Sanders

Bellingham, WA

FLETCHER EVANS
IS A
CHRISTIAN
SCIENTIST.

**FLETCHER EVANS**
FOUND by Erin Goodell
Seattle, WA

Oh my goodness, I really do
miss you. When you didn't sit
by me when we ate I was sad
bt this okay. I get the feeling
that Bryn might have a crush
on you. Kinda buggs me really.
When I think of you my chest
gets really heavy and I start
getting bigger breths.
It's going to be hard when you
move. I never thought I could
feel this way about someone.
wow this makes me feel like
your off at war in the olden
days and me writing love letters.
        I P

FOUND by Case Lettinga
Grand Rapids, MI

45 +
AGING HIPPIES VOLLEYBALL!
3:00 PM THURS SAND COURTS

1
2
3
4
5
6
7
8
9
10
11
12
13
14
15
16

I hope one day to see this sport on ESPN.
— DAVY

YEAH, I'M LOOKING FOR A LITTLE SOMETHING SPECIAL FOR MY AGENT SOMETHING SUBTLE, YET PAINFUL THAT SAYS HEY, REMEMBER ME. FUCKER.

A LITTLE SOMETHING SPECIAL

FOUND by Brian McCloskey
Venice, CA

While sorting through some of my deceased fathers' personal items, I came across this photograph. On the back there is a Los Angeles, CA address and "July 1975", a date that precedes my parent's divorce.

Thinking that this could be a long lost relative, I showed it to my mom. She responded by saying it might be the secretary my father had an affair with. What affair?! The family stories always differ, so I didn't pursue that question.

Anyhow, my father did not seem the type to have an affair, too bound by duty, family and responsibility, but it was the 70's in California!

I like to think this oh-so-70's babe was saying to my dad, "Ease Up, Ed, and enjoy the ride."

— Kara

this photo FOUND by Kara Barton, Los Angeles, CA

175

# JUSTIN DAVISSON meets Zippy THE PINHEAD

O.K., that there is Justin's original letter!!

Zippy

*I*n 1987, Justin Davisson did what any bright, creative, enthusiastic 17-year-old metalhead obsessed with the comic strip *Zippy the Pinhead* might have done—he wrote a letter to the strip's author and creator, Bill Griffith.

A few weeks later, Justin's letter was found tumbling down a windy street in San Francisco—apparently, it had never reached Bill Griffith. For fifteen years, the woman who found the letter kept it in her desk drawer; then one day she handed it over to me and my friends at *FOUND Magazine*. We published Justin's letter in our *FOUND* book. And after a fair bit of time tracking Bill Griffith down, stalking him, and haranguing him, we finally got him to read Justin's letter.

Now, almost 20 years later, Bill Griffith and Zippy respond!

Read on, my friends.          —DAVY

Justin Davisson at age 17

To All,

Could you please send me # a complete catalog of Zippy and merchandise. Bill Griffith - if you read this - here's some idea you should use for the ~~pro~~ peroxial pinhead - Zippy joins a heavy metal band, Zippy meets David Letterman, Zippy meets ~~Sally Jesse~~ Donald Trump, Zippy meets Charles Manson, Zippy goes to Carmel & meets mayor Clint, Zippy meets Jim & Tammy Faye, Zippy meets Gary Hart, Zippy meets Donna Rice, Jessica Hahn, Fawn Hall & has affairs with all of them in one night, ~~She~~ Zippy meets Gumby & Pokey, Zippy meets Rocky, Bullwinkle, Fearless Leader, Boris Berriot, & Natashia, Zippy meets the Noid, Zippy meets Teddy Ruxpin, Zippy meets Sean Penn & doesn't get hit!, Zippy meets the Pope & takes his place, Zippy meets Hulk Hogan & becomes the new World Wrestling Federation world champion, Zippy meets his sanrio heir apparent - Zee-pee, Zippy meets Jerry Faldwell & Oral Roberts, Zippy meets Ozzy Osbourne, Zippy & Claude go back to ~~Haight~~ Haight-Ashbury & People's Park in the summer of 1967, Zippy meets the Freak brothers & gets his stomach pumped after too much partying with the Fat Freddy, Phenias, & Freewheelin' Franklin, Zippy meets Sledgehammer!, Zippy meets Morris the Cat, Zippy meet Steven King, ~~A~~ Zippy meets Bugs Bunny, Zippy meets & goes bowling with Fred Flintstone, Zippy meets ALF, Zippy meets Joe Bob Briggs, Zippy meets Siskel & Ebert & Rex Reed, Zippy meets Pee-Wee Hermann, Zippy meet Elvis, Zippy meets Joe Montana, Zippy meets Howard Cosell, Zippy meets pit bulls & free way gun shooters, Zippy meets ~~Mikeal Gor~~ the Gorbechev's in the U.S.S.R., Zippy meets Richard Simmons, Zippy meets Judy & Audrey Landers ~~(Lucky~~ (Lucky Pinhead!), & Wow!, The best of all Zippy meets the 3 Stooges! We don't get ~~Zi the Zi~~ Zippy in any of the local papers except the Bay Area Spectator which is, supposedly illegal for me to buy. When is the Zippy movie due out, I heard Randy ~~Quaid~~ Quaid was going play the Pinhead I heard that a few years ago. they gave out free Zippy t-shirts for eating Ding-Dongs, ~~&~~ & Taco Sauce, are there going to be any more events like ~~that~~ in the →

CONTINUES!

Bay Area, I have had the delicacy, delicacy before y It's so quite good. Next year I get to vote. I'm got voting for Gary Hart - he can't keep his parts on & I'm not about to vote for Albert Gore because his wife is head of the Parents Music Resource Center & they're not my favorite people in the world. I definitly want a real Pinhead in the office. Who is going to be nice president. Tuesday I have Weld, Griffey, Claude, Tuxedo Sam, Mr Bushmiller? I want to have a Zippy picture painted on my guitar one day. On yeah I almost forgot, Zippy meets Robin Leach, Garfield, Spudds Mackenzie, the Peanuts gang, Richard Nixon, G. Gordon Liddy, Dr. Demento, Cheech & Chong, Marget Thacher, Sammanth Fox, Queen of England, Mormar Kpaddi, the I yathola, Rambo, George Zimmer of the men's where house, Vanna White, Cal Worthington Jr, Gary Hart, Malcam Forbes, Liz Taylor, Joan Rivers, Eddie Murphy, & a pack of weasels, & the California Raisins. Thanks A lot,

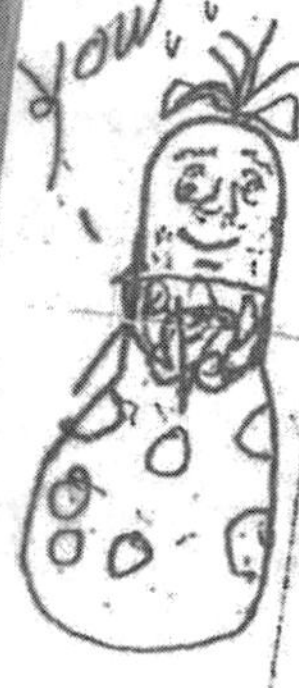

Justin Davisson - The only person in town that knows anything about - Zippy the Pinhead

yow!!

Justin Davisson
422 Huntington Pl.
Pleasanton, CA 94109

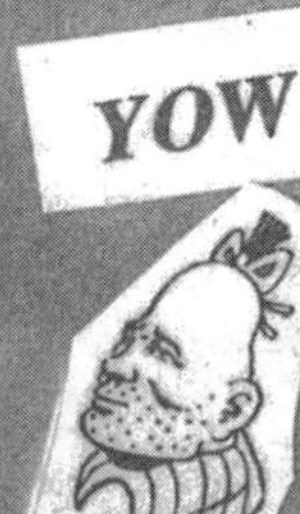

P.S. - How bow 'bout Zippy meets Godzilla, King Kong, Robocop, Alfred E. Neuman, the Fat Boys, ollie North, William Deaver, Cherry Pop-Tart (or the cartech character), Alice Cooper & Frank Zappa.

Zippy in 1988
Put A Real Pinhead
in the White House

In 1987, Justin Davisson hoped that his ideas would inspire Bill Griffith to create a comic strip. Almost 20 years later, they did!

The final and most tantalizing step was to reunite Justin with the letter he wrote in 1987, and show him Bill's new comic.

I tracked Justin down in California. He's 35 years-old now, and works at an alt-weekly newspaper in the Bay Area. I put together a little surprise package for him, sent it out, and called him at work a couple weeks later.

Justin told me that he'd got the package and been completely stunned. He didn't even really remember writing the original letter. "I can't believe how crazy I was back then," he said. "And I can't believe the whole thing came full circle. It's a *trip*!"

"The funny thing is," Justin went on, "I'm still a Zippy fan. Just last year I went to see a play in the Mission District that was entirely based on Zippy comics. To know that my letter was found somewhere—and that Bill Griffith read it and drew a strip based on it—it's insane; it staggers the mind."

—DAVY

Justin Davisson at age 35

Dear FOUND:

This list appears in the back of a daily planner I found lying in the street near my house just outside Harvard Square in late December of 2003. There's an undeniable, poetic quality about this list, and like any good poem it is very much a part of its moment. To me it has all the markings of a New Year's resolution, casting aside the old and taking on the new. These odd but insightful choices strike me as rather daring -- the writer chucks out the founding blocks of every language, "yes" and "no," in favor of more interesting, though possibly made-up, words like "untacular."

Needless to say, this is an inspiring work. My girlfriend Sara and I have decided to create our own "phase in/phase out" list. Currently, I am phasing in the word "rubicund," and Sara is phasing in "mimeograph."

Other entries in the planner note the time of Latin, Pre-Calc, and other AP, college-bound courses. I like to think this kid is pruning her vocabulary in preparation for the erudition of college-age hipsters. No doubt she will be sorely disappointed, and she'll be the only one cool enough to use "thou" in everyday conversation.

Sincerely,
Rekha Rosha

Rekha Rosha
Cambridge MA

Words to phase out

Nice ← i suck
stupid
forever
definitely
word)
best
gross
wonderful
interesting
insane
random
key
totally
*like
jesus
jesus christ
OMG
enjoy
enjoyable
Yes
No
lifestyle

I'm not writing this to jump on your back, but as a sister in Christ I hope you will see what I'm saying.

Some idds I see in you that you need to get rid of:

need for attention
trying too hard for attention + friends
money
loneliness
doubt
self-focused ⎤ you are God's
self-hating ⎦ vessel, God's creation.

Words to phase in

groovy
indubitably
qualms
dire
devious
fabulous
bleeding
bloody
jeff
cross
thou
untacular
tomfoolery
cerulean
umber
killer
radiant
flaxen
solid
tight
~~extraordinarius~~
so it goes

is nothing and I don't think it to be fair to you. I wasn't looking to fall in love with anyone it just

are for a long time. Believe me, I would love the opportunity to be with someone who truly

Mom,

Fluffy is dead. I found him in a puddle when I pulled up next to my spot. I laid him on the picnic table because I didn't want to leave him lying there. Rocky stayed the night b/c I missed him. Let me bury fluffy. It might get rid of my bad luck w/ animals. I need some gas $ so if you could leave me $10 & a

blanket for fluf I would appreciate it.
I ♥ u
♥ Wiz

1. Rats loafing
"        "        — medium
"        "        — long
"        "        — close up
3. Clowns stalking
4. Clowns killing
5. Clowns cheering
6. clowns stealing car
7. clowns rat patrol

to ____
you. I never would
intentionally, but thank
you for being there for
me. It truly means a lot!
Molly

# Chimay.
### Notes du jour.

1) take a shit.

2) do laundry

3) masturbate

4) watch t.v.

5) masturbate again.

March 24, 2003

Whats up Kim,

Hey its your nigga hitting you from Chicago, I wrote you a while back, but I dont know if you read it or not, but I know it didnt come back. Well if you aint get it oh well.

My name is Dorian aka DJ. Ma Ive been holding you down in Chicago. Every one been bumpin your shit, you did a good Job on your new C.D. You need to pat your self on the back, also give it up to "Bee Hive". Man I wish I could be on your promotion team or something. Im a 22 year old electrician Local 134. But one day I will promote artist, give ideas for videos you know shit like that. Well enough with that Congratulations on your C.D. Its like you really felt me. I was wishing you and twista came with some shit. In a matter of fact today I saw Twista in Kenwood Liquors, him and his buddy money T, well when I rode up I was bangin thuglov that shit tripped me out. So when I went in I gave him his props, I live in the Jeffery Manor and twista is in the hood all the time.

Today is March 24, 2003 and you'll be at the House of Blues friday. I wanna come see you bad, but I have to work. I was going to take off but these white folks at work be trippin. Well Im happy you did business with Styles and Swizz. Shut the game down baby especially that Hater EVE. She was cool at first. Then she just flipped her whole stello. But you 10 steps ahead of all those hoes. A I saw you on In The Basement. I hope you aint giving my love away to tigger! Im just kidding ☺. You showed Chicago luv Thanks! Plus you spoke on some good shit.

So you up on that illuminati, 666, New World Order shit? I think you are. Spit some knowledge about that, I wanna know what you think. But Kim my hand is starting to hurt plus Im starting to get writers block. You are the Queen Bee fuck all the haters. Hey you know black folks always want something. If there is any chance you can hook it up for me to see you in concert?

Also before I leave I wanna say sorry about BIG my pops died March 9, 1987 on my 6th birthday so that a very special day for me too. So if your in Chicago and you wanna kick it

with your biggest fan and be on some real shit, then get in touch. Tell Hillary & The Bee Hive keep that shit coming. Thanks for taking time out on your busy schedule to read this letter.

Love Ya
    DJ
    chicago Luv

P.S  Excuse me if I spelled some stuff wrong, Im not dumb. Also Im leaving you my telephone # and address just in case you wanna shoot the shit.

Dorian Boykin
9549 S Bennett
Chicago IL 60617

773-281-0427
    or
773-962-9075

The Provincial Flag

DAVY REPORTS!!

**I**'ve always loved geographically-specific rap—songs that are intricate in their descriptions of a particular town or neighborhood. As a kid I listened to so much Too $hort that if you were trying to find your way around Oakland, California, I could've probably given you directions. Petey Pablo's big radio hit "Raise Up (Spin It Like A Helicopter)" seemed to shout out every city in the U.S., which surely boosted its airplay around the country, but what I prefer is the album version where instead he drops the names of every state prison and forgotten hamlet in his home state of North Carolina. Songs like Petey Pablo's "919 Motherfucker" make me burst with regional pride for places I've hardly ever been. So when I recently learned of Halifax, Nova Scotia's prolific underground rapper and producer Classified, it made sense that his rhymes about life in the Maritime Provinces would captivate me. I talked with him today on the phone and discovered that his entire career began with one very special find.

**Classified:** Yeah, this was twelve years ago. I was into hip-hop, I was eager to start messing around spinning records, but I couldn't afford a real set of turntables. The cheapest turntables I could've bought anywhere was a couple-hundred bucks. I just didn't have the dough.

Then one day, me and the girl I was dating, we wandered into this little junk shop, a place called Frenchy's, just one of those crappy sad-sack second-hand shops in some little town in the country. And there it was—a set of turntables that looked like no tables I've ever saw before. Must've been from the '60's or '70's, just an enormous slab of wood with two record players, a monstrosity, an old antique piece of junk, really. The guy wanted ten bucks for it. I gave him ten bucks. At the time, I thought, "Hey, this is something to start with."

Twelve years later, I've recorded ten albums of my own and a bunch of others for people I know, all with those same tables. Same needles, even! I think it means something to be working with these turntables that already had their own history. Who knows where they came from? I love wondering about that. One hell of a find—and I had no idea at the time.

CLASSIFIED

**Davy:** Yeah, for me too it happens that way. Every few months I'll get a bunch of t-shirts for like sixty cents each at Value Village, and at the time I can never predict which one's gonna become a real favorite. But one always does. Or this headboard I've got for my bed. Found it in an alley in Chicago. It's a big wooden headboard, and it makes the pair of mattresses I sleep on seem more stately, like a real bed or something, not just a mattress on the floor. Now I can't imagine my bed without it. I guess it's like that with all stuff you find at thrift stores and garage sales or in the alley—something sparks your interest enough for you to nab it; then months, maybe *years* later, you realize how lucky you were, you've got this treasure.

Nova Scotia Communications & Information

**Downtown Halifax** is a blend of the new and old. It is th_ of the modern Scotia Square shopping center, center, an Halifax City Hall, foreground, which dates from 1887.

**Classified:** Does something count as FOUND if you know who it belongs to? Like a note or a picture of someone you know?

**Davy:** Sure. I feel like if something gives you a glimpse into someone else's life—whether you know 'em or not—it counts as FOUND.

**Classified:** Cool. Because a few weeks ago I found this picture of my dad. I was digging through some shit in the basement, and I found this picture—oh my God. It was him and his band when he was fifteen years-old. My dad's always been in bands—rock bands, cover bands, dance music. He's the one got me into music, fucking around with his instruments in the basement. I knew he'd been playing since he was a kid. But I never dreamed I'd find a picture like this, crazy hippie hair, just looking ridiculous. I showed it to him, like, "What the hell's this?" He tried to act like he was proud of his old teenage look, but I could tell he was like, "Man, what the fuck was I thinking?"

That's what's great about FOUND stuff—it's proof of something. It could be a stranger's note but it's still proof of a certain emotion. It's made concrete. When somebody's letter or journal or photo album is in your hands, it brings them to life. You feel like you know them. I know my dad better after seeing that picture. He could've told me about his high-school band, but I would've pictured something totally different. This is such specific evidence. He will no doub_ be blackmailed.

FOUND Magazine. Fucking around in the bas_

Classified's latest album is called *BOY-COTT-IN THE INDUSTRY*. The record is hittin' top to bottom, but if you want to check out the most geographically-specific track, it's a song called "The Maritimes." I think you can listen to it or even check out the sweet animated video on Class' website: **www.classifiedlive.net**

# City of Westminster

**Department: Education and Leisure**

| | | This matter is being dealt with by: |
|---|---|---|
| | Deidre McGrath B.A., M.I.P.D. | Amanda Duffy |
| **Director** | David Ruse A.L.A., M.I.P.D., M.I.L.A.M. | |
| Assistant Director (Leisure and Libraries) | Amanda Duffy B.A., A.L.A. | |
| Westminster Libraries Information Services Manager : | | Direct Line: 0171 798 3131 |
| | | Fax : 0171 798 2040 |

Your reference :
My reference :

Date
19th August 1996

Dear Sir,

I understand from the Library Staff that last week you were verbally requested to leave the library and not return until your personal hygiene becomes acceptable. In spite of these requests you have continued to come into the library.

Your physical condition is in violation of Section 4 of the City of Westminster Public Libraries and Archives Byelaws. You will be excluded from the use of any library of the library authority until you no longer contravene this section of the Byelaws.

Yours sincerely,

*Amanda Duffy*

Amanda Duffy
Information Services Manager

**SECTION 4**

**FOUND by Kelly Sweeney**

London, England

This note was folded up and stuck beneath a table leg at an outdoor café on Tottenham Court Road.

– K.S.

186

NAME (LAST, FIRST, MIDDLE) OF PERSON GIVING STATEMENT

Edward A.

DOB / AGE 05.23.58

RESIDENCE PHONE (DAY / NIGHT)

BUSINESS PHONE (DAY/NIGHT)

BRYANT ST

ZIP CODE

BUSINESS ADDRESS / CITY IF NOT SAN FRANCISCO SFPD

ZIP COD

DATE OF STATEMENT 03-20-03

TIME STARTED 2040

TIME COMPLETED 2050

LOCATION WHERE STATEMENT TAKEN

STATEMENT TAKEN BY (NAME / STAR)

IN PRESENCE OF

AT SCENE ☐ OTHER: OFFICE

WHILE WORKING A CROWD CONTROL ASSIGNMENT ON 03-20-03, OUR PLATOON WAS ASSIGNED TO STOP A RIOTOUS CROWD WHICH WAS E/B ON MISSION ST. FROM 7TH ST. OUR PLATOON FORMED A SKIRMISH LINE ACROSS MISSION ST. AND PROCEEDED W/B. WHEN THE VIOLENT MOB OF RIOTERS CAME INTO CONTACT WITH OUR LINE I VERBALLY TOLD SEVERAL OF THE CONSPIRITORS TO REVERSE DIRECTION OR THEY WOULD BE STRUCK. MOST OF THE MOB BEGAN TO MOVE W/B ON MISSION ST. BUT SOME INSISTED ON TESTING MY RESOLVE. ONE WHITE MALE 22 YRS OLD, BLACK JACKET, PANTS & BANDANA OVER FACE ATTEMPTED TO GRAB MY BATON. I SKILLFULLY PARRIED HIS MOVE AND STRUCK HIM TWICE IN ZONE ONE OF HIS BODY. THE COWARD THEN RAN INTO THE CROWD.

**ZONE ONE**

**FOUND by Seth Meisels**

**San Francisco, CA**

The day after George W. Bush declared that war on Iraq had begun, huge protest marches swept through downtown and the Mission District. I found this in the street a few days later.

—S.M.

I DECLARE, UNDER PENALTY OF PERJURY, THIS STATEMENT OF _____ PAGES IS TRUE A_____ Y PERSONAL KNOWLEDGE.

SIGNATURE OF PERSON GIVING STATEMENT

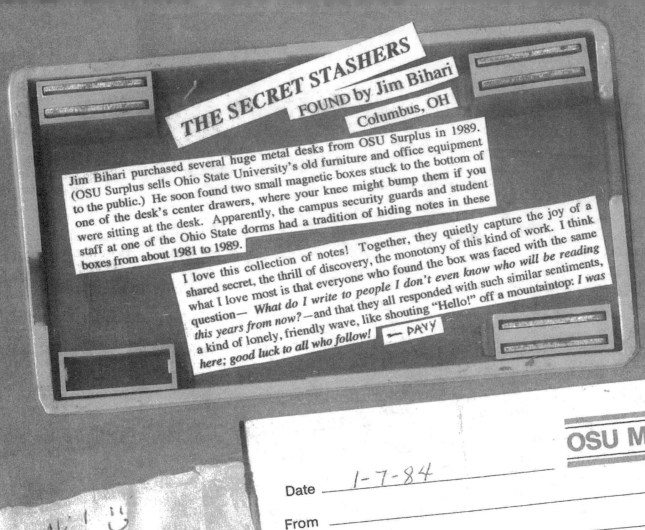

**THE SECRET STASHERS** FOUND by Jim Bihari
Columbus, OH

Jim Bihari purchased several huge metal desks from OSU Surplus in 1989. (OSU Surplus sells Ohio State University's old furniture and office equipment to the public.) He soon found two small magnetic boxes stuck to the bottom of one of the desk's center drawers, where your knee might bump them if you were sitting at the desk. Apparently, the campus security guards and student staff at one of the Ohio State dorms had a tradition of hiding notes in these boxes from about 1981 to 1989.

I love this collection of notes! Together, they quietly capture the joy of a shared secret, the thrill of discovery, the monotony of this kind of work. I think what I love most is that everyone who found the box was faced with the same question— *What do I write to people I don't even know who will be reading this years from now?*—and that they all responded with such similar sentiments, a kind of lonely, friendly wave, like shouting "Hello!" off a mountaintop: *I was here; good luck to all who follow!* — DAVY

Hi! :)

I found the secret S
Box on 6/6/81. HAS
ANYONE else MIKE BIA[N]
Yepper! I took me long enough.
been around this office for a year

1  Yes 11.2.81 by J
2  YES 11·19·81 by RO
3  YES 11-22-81 by ES
4  ☺ found! CAG (so [little]
5  NO I can't find it. Will someone
   please tell me?
6  YEA! KK 12/9/83
7  Shazaam! DB 12/9/8[3]

**OSU Memo**

Date ___1-7-84___

From _____

To _____

Congratulations! You have just found one of the deep, dark secrets of BAOS. I'm one of the newer members of this year's staff. I was hired in September. Another "rookie" also knows about this secret Dave. I seriously doubt that any of the old staff knows this place exists.

Well, so much for small talk. Win[ter] quarter began 3 days ago and I am already overwhelmed. It is going to be a fun quarter!
Kathy

Hey, I found the secret stash boxes on my 1st double shift! Good luck to the rest of the office staffers in their treasure hunting for the stash!
Karen Price
10/25/86
7:27 a.m.
[...] since 3 a.m.

188

Hey. I found it!
7/1/85
6:45 pm

Actually, I found it yesterday but I couldn't put a note in because too many people were around. This is neat. I'm working at Bursell for the summer. For the past 3 years I've worked in Siebert and Petersen. I always thought (and still do) that South Campus was the place to be. O.K. I guess you guys up north enjoy college and have a nice life!
Katie Kubik

Alright So It took Me Awhile but I finally found it!
P.S. I was Looking for the missing $20.
Linda LeC___
1 - ___

9-84
___rge and I found it! Kim
(II) (10:57 am)

I saw Kim & George find the box. Tanya
(10:58) 10-9-84

11/27/88

I've known this was here since '86 but I never bothered to write anything. Well, here's my contribution.
Kris Johnson (ROM)

**OSU Memo**

Date: 2-24-86
From:
To:

Who will be the next to find the "box of thoages". Here lies the greatest staffers accomplishments, finding the box. Can't you feel a plethora of enjoyment now.
Tim Yeager
Barrett Security
84-85

I am now officially a part of "The Secret Stashers"
Is this a Secret Squirrel thing or what?
Cool!

My name is Harvey, and I'm working BAOS for the summer of 1988. I'm from the Blackburn-Haverfield-Noskers complex. The place is Boppin' Hoppin' Non-stoppin'! Come and visit sometime.

Don't ask me why I was under the desk when I saw the boxes, I couldn't imagine what they were - BAOS archives - until I pried them away from the drawer.

Funny, there were no rumors of "the secret stash" at all this summer. That's good. This should only be for the elite privileged!

Word of caution to you future stashers: Beware of the Lounge Lizards! (They'll drive you up the wall everytime.)
Harvey
7:00 a.m. 7/26/88

3455 charing cross • ann arbor, mi • 48108

I found it and I've only been working here a week!! (I hope the boredom picks up) Good luck to all future finders of the box!!
Mike Flagg
9/20/86

G.
This is cool! Just think if the Russians got hold of this stuff. Security Staff.
Tim Y.
10/13/85
will be

What a spaz! I found the secret stash box on 11/10/87
Cindy Koury

189

**OSU Memo**

Date: Nov. 20, 1988
From: Secret Staff
To: BAOS

Hi Guys—

Well you found it. These are all the old notes. If you'd like to leave a note date it & put it in the other box. Try to keep the notes in order. Thanks

**OSU Memo**

Date: 7/26/86
From: Geoff Furse
To: You Future Secret Stashers!

So far, all these secret stash notes have been pretty boring. No good gossip or nothin'. How 'bout some imagination? Which of these royals will be together come 1990?

Jim Morrison / Beth Weeks
Brian Allen / Liz Wolters
Mike Jablonski / 2 girls (at the moment) (one lucky guy)
Michele Molano / ???

Good luck to all of you who have the opportunity to read this in the future!

Can you believe it? I've worked here for over a year and I just now found the secret stash!! Sally can't believe it. Oh well, so I'm a little slow sometimes.

Karen Chism
11-11-82

Oh boy what a thrill to find this. I'm so excited! I've been here for 9 weeks and my knee found the boxes. I really like being the NSM here. Its a fun job. NSM is the Night Service Manager for you future finders.
2/8/89 9:00 p.m. Vaughn (Vaughn Bud Bird)

2-10-89

Ouch! You guessed it I found the mystery boxes! What an exciting thing to happened on my grave shift

Janet Wren
9:00 p.m.

I found the boxes (secrets) on October 23, 86 @ 6:00 in the morning just because I was putting on my shoes

Tracy Frost

Well, I finally found the Secret Stash box thanks to a few staff members who made me look for it.

Stephanie Gruveas
11/28/88 4:15 p.m.

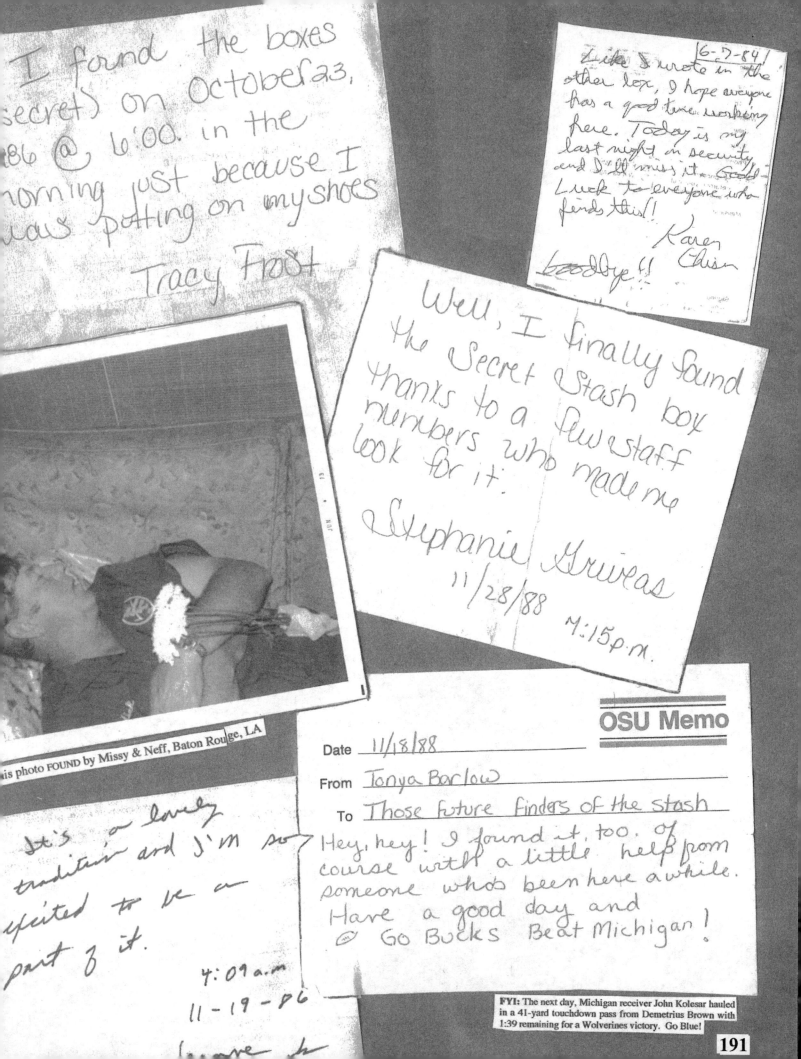

his photo FOUND by Missy & Neff, Baton Rouge, LA

It's a lovely tradition and I'm so excited to be a part of it.

7:09 a.m.
11-19-86

**OSU Memo**

Date 11/18/88

From Tonya Barlow

To Those future finders of the stash

Hey, hey! I found it, too. Of course with a little help from someone who's been here a while. Have a good day and @ Go Bucks Beat Michigan!

FYI: The next day, Michigan receiver John Kolesar hauled in a 41-yard touchdown pass from Demetrius Brown with 1:39 remaining for a Wolverines victory. Go Blue!

191

**Davy:** Hi damali. I remember you told me a great story once about a crazy find you had in college.

**damali:** Oh, I know the story you mean. Yeah. Actually, it was right after I finished college when I was living in the city as an honest-to-goodness citizen.

**Davy:** Which city?

**damali:** Providence, Rhode Island.

**Davy:** A-ha! A great city for FOUND stuff.

**damali:** Yes, and the second of two cities I lived in where the mayor had been convicted of a felony and re-elected. Well, in Providence I had this friend named Cinimon. She spelled it C-I-N-I-M-O-N, not like the spice. Cinimon was the obsessive type, a bit of an odd bird. Once she made me a pair of earrings and gave them to me on a loaf of bread she had baked and decorated in the shape of my head, hair and all. Anyway, for a week or so, Cinimon had been going on and on about Gary Oldman. She couldn't get enough of him. She had mostly been going on about his performance in the movie *Immortal Beloved*, which is a story about Beethoven going crazy over his girlfriend or something. She told me a thousand times how I had to see the movie. I'm a big fan of Beethoven, but wasn't that interested in seeing his mental deterioration on film. And we all know Beethoven was black, so Gary Oldman... whatever.

**Davy:** Beethoven was black?

**damali:** Yup. But if that's how you have to play it, I understand, Hollywood and all... Anyway, I spent a week hearing Cinimon rave about Gary Oldman in *Immortal Beloved*.

The next week was June 1st—the traditional Dumpster-diving day for Providence. That's when the art-school students move out of their houses and leave tons of goodies and crap behind. So Cinimon and I had planned to go check things out. This was my first Dumpster-diving experience. I mean, I had found stuff in the trash before, but this was an organized, all-day, full-body-in-the-trash, beat-the-next-dude-to-the-good-stuff, Filene's Basement kinda deal. So we put on our grubbies and left early.

Cinimon wanted to find mannequins—she had a thing for them. They were, like, a special commodity, highly sought after on June 1st, so much so that at one stop we asked someone if they had seen any and they said furtively, "No, those are probably all gone." I think they were looking for some themselves and didn't want us to jack their bounty. Mind you, the whole time we're driving 10 miles an hour up and down the streets in our borrowed mini-van, Cinimon is still going on about Gary Oldman, she just couldn't stop talking about him, she was fixated.

We get to a major dumpster—like an actual dumpster—blue, steel, smelly and full of stuff. We actually ran into someone else I knew there. That happens on Dumpster-diving days. As I was saying hello, Cinimon dove into the rubble. She was a large beautiful white woman with long dark red hair in a big flowing black dress and combat boots. She pulled up her skirt and tumbled in one leg at a time.

As I stood talking to my acquaintance, I hear a scream from the piles of rubbish. "*GARY*!!" Cin's head pops up. She is holding a picture of Gary Oldman. No kidding. It's the cover of the soundtrack to *Immortal Beloved*. She was out of her mind with glee. I have to say I was pretty shocked myself. He must have heard her pining after him. "Gary! Can you belive it, damali? It's *Gary*!" I don't think I remember Cinimon ever being as happy as she was at that very moment. It still makes me smile.

*eyes to the ground*

**Davy:** That's fucking amazing! Wow. So, did you find anything else that day?

**damali:** Yeah. We drove to other piles of trash. By this point I had picked up a huge scarf, which we decided I could wear as a skirt, a pair of pants, and some drawing materials, a large spiral-bound sketch pad and some colored drawing tools of some sort. Cinimon had plastered the Gary Oldman picture to the dashboard of the van. As we cruised the streets she kept patting the picture it and cooing, "Gary will lead us to where we need to go next. Won't you Gary?" I guess so, because that day we found two full mannequins for Cinimon's collection. Okay, finding an arm or a leg is shocking, finding half a mannequin is a coup, but finding two full mannequins, it's like a Dumpster-diving miracle. Cinimon, she was beside herself with delight and faith in our angel, Gary Oldman.

**Davy:** Man, good thing it was Gary Oldman from *Immortal Beloved* leading you around town. I don't think Gary Oldman from *True Romance* would have been as charming a guide. It's a crazy story, though. Like, what are the chances? Gary Oldman, just there in the Dumpster, waiting for Cinimon to rescue him.

**damali:** There's really something spiritual about finds. I think people feel that if they find something on the street or in the trash, it's especially meant for them. That there was a mystical factor in their finding it. I think I've even seen people look around just to make sure it's them the find is for—just to make sure that they are truly the lucky one. It makes the object feel special, sure, but most importantly it makes the finder feel special and connected to something larger. That's what Cinimon seemed to be feeling.

As for me, the Dumpster shopping was excellent. I was working a new office job and I didn't have clothes for an office, having been a student and a house painter before. I remember telling my boss excitedly that I had gotten the clothes during the traditional Providence Dumpster-dive. I modeled them proudly. "Like my pants? Guess where I got them?" I grew up in hand-me-downs, what's the difference? And hey, I was excited about being part of a Providence tradition. Plus we were a non-profit. I thought he would appreciate the re-use mentality that I so creatively brought to my professional image.

Instead, he said grimly, "That's fine, damali, but please don't wear clothes you found in the trash to the board meetings." He wasn't impressed after all.

Every board meeting, I wore one of my Dumpster outfits. My boss always gritted his teeth and made comments, half-joking, half-serious. He kept telling me not to wear clothes I found in the trash to the board meetings. Though each time, he knew I would do it again, and I did. I figured, if no one else, Gary Oldman would back me up.

**Davy:** The Gary Oldman from *True Romance*?

**damali:** Yes. ⚡

damali ayo is an artist, writer, and performer based in Portland, Oregon, and author of the very funny, thought-provoking book How to Rent a Negro. Learn more about her kick-ass work at www.damaliayo.com.

er to:

# DOLLY PARTON
## WE WOULD LIKE TO MEET WITH YOU!!

Korney Muffkin™

Speedy Muffkin™

Cowboy Muffkin™

Cowgirl Muffkin™

Dear Ms. Dolly Parton,

My name is Dennis Donohue. I am the creator of the Muffkins™ and writer of their adventures which began in 1990.

The Muffkin™ characters and a great deal of their stories are derived by me through dreams. In real life the character Carpacho™ was my dearest of friends, Christo. He was my first employer and like a father to me. Christo passed away in March 1990, and that's when the dreams began. Ms. Parton, you were introduced into the dreams by Carpacho and some of the Muffkins™. Since your introduction I have been repeatedly shown the same scene and realized that it will continue until I reach you. In this scene you cross the Magic Walkway that is leading to their village, transforming to their size and sing two songs. I have the song titles and all

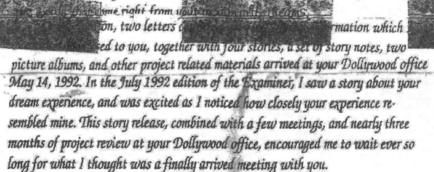

the words _____ right from your mouth in the dreams.

_____ton, two letters _____ _____ information which _____ to you, together with four stories, a set of story notes, two picture albums, and other project related materials arrived at your Dollywood office May 14, 1992. In the July 1992 edition of the Examiner, I saw a story about your dream experience, and was excited as I noticed how closely your experience resembled mine. This story release, combined with a few meetings, and nearly three months of project review at your Dollywood office, encouraged me to wait ever so long for what I thought was a finally arrived meeting with you.

Macho Muffkin™

Carpacho™

Ms. Parton the people at your Dollywood office really loved the project and I received a wonderful letter from them stating so. However you are the one I still need to meet. I believe that creativity and certain forms of vision are acquired at birth. I know you possess these qualities because they are your gift from God that has led you to the top.

Praying that we will soon meet and God bless
Dennis Donohue
8222 Wiles Rd. #166
Coral Springs, FL 33067
305-974-7770

The characters herein are from the as yet unpublished stories of the
Muffkin Adventures " The Little Bakerman And His Magic Corn"

Muffable Muffanimals™

Creator and Writer Dennis Donohue

Muffkin™ Wiz

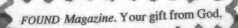

FOUND Magazine. Your gift from God.

Friday Nite at HardOn Hotel

Dear Gary:

FINALLY the kid has some time to write..........Finally got that goddam broad off my back, details to follow, Finally got the new roof on the porch, and new shingles put on one side of the house, and now we can take care of some long over due business.

The thing that really messed me up was that girl. The story from the beginning, and about the twentieth time I8ve typed it out: Mid August. Girl calls station to win in one of our contests. I have nothing to do so I talk to her for awhile and explain to her how she can hear me intro a record on the radio while I am talking to her on the phone. She suggests we get together for lunch. Sight unseen, right? No, I wait until she comes in to pick up her prize, and she looks pretty nice. So, about three weeks later after Bon & kids came and gone, I took her out to lunch. Three days later I took her to a movie, and the day after that to the WHAM/WHFM99 Picnic. Then the 'I was thinking of you' cards started arriving at the house. I wanted to go out, drink beer and have a good time. She wanted to go to 'her road' and make out. WRONG! Calls at the station, attempts to get me to screw her, which were skillfully rebuffed, the whole bit. She was very worried that this was a 'ride' and she didn't want a ride. I pointed out that I had the world by a string and wasn't about to go getting involved long-term wise, since I could get sent to one of the chains other stations. She told me the last time a guy zapped her she attempted suicide and she'd try it again. Now I was sure i had a sickee on my hands, and when the 'Ilove you' notes started arriving in the mail, I decided it was time to call it quits whilst I was ahead. That night I met her and said 'No More' her last words to me as I dropped her off at home were: "I'm gonna have you any way Ican, so if you want to play this way, you'll pay." The next morning, my mother, who didn't know a girl existed got a call from her saying she was pregnant, I was the one, she felt Mom ought to know, and she wasn't going to hold me responsible. You can imagine the reception I got when I bopped home from work. "Hi Mom!" "Paul, answer one question the absolute truth now: Are you the father of that child?" "WHAAAAAAAAAAAAAATTTTTTT?" An hour later, my PD calls me &from work, says the cops are looking for me, and I'd better get down to the public safety building. Well, I go down there to find the girl had been there with her uncle and signed a complaint saying I had beat her up the night before and dumped her along the road. And, she had the bruises to prove it. She had told me she was nineteen, told Mom she was 18, and the age on the complaint was 17, which later rpoved to be correct. Now, this 'uncle' I had heard about from her. He wasn't really her uncle, but rather an older guy who sort of as she put it: "Looked out for my life". She alluded to mafia connections, and also hinted tha if I ever 'zapped' her, uncle Augie would be most happy to put me in the hospital for a year. Now, Gary you know damn well I do not beat up girls. Hell the night before she almost invited me to but I didn't. So, I waited for a few days, during which Oliver the PD said:" Paul, she scared you and that's the last you'll ever hear from her." The station stands behind you all the way in any case." which was nice. So, a warrant was never sworn out for my arrest. I rslaxed and put the roof on the proch. That week several mysterious calls were received at the station by the office girls, and her car was observed by me and other staff members driving by five or six times, when I was in the bulding. Friday night -one week after the trip to the police station- I got in the car @ 10:45 to run down to FM99, and then to the Y. She was parked four houses down the street, lights out waiting. She followed me all the way to the Y, got out of the car, and told me she was sorry she had to do things that way, but, what was I going to do about this little problem of ours? She had a guy in the car with her, who looked about 17-18, maybe he was a real ugly girl. Anyway I told her to get lost, we had no problem, maybe she did, but not 'we' and if she wanted to fight dirty, I could fight dirtier than she ever dreamed. Christ she would have ruined my career and put me in prison for ten years for some other jizz-face's mistake with her, the little trollop. Anyway, I edged around her and went into the Y to get the off-duty cop to arrest her for harassment. She disappeared very quickly. The next morning-how hshall I put this?- she received a phone call from my attorney (?) who told her in no uncertain terms that any firther contact with me would land her in court against me, and the entire Rust Communications group, as she was hampering the operation of a large radio station. She denied ever following

CONTINUES ON NEXT PAGE →

, denied calling the station, even said she expected to get married.. Later, that same day, I recalled she mentioned a priest's name who was kind of palsy with her. So, our family got in touch with the priest, who said, he was counseling her as she was in a state of depression. After we spilled our story, he decided the girl was psychotic needed professional help, and intended to get in touch with her parents. See, thing is, Pop & Mom are separated, Mom lives in Wayland, and she lives with her married sister in Rochester. And tha t's where my involvement ends. But boy, was my brain ever messed up for a month there. I couldn't eat, couldn't work, couldn't do shit. I was jumping every time the phone rang, or saw a car that looked like hers behind me...........
Now the rule is: Everything in a skirt is a threat. The hits are better than real people. You try to be a nice guy and let her down easy, and she turns out to be a lying paranoid lunatic. If she's pregnant, and I doubt it, it ain't me friends. That I can assure you. Not that she didn'ttry.
Enclosed find your goodies from GB.

Job rolls right along. Oliver our very strong PD° strong in the sense that he wants to over see every damsn little thing that goes on at that station, has recently become music consultant to WHAM, and is in charge of the chains two new stations, WRNL AM & FM in Richmond. So, he has little time for anything at FM99. Not that he's delegated any authority. Oh, he yells that he's gonna delegate some authority in one breath, and two minutes later says if you want something donwe right, you have to do it yourself. So, when he's not around which is often, we go on ahead and do things our way. He d shit purple putty balls if he saw how we have the monster setup: completely different from the correct Oliver way. But he hasn t looked at the machine in three weeks. It still sounds the same on the air, but we sneak a lot of stuff by him, simply to get it done when he would shove it back three weeks. This crazy company, the owner of the chain, a real elctronics feak, spends three weeks building a psychadelic light panel for the monster room, while we struggle with one set of non-stereo headphones. This past week our antenna fell apart and knocked us off the air for a day and a half with the chief eng. out of town. The brass won't admit it, but there is, since a rating period on, a possibility of sabotage. Our tower is right on the glide path into the airport, and it wouldn't be too hard for someone in a private plane to drop down to 400 feet, and put a couple bullet holes in the antenna. When the $50 ans hour tower specialists climbed up there, they found holes in the whole antenna, either cause by bullets, or electrical arcing. This was a once in a hundred years type thing, You shouldn't think this a real rinky dink operation. The only reason we shut down was to save the $10,000 transmission line. This way we only have to be $3000 worth of new antenna and have it flown in from the midwest. But what a rotten thing to have happen during a rating period. We are running from a temporary antenna @ about 5000 watts instead of 50,000 until the repairs are made.
Oliver's been sounding everybody out about going down to WRNL. Money's better, but hell, Richmond isn't exactly east of Eden, altho I'd be 1½ hrs. from my people in DC. We think he's just breaking our balls anyway. With that guy, terrific guy he is to work for , you never know when he s serious or having fun with you. I couldn't leave home anyway-draft. Tonight before I came up here we were all over at the station writing jingles for the new station. Yeah, writing the music and lyrics. I wrote: "Gonna set the night on fire;WRNL!" Monday He will take all the stuff we wrote and go to the jingle company in Dallas and have the singers sing it. About $5000 worhh of 'image'.
At home with Mom:  Leaves are mostly raked up, house is still a goddam mess, altho I have noticed Mom doing a lot of throwing out. We had the cracks in the front porch repaired new shingles put on one side of the house, we are making plans to redo the bathroom, etc. etc. Most of this stuff supposed to be done by XMas. IBm still sleeping in a room acorws the house from my clothes closet, and my stereo stuff and tapes are spread out over half the living room, so I told her I no longer gave a rat's ass what she did with the house, just give me a damn room to fix up and set up as my office. Which we will start on as soon as things are battened down for the winter outside. What she doesn't know is that it will be off-limits to her.......she has a tendancy to get very inquisitive about papers and stuff I leave lying around. I think she really means to clean it up this time, but I won't believe it till it's done. All for now. Keep on truckin'. Springtime will hopefully bring a new car, such as Dodge Challenger or Javelin AMX. ← Opinion, please.

*Paul*

Repercussions:
Sex life
stress          sleep sitting up
Pain
no waitressing
need more rides
exhaustion
Rude yuppies
Coffee from A.B.
Can't stop smokeing 2+3 packs a day
Unable to find information
leading to confusion.
Chronic aches
Ankle * (kid injury, rebruised)
knee       (the good one, makeing me limp now)
shoulder (the tray one - hurts a lot to
     work when I have to.)
Apt no longer habitable
man disrespected me
neighbor fucked w/ me
DUI
                                    you can~
Putting up w/ yuppie scum    RUOK?

Will power jeopardized

BEER ♡

REPERCUSSIONS

FOUND by Mark Forman

# The Twilight Zone

ROD SERLING
1490 MONACO DRIVE
PACIFIC PALISADES, CALIFORNIA
January 8, 1965

Mr. Charles R. Washam
Livonia, Michigan

Dear Mr. Washam,

I am in receipt of yours of December 29th.

I will attempt neither diplomacy nor subtlety, sir, when I tell you that your suggestion that I stole "A Carol for Another Christmas" from some obscure piece which you unsolicitedly sent to my office, must be a new heighth of pretension - if not insanity. "Carol for Another Christmas" was obviously based on the Charles Dickens' story. Its suggested dramatization came from Joseph L. Mankiewicz who produced and directed it. As my secretary indicated to you upon returning your script, I do not read unsolicited material ever. I don't read it for the very reason that too often people write in accusing us of predatory plagiarism when such is certainly not the cas

Since I have never read your material, I'm in no position to know when it was submitted in relation to the conception of "A Carol for Another Christmas," but I trust this letter is sufficiently harsh to suggest to you that the plagiarism you are so concerned about is a figment of your own imagination. But if this assurance is unsatisfyin and insufficient, feel free to take this to a lawyer and l your legal representatives contact me directly.

Sincerely,

Rod Serling

RS/ml

## MO' MONEY, MO' PROBLEMS

### FOUND by Brother Mike Rothbart
Madison,

You know how it goes—you create a wildly popular TV show, and before you know it, old acquaintances are coming out of the woodwork, asking for shit.

I've got no clue how dozens photocopied letters to and from R Serling ended up in a manila folder the floor of a city bus in Madison, b that's where my brother Mike fou them. To me, they provide insight i the odd balancing act that folks who experienced unexpected success m often try to perform—dodging bull from the hataz while still doing their b to represent.

I'm especially taken with the correspondence between our man Rod and his old college classmate Frank Thompson, Jr. Who's being the jackass here? From the friends I've shown this to, there's an even split. But I got to say, I admire Rod's even-handedness and humor. Just another day responding to mail... in the Twilight Zone.

—DAV

**ROD SERLING**

CLASS OF SERVICE

This is a fast message
unless its deferred char-
acter is indicated by the
proper symbol.

# WESTERN UNION
## TELEGRAM
®

The filing time shown in the date line on domestic telegrams is LOCAL TIME at point of origin. Time of receipt is LOCAL TIME at point of destination

758A PST APR 3 69 LA089

L SMA013 (B AHB008) PDB FAX AH NEW YORK NY 3 925A EST

ROD SERLING

1490 MONACO DR PACIFIC PALISADES CALIF

ROD DEAR SAW PLANET OF THE THE APES YESTERDAY IT SCARED THE
HELL OUT OF ME. BRILLIANTLY DONE AND YOU ARE BUT SENSATIONAL.

LOVE

JOAN CRAWFORD

(926).

1201(R2-65)

November 8, 1961

Mrs. Helen Luboff
2807 Ocean Front Walk
Venice, California

Dear Helen,

I rather think our correspondence has reached the point of
vastly diminishing returns. What is stunningly apparent is the
pattern of your neurosis. Changeless, consistent, repetitious.
Orson Welles quoted your poetry in a press conference; I lifted
phrases from your book and used them in an Emmy acceptance;
neighbors detest you; police persecute you; old friends abandon
you. Good God, Helen, is the obvious not even suggested to you
yet? You are laboring under such an incredible illusion that
it's a sizable wonder that you don't perceive any of it. No one
has stolen anything from you, Helen. Nothing that you've written,
or at least that I've seen, is worthy of theft. That you label
your own work as an "epic" is not a valid judgement. It is simply
a presumption on your part that within the framework of your
emotional problems seems more to be pitied than censored. Your
constant rantings about this manuscript and that publisher and
that television script - again, how long does this self delusion-
ment go on? You have had nothing published, nothing produced,
nothing printed. Perhaps your flailing accusations of plagiarism
assuaged your frustrations and your hurt, but they are unworthy of
you and unfair to your appointed recipients.

I would count it a personal favor if you stopped badgering me.
No more long, lyrical letters. No more ugly and unfounded accusations. No more ridiculous protestations of your own honesty and
talent and the dearth of these two qualities amongst those surround-
ing you. And please, in the name of simple pride, do not expose
others to your highly personal problems, including some incredibly
damaging accusations made against your own husband. None of this
is my business and I don't want it my business.

You have my sympathy because I know what has been your pain
and unhappiness, but I also know the energy expended in your myriad
assaults, judgements, pronouncements and poetic explosions, might
better be withheld and put to more practical and creative use.

Sincerely,

Rod Serling

RS/ml

2827 North 52nd Street
Lincoln, Nebraska 68504

Mr. Rod Serling
Writers Guild of America, West
8955 Beverly Boulevard
Los Angeles 48, California

Dear Rod Serling:

Since I doubt that we ever really knew each other at Antioch College, though we sat together in Vivian Bresnehen's course in Shakespeare's tragedies, I'm uncertain how to address you. I will say that I read the science fiction play you wrote for her class (it was an assignment, I think) and said to myself, "For God's sake, I hope Serling never tries to become a playwright." Well, somebody had to do it.

After eleven years as a college teacher of English, I've cut out and am trying to make it as a writer of fiction. Fiction I wrote under Nolan Miller; even a novel, in his novel workshop of 1947-1948. But I gave it up completely until three years ago. Teaching my last at the University of Nebraska this past spring, I've been hard at it full time since this summer. I have an agent now, Scott Meredith in New York City; he says my work is professional and just about to sell. I'm that close; I'm sure you know what I mean.

The old problem arises: money. Karl Shapiro, who has been at the University of Nebraska for several years and whom I've known for a long time, is trying to raise money for me. I'm canvassing my friends. Who do you know that might be interested? I shudder to think how many times you've been asked. But the only way to make it from good work to good and salable work is to be singleminded and selfish, I've discovered.

Nolan knows I'm writing again. I sent two stories to The Antioch Review last spring and summer: one he thought lousy (so do I, now); the other he liked but had then an oversupply of acceptances. Other than being reminded of your existence by various television series and admonitions about preventing forest fires, I thought of you again when we visited Mike and Celia Hektner in Denver this summer. We made connections with them again, after years of no communication. I was best man at the wedding; that's a long time ago!

If you can help in any way, fine; if not, well, that's the way of the world.

Sincerely

*Frank Thompson*

Frank H. Thompson, Jr.

TREASURE HUNTERS

November 9, 1965

Mr. Frank H. Thompson, Jr.
2827 North 52nd Street
Lincoln, Nebraska 68504

Dear Frank Thompson,

Your own candor prompts a comparable candor in return.
And if I've misread your letter, you have abject apologies by
way of a preface. But if I read it properly - you're asking
me if there's any way you can get money to help support you
while you free-lance. Call it patronage or what-all - this
seems to represent the sense of the request. Frankly, Frank,
I find this unusual, if not singularly without precedence. I
know of no instance when a writer solicits financial aid to
support his own career. Most writers I know hold down crummy
eight-to-five jobs and then do their free-lancing on kitchen
tables late at night. This is hardly the best of all possible
worlds and doesn't necessarily prove conducive to the most
qualitative writing. But necessity dictates the situation and
we all of us have to live with it.

I know this sounds harsh and even patronizing - coming
from the affluent Hollywood gentleman to the struggling writer
in Nebraska - but again, candor dictates that I tell you you're
on the wrong highway. Hell, man, you've put yourself in a very
special bind if, indeed, you avail yourself of others' aid. It
can't help but be reflected in your writing, because it's
writing that evolves from a combination of guilt and a constant
awareness - not to say, preoccupation with - obligation.

I think your best bet is to take the bull by the horn
or the typewriter by the keys and get the hell to work whenever
the free time is available. This is what I did. This is what
all my friends do. They don't solicit financial aid because it
is neither realistic nor is it particularly helpful over the
long haul. Conceivably, it can eat away at your pride and as
I've already mentioned - can set up some pretty ugly roadblocks
to creativity.

And apart from your thinking that I'm a son of a bitch -
what else is new, Frank?

Best to you and good luck,

RS/ml

Rod Serling

201

Mr. Rod Serling
1490 Monaco Drive
Pacific Palisades, California

Dear Rod Serling:

If I don't reply right away, the desire to do so will vanish very quickly. There's no reason to reply at all, really, since no personal relationship has ever existed between us. But candor twice seductively invites candor a third time.

I recognized immediately the neat allegory your advice made use of. The hero: the determined young man who holds down a crummy eight-to-five job and free-lances on a kitchen table late at night. The villain: the would-be writer who pretends to work but expends most of his energy in trying to con people out of cash he doesn't deserve. Why, the allegory even hints at certain "archetypal patterns." Man, where have you been? Is Pacific Palisades that far away? Nobody, but nobody, takes this seriously any more. You couldn't even sell it to television or the movies. How about Washington and the cherry tree? Or Honest Abe and that log cabin? The starving writer in the garret? Oh, come on. I don't know what kind of writer friends you have, but the ones I know made it however they were able. You know of no instance of a writer soliciting money to support his own career? You must have stopped listening to your friends; you must have read your literary history with blinders on. And compromise? I haven't found a human being yet who can avoid it; it's the human condition that everyone talks about.

Oh, I know why you answered as you did. Aspiring writer presents himself to successful one; for the one who has succeeded the temptation is irresistible. How he has made it now, looking back, seems inevitable. Of course he made it by hard work and struggle; of course he made it own his own talent and guts. Go and do likewise. Here's the formula. Have you ever read Horatio Alger? I have, and you should. The hero, in all those more-than-a-hundred novels, works hard, saves his dough, is unbelievably virtuous, and then by chance meets an old codger who gives him fifty thousand. Rags to riches—it's a myth, you know, not fact. But we never read the last part of the book, or conveniently forget it.

You had no way of knowing, but when I ask my friends for something they know how to take it because I so seldom ask. In short, I don't need your dime-store advice; it appears every month in Writer's Digest and other mags, deliberately aimed at those people who won't make it. I sincerely hope you had something else on your mind when you were dictating the letter to me; just on the level of theater it was an unconvincing performance.

Page 2

Do I think you're a son of a bitch? I think you're playing the role of one because that's the role for elder statesmen in the field to play. It's a little like Nolan Miller's "hardcock facts" he was peddling to me last winter. A little hearty, man-to-man talk, with a "hell, man" here and a "son of a bitch" there. Well, it's like seeing the "I Love Lucy" re-runs for the fifth time. I like Nolan anyway, and if I ever met you I'd probably like you too.

I'm working, as usual, and will continue to. I make a few bucks here and there, mainly by editing book manuscripts. Some friends have come through with a little dough; others will come through with a little too. My agent makes approving noises.

Do us both a favor and don't reply to this. You've got your work to do, too. Besides, you get tired of playing the advice-giver, I'm sure. You gave me good luck; I give it also to you. I hope you continue to do good work; I hope you make even more money. I really do.

Sincerely,

Frank Thompson

Frank H. Thompson, Jr.

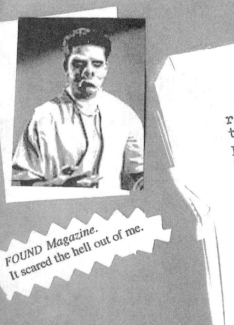

Mr. Frank 52nd Street
2827 North 52nd Street
Lincoln, Nebraska 68504

Dear Frank Thompson,

I think I must have fallen asleep during the second act – or maybe I didn't even get to the theatre – but somehow the curtain doesn't make any sense.

As I read the play, some guy named Thompson hits me up for money. I don't remember Thompson; I don't know what the hell he's written; I don't know anything about him. I get fifty letters a week that come from stock brokers, real estate men, Baptist churches in Sioux City, Iowa and from kooks who assure me that they're not kooks but that it's only fair that I spread the largesse around. Your letter was no less presumptuous and no less demanding then theirs.

But now comes the climax of the play. Thompson opens up the envelope and instead of money out comes advice. He gets red hot and fires away at me in high and righteous dudgeon because I have the temerity to suggest that writers as a rule do not fade away without subsidy.

Allegory, Thompson? My ass! My reference to kitchen table writing wasn't meant to be subtle. It was what I did throughout four years of college and four years thereafter. I had some pretty talented writer friends who did the same thing. One of them was Frank Gilroy who just won himself a Pulitzer. Not one of these guys ever resorted to figuring out tactful methods of dunning via correspondence. You know what they did? They wrote. And would you believe it, Thompson? Nobody starved. Nobody chopped Lincoln logs. Nobody lived in a garret. What sours your craw, Thompson; anyway? If a professional writer suggests that you spend your time writing fiction instead of pleas for aid, he is falling back into "archetypal patterns"? It isn't either-or. It isn't heroes and villains or honest men and con men. If you have to polarize it (and by God, this seems to be your particular compulsion) it is the guy who feels a sense of pride in making it on his own as opposed to the Frank Thompsons amongst us who seem to think that they are somehow anointed, who have some special talent and who demand the helping elbow of whoever's called upon instead of a foot in the ass that they deserve. You're quite right in that we obviously don't know the same writers – or more pertinently – we must not know the same kinds of writers. It strikes me that if you're repelled by "dime-store advice" or by Nolan Miller's patronizing "hardcock facts", these are the wells you shouldn't go to for your drink. The brass shows when you equate rejection with somebody playing a role. You're not important enough for me to put on special trappings to reject you. What I was trying to do was to turn you down with a reason; one that I believed and one that I thought might be helpful.

You talk about compromise but I don't think you know what the hell compromise is. In my book it's giving a little and taking a little and winding up with at least half a loaf as opposed to nothing. Writing to strangers for money on the other hand, I think is a sell-out. I think it's demeaning and prideless. But as to role-playing, Thompson, I think this is your long suit. The hard-bitten realist flailing away with righteous anger may provide you with therapy but I doubt very much if it will really compensate for your rudeness, your impatience, or the kind of distorted values that make you feel so bloody privileged.

I continue to wish you luck. I think you're going to need it.

Sincerely,

Rod Serling

BILL O'REILLY

Bestselling Author of THE O'REILLY FACTOR and THE NO SPIN ZONE

Who's Looking Out for You?

THE REAL BILL O'REILLY

FOUND by Patrick Proctor

Springfield, MO

A MEMOIR

BARBARA BUSH

THE REAL BARBARA BUSH

FOUND by Gillian Schilke

Kirkwood Café, Cambridge, MA

There's something so simple and pure about the way these book jackets have been defaced that's truly delightful.

— DAVY

Hey, okay, you had infidelities in the bookstores. But let's all be honest here—who among us hasn't?

—DAVY

I have Faith about Big and Little good and bad. When Sept. 11 happened I saw the Bright Side — More People weren't Killed. My faith is strong and unwavering. I have faith that if we are truly meant to grow old together — we will — That there will be, has been Good that has happened in My Life. My Glass is half full. It has to be Kevin or I have trouble getting through my Days.

I Need to tell You that I Continue to Remain Committed to our Relationship. I Beleive this is the Best thing for US. I Beleive we have fought too much for too Long — about Not Alot.

I am Not Minimizing what I have done. I had infidelities in the Book stores. I'm Sorry So SO Very Very Sorry. The Computer thing was stranger/harder for Me to Deal With/Understand.

Found
MAGAZINE

www.foundmagazine.com

"Jason Bitner will flip yo' shit"
—The Boston Globe

205

Date 9/12/96

Dear, Dian wa ...

My name Is Daniel S........,
When I was In ulster county, I went to
the dentist to get my teeth clean. At the time
I had on three bottom gold teeth. As soon
the dentist seen them he told me they were
not allowed In this facility. Then he ask me
If they were removable. I told him yes then
he said I could send them home or my
property. So I decided to send them In my
property. After that he told me It will follow
me wher ever I go. What I would like to know
Is If I could have my gold teeth back, because
I see alot of ▬ people here In Green
correctionl facility with there's on. If I can
It will mean alot to me. Thank you.

Daniel S......

95........ / N-1 .........

Don't upset
the warden

# D.C. Boys

Darik + Damion + Daddy Claycamp

Hi guys, how are you two doing? Daddy is doing ok, But I miss you two very much. I can't wait until I get to see you again. When we get to spend some quality time together we will do nothing but have fun.!!!!! I love you two very much and always will. IF you don't love me or want me to stay out of your life Just tell me because I want nothing But For my two Boys to be happy. Daddy loves you two very much and would never hurt you or if I could help it, No one else would ever hurt you. Write Dad a letter or draw and color me a picture, please.

love your Dad

Daddy Scott
Not Daddy Matt

Scott

Your one and only Dad

ONE AND ONLY

FOUND by Erin Tylski

Ashland, NE

**BRUSH WITH FAME**

FOUND by Robbie Doran

San Francisco, CA

Notice Dave Matthews' expression compared to the expressions of these two girls—they are so stoked and he is so not having it.

—R.D.

What exactly did he mean by "plugged in", "lemons", "spill-over" & "spaced"? I couldn't follow it!

**PLUGGED IN**

FOUND by Brother Mike

Madison, WI

**RAY'S TURF**

FOUND by Allison Devers

Oriental, NC

Ray is out of Town, so anyone can ~~ot~~ sit on their couch—until friday.

**BRUCE**

FOUND by Brian Larson

Redlands, CA

Bruce is hiding out in the wash. He probably stole something again!

WE ARE THANKFUL FOR
JEANNINE + LAURB
BECAUSE JEANNINE IS
SWISS AND HER FAMILY
SPEAKS SWISS-GERMAN.

Mrs L. Raymond White

5 Excelsior Blvd

Oakland.

Calif

*Christmas Greetings and best wishes*

*for the coming year*

*Pop*

Found this in a used book. Many cool things about this old Christmas card—1927 postmark, 2-cent stamp, no zip code—but the simple signature always tugs at my heart.

—A.L.

# IF IT IS LEFT IN THE SINK, LOOK FOR IT IN THE TRASH.

I found this note in our office kitchen's trash receptacle. I guess somebody left it in the sink.

—R.H.

**China's Flag** was adopted in 1949. The large star and four small stars stand for the Communist Party and its members.

**The State Emblem** of China is framed by wheat and rice, the nation's leading agricultural products.

I hear a lot of fantastic stories from folks who've got FOUND pets—discovered at the park, in the street, in junkyards, in Dumpsters, at the beach. There's a common thread to all of these stories, this sense that their pet is all the more precious because of how it came into their lives. They didn't just go to the pet store, they *found* this animal, or in a sense maybe their pet found them. It's like they were guided together. The serendipity seems to make it sweeter. And by finding their dog or cat or ferret or iguana and taking them in, they've rescued them from a bleaker, uncertain situation. No surprise, I love these kinds of stories.

So when I first talked to Kathleen Lavey, a newspaper writer in Lansing, Michigan, and she told me that she had two FOUND *daughters*, I was riveted. Here's the conversation we had:

**Davy:** Wow! So, where were your daughters found?

**Kathleen:** Both of my girls are adopted from China, and both were found abandoned on the street. My older daughter, Julianna Xisi, was left under a bush by the gates of an orphanage; my younger daughter, Ella Yuemei, was left on the sidewalk of a busy street.

**Davy:** Who found them?

**Kathleen:** An orphanage worker found Julianna, and Ella was found by a passerby on their way to work in the morning. China started their one-child-only policy in 1979. As I understand it, in many segments of Chinese culture—if you only have one child—you want a son. A son carries on your family's ancestral line. If you have a daughter, she has no obligation to support you in your old age. For peasants and small-town folks, it's especially important to have someone to look after you when you're old. Sons are better; that's what people want. A lot of baby girls are abandoned. Typically, mothers will drop their babies off in high-traffic areas and even hide out and watch to make sure someone finds them. A lot of them are left near orphanages, police stations, and hospitals.

**Davy:** When were your daughters found?

**Kathleen:** Julianna was found on January 2nd, 2000, she was plucked out of the bushes, reeled in from the cold. She'd clearly just been born the night before, New Year's Day. Now she's five years-old, about to start kindergarten. Ella is three. Ella was found in a box on the street, wrapped up in a little cloth, a little packet of powdered milk in the box beside her. She was already ten days old when she was found, which makes her story a little murkier. Stirs up a lot of questions.

**Davy:** Yeah—what were those ten days like for her mother? Trying to decide what to do, maybe terribly torn? It's intense. Do you ever wonder what it was like for this young mother to leave her baby behind?

## CHINA

**CHINA** is a huge country in eastern Asia. It is the world's largest country in population and the third largest in area. About a fifth of all the people in the world live in China. The country covers more than a fifth of Asia. Only Russia and Canada have more territory. China's vast land area includes some of the world's driest deserts, highest mountains, and richest farmland.

Chinese families traditionally valued sons far more than daughters. A husband could divorce his wife if she failed to give birth to sons. In some cases, daughters were killed at birth because girls were considered useless. Today, girls as well as boys are valued. This change came about partly because the Communist government strongly supports the idea that women should contribute to the family income and participate in social and political activities. Women do many kinds of work outside the home. Many young husbands share in the shopping, housecleaning, cooking, and caring for the children to show that they believe the sexes are equal. However, equality between the sexes is more widely accepted in the cities than in the countryside.

**Kathleen:** Every freakin' day! You know, the anonymity factor is a big reason why a lot of people adopt from China—there's no chance the parents will ever materialize and come looking to claim their kids. It's supposed to ease the anxiety and concerns about who the birth mother is. But it's had the opposite effect on me. I think about Ella's birth mother, and those ten days, and I feel such a kinship with her. It's hard to get my head around it. I love her, too. She gave her baby an opportunity in a culture where abortion is encouraged. Maybe she couldn't afford her, maybe there were social pressures, but I appreciate her generosity, going through with it, giving birth. I feel a kinship with her that transcends everything. Julianna's mother, too. These are the kids' other mothers. There's a little ritual I started with the girls, before they could even read and write. At church there's a place where you can write down prayers—so, we've been writing prayers for their birth mothers, for their health and safety, to let them feel our love.

**Davy:** Think you guys will ever go to China and visit the town where they were found?

**Kathleen:** We're planning to go. In five years, I think, when they're eight and ten; they'll be old enough by then to comprehend it all and remember it, but not teenagers yet, calling out what's great and what sucks. I've got the address where Ella was found. It's not her mother's house or anything, just a random building on a busy street. We'll go visit that address, check out that square of sidewalk where she was found.

A lot of us adoptive parents who've taken in kids from China are, well, okay, a bit over-educated and neurotic. And it's a question: what's the best way to preserve the kids' cultural identity? One way is language. Starting this fall, we're all learning Chinese together. All those years in college I struggled through Spanish—but Spanish was easy it turns out!

One thing I've heard is that the word we translate as "abandoned" in regard to these kids is more precisely translated as "placed in order to be found." Here's the way I hope all of this will make sense to my daughters when they grow up—they were born in a very poor place by people who couldn't take care of them; by the seeming randomness of being left somewhere and then stumbled over—*found*—they ended up growing up here in Michigan, with me.

We're all very lucky.

Kathleen Lavey with Julianna and Ella.

LIZ!
over the years, I have FOUND many great things:
1) The "ladies poker club" plans outside of Rite Aid
2) "Gummy boobs?" of Rite Aid
3) That I really do like airplanes.
4) That I really love living with you in our house with 3 cats.
5) That I love you, and want to spend my life with you.
→ You are my greatest find.
WILL YOU MARRY ME? ♥
Marc

p.s. page me later

Quoting Marc Leslie <mleslie@h        -richmond.com>:

So, can would you be adverse to me using an ad to propose to my girlfriend?

-----Original Message-----
From: FOUND Magazine [mailto:info@foundmagazine.com]
Sent: Friday, April 15, 2005 2:07 PM
To: Marc Leslie (Homeward)
Subject: RE: FOUND Magazine sponsors!

ARE YOU KIDDING - THAT WOULD BE AMAZING!!!!
we would absolutely LOVE to run an ad like that
keep us posted!
+davy

Quoting Marc Leslie <mleslie@h        -richmond.com>:

Okay, sweet.  I am all over it.  When is the due date again (I lost
that   second e-mail)??

I will be incorporating Found into it as well.  We both love Found,
and  I have been trying to find a cool, non-cheeseball way to do
that.

From: FOUND Magazine [mailto:info@foundmagazine.com]
Sent: Friday, April 15, 2005 5:59 PM
To: Marc Leslie (Homeward)
Subject: RE: FOUND Magazine sponsors!

cool marc - deadline is april 30th.
this is really fantastic!

+davy

Date: Mon, 2 May 2005 09:56:10 -0400
From: Marc Leslie <mleslie@h        richmond.com>
To: 'Davy Rothbart' <davy@foundmagazine.com>
Subject: RE: FOUND Magazine sponsors!

ad was sent Friday, and post office told me it should be to
you by Saturday.  Can you let me know when you get it?

Quoting Marc Leslie <mleslie@h        -richmond.com>:

Awesome.  It will be on the way this week.  What is the ETA for
when the
mag is coming out?  I need to figure out how to buy a ring and
stuff.

From: Davy Rothbart - FOUND Magazine
Sent: Thursday, May 05, 2005 3:35 AM
To: Marc Leslie (Homeward)
Subject: RE: FOUND Magazine sponsors!

got it, marc - looks great!

i'm actually gonna make the ad a bit bigger and possibly even give
it a whole page.  this is a mighty big thing you are doing and i
think it's awesome!  we can also try and get you a mag before
anyone else, so there's no chance of her stumbling over it at a
friend's house or something, you'll have more control over the
situation.  it's lookin like august is when it will be out; let's
keep in touch as that gets closer.

awesome!!
+davy

Date: Mon, 18 Apr 2005 12:46:59 -0500
From: Davy Rothbart <davy@foundmagazine.com>
To: Marc Leslie <mleslie@h        richmond.com>
Subject: RE: FOUND Magazine sponsors!

hi marc - the official date is july 4th for the mag's release, but
between me and you, i'm thinking it'll actually pop about 1 month
later... so you have a little time to investigate ring-buying.

i'm measurement-challenged, but any business card size will work.
2" x 3"??  if it looks like a driver's license or business card
size im sure it will be all good.

cool man!
+davy

Date: Thu, 5 May 2005 08:22:05 -0400
From: Marc Leslie <mleslie@h        richmond.com>
To: 'Davy Rothbart - FOUND Magazine' <davy@foundmagazine.com>
Subject: RE: FOUND Magazine sponsors!

Dude, that would be awesome!  I really appreciate it man!  I promise I
will wear my "The Booty Don't Stop" t-shirt under my tux at the wedding!

hey marc - that's awesome!!
ok, so good news and bad news.  good news is i made this thing into
a full-page spread, it looks good and i think it's pretty funny.
bad news is i'm just finally sending it to the printer next monday,
which means a few week turnaround and it won't be out til about the
1st or 2nd week of september.  they can fed-ex you a copy the
minute it rolls off the line, but it's still gonna be a few weeks.
i'm sorry because i know it must be weird to have to wait on
somethin like that now that you are all ready to go.  anyway, call
me or email if we need to work out a new plan, otherwise hang in
there!  just keep me posted my friend, and sorry for the delay, i
really really apologize.
peace - davy

Quoting Marc Leslie <mleslie@h        -richmond.com>:

No need to apologize.  I am stoked that it is a full-page spread!  That
is awesome!  Now, I have to figure out how to get Liz to look at the ad,
in some sneaky way.

No worries on the time.  It is weird to be ready to go, but I think that
1st week of September is totally fine with me.  Just let me know when
is fine.  I still have to ask her parents for their blessings, etc.
or 2nd week of September is coming, so I can get prepared.

Thanks for taking part in this.  You'll be in Richmond in late September
for a FOUND gig, so I hope to meet you then.  Liz met you a few years
back at some crazy backwoods reading/country music thing in Louisa
County, VA.

Thanks for everything.  This is gonna be so cool!!!!

this photo FOUND by Tom Dykas, St. Louis, MO

From: Davy Rothbart - FOUND Magazine <davy@foundmagazine.com>
To: Marc Leslie <mleslie@h        richmond.com>
Subject: RE: Question regarding my FOUND marriage proposal

awesome marc!!

i would also like to interview you (and liz) when im in richmond for a
documentary film i'm making about love!

please holla at me around sept.5th to check the status of things.  i dont trust
myself to remember with the craziness around here...

thanks for being so chill about the delay, etc.

peace! - davy

www.FoundMagazine.com

Jason Bitner

+ FOUND notes
+ FOUND photos
+ FOUND booty rap
+ FOUND heavy metal
+ FOUND answering machine messages
+ Find-of-the-Week – a new one every 7 days!
+ FOUND Magazine Tour Info
+ list of bookstores who carry FOUND
+ join our monthly e-mail list
+ get bit by bitner
+ good, kind people visit the site daily
+ find more finders – e-mail your friends about foundmagazine.com!

the ALL-NEW **foundmagazine.com**

stop by anytime!

*Dear Ms. Lavigne,*

I fucking love your music! Of course there's back-story to this, as well, there's damn-near-always some sort of backstory. I've been a fan ever sense I first saw the Complicated video, about two years ago, when the title only listed your first name. And then when Sk8ter Boi was first played on Mtv, at least the first time I caught the video, I sat up all morning waiting for it to play again, because it was a lot of fun and it pretty much rocks. All the while, I'm sorry to say that even though I definitely recall holding your album in my hands, on at least three occasions, I've yet to pick up copies. As much as I'd love to run right out this afternoon, I can't afford to do that today.

As for the past, normally I don't buy music that gets played on Mtv, with a few exceptions. I only have so much money, unfortunately and there are other albums I'm usually more interested in owning. I do love your music, though and over the last three days I've been listening to it near incisively, to the point where I had to stop, set it aside and think to myself, "Okay, that's enough Avril Lavigne for now." (And I completely misused the word "incisive", but whatever.)

Last weekend, actually, I managed to come up with what seems like a pretty outlandish fantasy. One that even jumps back a few years, to the time when I first heard your music and while I'd guess you've heard of me, this does seem pretty outlandish, abet in a beautiful way - extremely beautiful. I was incredibly moved, imagination or not. The origins of this, again, stretch back to 2002. Listening to Complicated back in 2002, parts of the song seemed to hit close to home, of course I know that's a point with so much music. And then Sk8ter Boi, too. At some point Sk8ter Boi was playing in the background, and as the music skimmed by through my ears, I thought for a moment that it sounded like you sang, "Andy."

I'd imagine, at that moment a grave look came across my face Avril, because I remember thinking, "That's paranoid, dude." Then, afterwards I pretty much forgot all about it, not that I forgot about your music, it was only a handful of months ago when I held a copy of Let Go in my hands. I picked it up at Easy Streets records, in West Seattle, however ended up buying something from And You Will Know Us by the Trail of Dead. (like that's not cryptic.) Although, hopefully a consolation, because it's not as though I switched out for something lacking in quality.

I was even excited to hear Carissa's Wierd play Complicated, at their farewell show last November. Carissa's Wierd is probably one of my favorite bands. I can hardly wait for the live album's release on the 9th. Is Complicated going to be on there? I sure-as-fuck hope so. I feel bad because I screamed, not during Complicated, but at some point during the show I screamed between songs and that was pretentious. Then, when I heard they were releasing the live show, I felt bad. I'd had a bunch of drinks and I don't know, just screamed really loud. Hopefully they were able to edit that out, or even better, decided to leave it in. That would be pretty cool. I'm sure it's something that I'll play for my Grandchildren someday, if I make it that far.

Afterwards, I bound up into the Crocodile's private booth, because I saw someone up there that I (vaguely) know and one of the first things I said was, "Holy shit, they played Avril Lavigne!" I thought that was fucking awesome. And he was like, "Yea, I've been meaning to talk to you about that." It struck me as odd, actually, but I thought he was just being sarcastic and that's probably what it was Avril. I really didn't think much more of it at the time, not until last weekend.

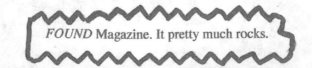

:Religous beliefs

PLEASE THROW YOUR
OWN GARBAGE AWAY
Thanks MAIL PERSON

Kleenex
cascade
hand soap
TP
Prostitute

ASK FOR
RUSTY

pee on me
I am
a Bathroom

JENNY

POISON

EARTHQUAKE

FIRE

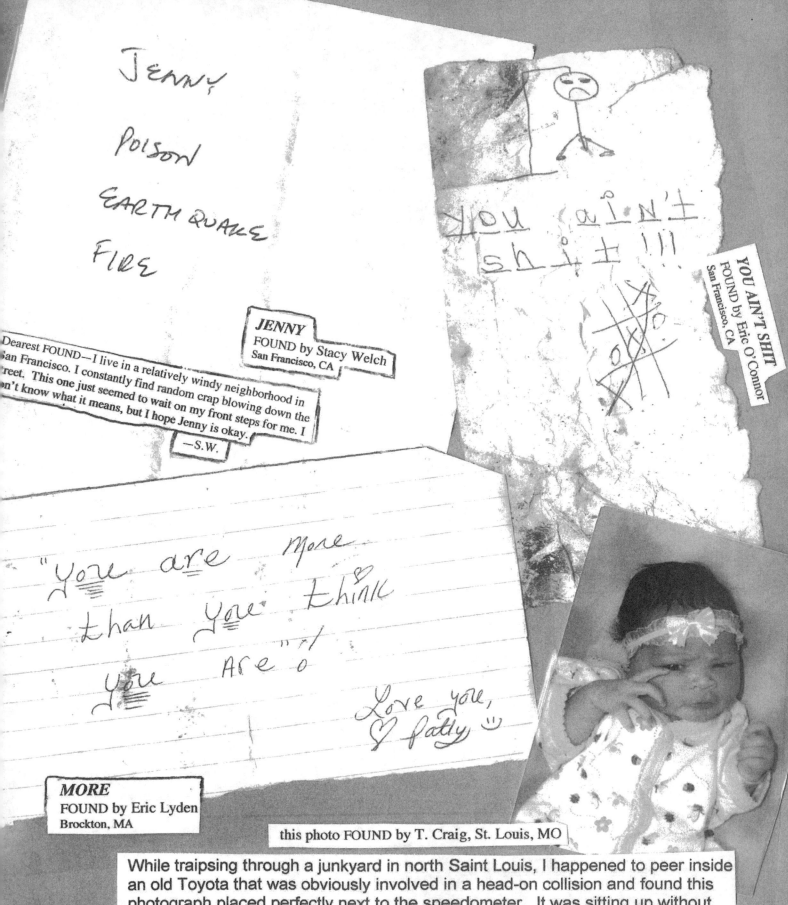

YOU AIN'T
shit!!!

Dearest FOUND—I live in a relatively windy neighborhood in
San Francisco. I constantly find random crap blowing down the
street. This one just seemed to wait on my front steps for me. I
don't know what it means, but I hope Jenny is okay.

—S.W.

"you are more
than you think
you Are"

Love you,
patty

this photo FOUND by T. Craig, St. Louis, MO

While traipsing through a junkyard in north Saint Louis, I happened to peer inside
an old Toyota that was obviously involved in a head-on collision and found this
photograph placed perfectly next to the speedometer. It was sitting up without
the aid of tape almost suggesting it remained unmoved from the moment it was
placed inside, through the unfortunate crash, and finally to the car's final resting
spot perched atop old tires with it's guts hanging out everywhere. I felt good
about the find until my imagination got the best of me: why would somebody
leave their infant's picture behind?

—T.C.

# FOUND magazine
3455 Charing Cross Road
Ann Arbor, MI 48108

before you party

SEND

IN

YOUR

FINDS!!!

email is: info@foundmagazine.com. Peace!

11/28/03

3:30 pm

Jes, if you ever
wake up...

Things I need you to
do before your party tonight:

1 Clean house
2 Kill cat (or just put him in your room)
3 Get the dank from Pat
4 Get the swag for your sister
5 Pick up the kids (2) budweiser
6 Pick up my dope from charles
7 get my new needles
8 ~~Get the beef~~ dad said it
   meet me at Max n Ermas
   at 9 and eat tortilla soup.
9 Party
10 dome                    love Jamie

Ann Arbor, MI

FOUND by J.C.Wilson

I work at Max & Erma's and found this under the table crumpled up. You never would have believed it - these two people... The funniest thing if you saw that they didn't even order tortilla soup! about it was      —J.C.W.

BEFORE THE PARTY

**1.**

**BACK COVER FINDS:**
Leaf FOUND by Aidan MacAulay (2 1/2 yrs. old), N. Vancouver, B.C.
Keyring FOUND by Meredith Braden, San Diego, CA

**2.** FOUND!

SNAKEPIT

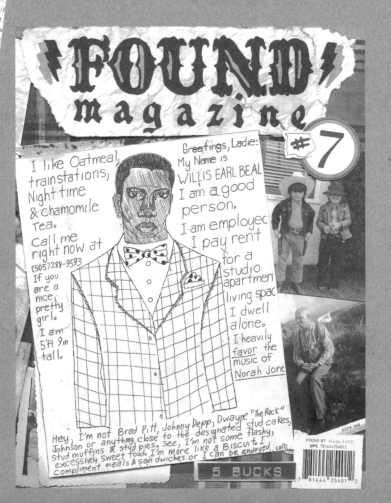

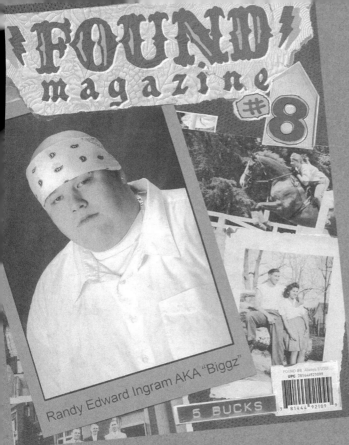

FOUND magazine #8

Randy Edward Ingram AKA "Biggz"

5 BUCKS

UPC 781446923099

FOUND magazine #9

my husband let me have a boyfrie
the last two years we were
together

Gift C.D.

Marky Mark (Hello Luna)    Me (That's Betsy)

For Caitlin

I Love Yuo ♡

5 BUCKS

FOUND #9 Always 5 USD
UPC 781446923161

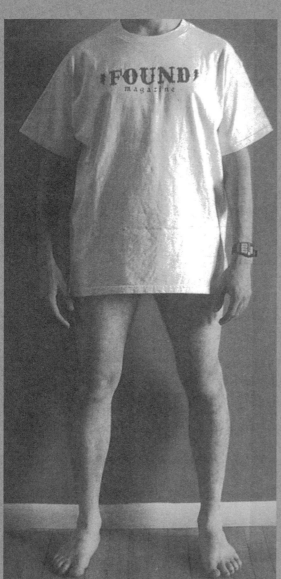

WEAR YOUR HEART ON YOUR SLEEVE IN A FOUND T-SHIRT!

FOUND

MY HEART IS AN IDIOT

Essays

DAVY ROTHBART

PICADOR

FOUND's Davy Rothbart proudly displays two hand-decorated copies of the first printing of FOUND #1, June, 2001.

WE CAN'T DO IT WITHOUT YOU...

KEEP YOUR EYES TO THE GROUND AND SEND IN YOUR FINDS!

FOUND ON STREET WHILE WALKING DOG

FOUND magazine
3455 CHARING CROSS RD.
ANN ARBOR, MI
48108-1911

FOUND ON SIDEWALK BY HIGH SCHOOL NEAR OUR HOUSE